The Word-Faith

CONTROVERSY

Other books by Robert M. Bowman Jr.

Orthodoxy and Heresy
Understanding Jehovah's Witnesses
Why You Should Believe in the Trinity

001 by Robert M. Bowman Jr.

lished by Baker Books
vision of Baker Book House Company
Box 6287, Grand Rapids, MI 49516-6287

ted in the United States of America

0-8010-6344-2

ry of Congress Cataloging-in-Publication Data is on file at the Library of Congress,
ington, D.C.

s otherwise indicated, Scripture quotations are taken from the NEW AMERICAN
DARD BIBLE ®, Copyright © The Lockman Foundation 1960, 1962, 1963, 1968,
1972, 1973, 1975, 1977, 1995. Used by permission.

versions cited are New International Version (NIV), copyright © 1973, 1978, 1984 by
ternational Bible Society, used by permission of Zondervan Publishing House; King
Version (KJV); and Revised Standard Version (RSV), copyright 1946, 1952, 1971 by
vision of Christian Education of the National Council of the Churches of Christ in the
Jsed by permission.

rrent information about all releases from Baker Book House, visit our web site:
http://www.bakerbooks.com

The Word-Faith
CONTROVER

Understanding the
Health and
Wealth Gospel

Robert M. Bowman

BakerBooks

A Division of Baker Book House Co
Grand Rapids, Michigan 49516

Contents

Preface   7

Introduction: The War of the Words   13

Part 1: **The Roots of the Word-Faith Movement**

1 Understanding the Word-Faith Teaching   23
2 The Man behind the Message   35
3 A Metaphysical Mind-Set?   43
4 Kenyon's "Pentecostal" Context   57
5 Fathers of the Word-Faith Movement   85

Part 2: **The Shoots of the Word-Faith Teaching**

6 Real Men Don't Use Reason   97
7 Does God Have Faith?   105
8 The God with a Bod   115
9 Big God, Little Gods   123
10 Dominion and the Devil   137
11 Confessing Jesus—A New Twist   147
12 The Fall and Rise of the Born-Again Jesus   159
13 Just Like Jesus?   179
14 The Faith Debate   193
15 On Being Healthy, Wealthy, and Wise   205

Conclusion: By Their Fruits   219

Notes   229
Select Bibliography   243
Name Index   249
Scripture Index   251

Preface

Christianity in its essence is about *faith*. At the heart of the Christian religion, gospel, doctrine, and worship, is faith—faith in God, in his Son Jesus Christ, in his word revealed in Scripture. Ironically, though, there is debate today within Christianity as to the meaning of faith. Where there should be crystal clarity, there is instead confusion, as discordant views are simultaneously trumpeted for all the world to hear.

Actually, several ongoing debates about Christian faith are taking place in the church today. Some of these go back a long way. Catholics and Protestants, after nearly five centuries, are still debating the validity of the Reformation teaching of justification through faith alone *(sola fide)*. Liberals and conservatives (categories cutting across the Catholic-Protestant divide) have for about two centuries been debating whether Christian faith requires one to believe that the Bible is supernaturally inspired and to believe that Christ's virgin birth, miraculous life, and bodily resurrection are literal, historical facts. I will not be discussing these two very important debates in this book. As a conservative Protestant, or evangelical, I affirm the Reformation teaching of justification through faith alone and the conservative view of the Bible and Jesus Christ.

The Topic of the Debate

Within evangelical Christianity, another debate rages that is the focus of this book. It is a debate in which all participants affirm a conservative view of Christ and the Bible and a Protestant view of justification and salvation. Yet, it too centers on faith. The focus of this debate is on what is sometimes called simply the Faith teaching. The advocates of this teaching are Pentecostal preachers and teachers who are best known for their message of bodily health and financial prosperity through faith. If we believe—

and if we *confess* or say out loud that we believe—these teachers assure us that we can and will enjoy both health and wealth. This idea of "confessing" that one has these blessings in spite of appearances gave the teaching the name "positive confession." Likewise, it is because of the idea of speaking words of faith that the teaching is known as the "word of faith" or "Word-Faith" doctrine. Some of its critics, because of the movement's views on health and wealth, have labeled it the "health and wealth gospel."

The faith-healing and prosperity-gospel aspects of the movement are what give it both its intense appeal to many and its extreme notoriety to many others. What most people do not know is that the "health and wealth" promise is merely the tip of the theological iceberg. It is the teachings about faith, words, and confession—and what these teachings in turn imply about God, human beings, Jesus Christ, and the nature of the Christian life—that have turned out to be the most controversial aspects of the Word-Faith movement.

In the Affirmative: The Word-Faith Teachers

The architect of the Word-Faith teaching in its complete and current form is Kenneth Hagin, a televangelist based in Tulsa, Oklahoma. Tulsa, in fact, is the center of the Word-Faith movement. The International Convention of Faith Churches and Ministers, a Word-Faith denomination founded by Hagin and others in 1979, is based in Tulsa, along with Hagin's Rhema Bible Training Center, which is the movement's principal ministerial school. Oral Roberts's ministry and Oral Roberts University (ORU) are also located in Tulsa. Although Roberts is not a Word-Faith teacher, he has greatly influenced its development. T. L. Osborn, another popular teacher whose ministry is closely related to the Word-Faith movement, is also based in Tulsa. So is Harrison House, a publishing company that prints works by such Word-Faith teachers as John Avanzini, Charles Capps, and Frederick Price.

The other leading proponent of the Word-Faith teaching is Kenneth Copeland, a televangelist who embraced Hagin's views and has his own ministry based in Fort Worth, Texas. The Dallas–Fort Worth twin cities are another bastion of Word-Faith ministry, serving as the home base for Word-Faith teachers John Osteen and Robert Tilton.

Hagin, Copeland, and many of the other prominent Word-Faith teachers are recognized internationally through their television programs. Most of these televangelists broadcast their programs on the Trinity Broadcasting Network (TBN). TBN is headed by Paul Crouch, himself an advocate of the Word-Faith teaching. Not all of TBN's programming is Word-Faith, though. For example, TBN carries Charles Stanley, a popular Baptist preacher, and Hal Lindsey, a prophecy teacher best known for his megaseller *The Late Great Planet Earth*. Still, the programming on TBN is dominated by teaching that is either Word-Faith or very sympathetic to it. Through TBN, the Word-Faith teachers have found a forum for speaking to Christians of all denominations.

In the Negative: Critics of the Word-Faith Teaching

The debate over the Word-Faith teaching began in Tulsa in 1979, in the same year and in the same city in which the International Convention of Faith Churches and Ministers was established. In 1979 Charles Farah, a professor at ORU in Tulsa, published a book critical of the Word-Faith teaching titled *From the Pinnacle of the Temple*. The title alludes to Jesus' experience in the wilderness, in which the devil had tempted him to throw himself down from "the pinnacle of the temple" as a test (Matt. 4:5; Luke 4:9). Farah contended that the Word-Faith movement promoted similar presumptuousness by teaching people to expect that God would heal them even if they failed to seek medical help for serious conditions.

In 1982 one of Farah's students, Daniel R. McConnell, completed a master's thesis at ORU critiquing the Word-Faith movement. McConnell's thesis was startling: The Word-Faith teaching was not authentically Pentecostal but was instead a kind of cultic Trojan horse. According to McConnell, the Word-Faith doctrine had originated in the mind-science cults of the nineteenth century and had come to Pentecostalism through the writings of an early twentieth-century radio preacher named E. W. Kenyon. McConnell identified Kenyon as the real father of the Word-Faith movement. He argued that Kenneth Hagin not only learned his doctrine from Kenyon, he even plagiarized a good deal of Kenyon's writings in his own books.

McConnell's theory that the Word-Faith doctrine had been imported into Pentecostalism from the mind-science or metaphysical cults did not gather dust on a shelf of the ORU library. In 1985 evangelical author Dave Hunt published *The Seduction of Christianity,* a wide-ranging exposé of the alleged infiltration of cultic ideas into Christianity. A major example of this infiltration was the Word-Faith movement. Hunt drew on McConnell's thesis to substantiate his claim that evangelicals and Pentecostals were being seduced into believing heresies and cultic doctrines. For Hunt, this seduction will be instrumental in bringing about the great apostasy that he believes will decimate the church and prepare for the coming of the Antichrist.

Hunt's book sparked intense debate about the Word-Faith teaching and related trends in the Pentecostal and charismatic movements. The debate

has followed a fairly well-defined pattern. Critics of the Word-Faith movement have followed McConnell and denounced it as a metaphysical wolf
in Pentecostal clothing. (Even those who are sharply critical of Pentecostalism have made some use of this argument.) The best-known critic
articulating this perspective is Hank Hanegraaff, whose views have received
wide circulation through *The Bible Answer Man* radio program and through
his 1993 book, *Christianity in Crisis*. Advocates and sympathizers of the
movement have defended its teaching as both Pentecostal and biblical,
while still acknowledging that the movement has suffered various excesses.
(This is a safe criticism that even the most ardent advocates will make.)
Leading this defense has been William DeArteaga, whose book *Quenching
the Spirit* has gone through two editions and has been widely and warmly
received in Pentecostal and charismatic circles. DeArteaga, who is sympathetic to Hagin but is especially impressed by Kenyon, argues that the critics of the Word-Faith teaching are modern-day Pharisees opposing the
movement of the Holy Spirit.

No Easy Answer

At the 1994 annual conference of the Evangelical Ministries to New Religions (EMNR) in Philadelphia, I participated in a panel discussion about
the Word-Faith movement. The moderator asked each of us to begin by
stating how we would classify the movement. Several panel members gave
as their opinion that it was cultic or heretical (terms that were and are in
this context used more or less interchangeably). One panelist went so far
as to say that the movement was *worse* than cultic—it was in fact *occultic*, a
demonically inspired deception seducing people into something more akin
to magic or witchcraft than to Christianity.

These answers were direct and clear, articulated simply and forcefully.
I would have been happy to give a similarly simple answer to the question—but in all honesty, I could not. In fact I could not come up with an
intelligent-sounding technical term with which to categorize the movement. Instead, I found myself giving the rather inelegant answer that the
Word-Faith movement was *a mess*. It is, I explained, neither soundly orthodox nor thoroughly heretical. It could not be categorized without qualification as either Christian or cultic. Some of the leaders did teach some
heretical ideas, but none of them seemed to advocate those heretical ideas
consistently, and most of the people in the movement did not embrace
those heresies.

Furthermore, I argued, the Word-Faith movement was not the result of
an infiltration of Pentecostalism by the metaphysical cults. Rather, the

Word-Faith movement was a radical form of Pentecostalism. Little if any of the objectionable elements of the movement's teachings and practices did not have precedent or roots in classical Pentecostalism. The claim that the Word-Faith movement was cultic implied that Pentecostalism itself was cultic at its root. This was an implication that I, though not at all Pentecostal or charismatic, firmly rejected.

My inability to give a simple answer to the question of how I would classify the Word-Faith movement is not the result of any general aversion to simple answers. Some issues are black and white. Some questions must be answered with a simple yes or no. There are professing Christian groups that are properly classified without hesitation as heretical. Religions such as the Jehovah's Witnesses or Christian Science are legitimately labeled as *cults* in the theological sense of religions that profess to be Christian but that deny essential truths of the Christian faith. But I thought then, and I think now, that such a simple answer is not the right answer in this case.

In this book, I am going to be making the case for the following conclusions:

- The roots of the Word-Faith movement are in evangelical and Pentecostal Christianity, not in the mind-science or metaphysical cults.
- The questionable and erroneous assumptions in the teaching of E. W. Kenyon did have some precedent in the mind-science cults, but they also had precedent in the evangelical faith-cure movement of the nineteenth century.
- Although Kenneth Hagin did take much of his theology from Kenyon, and indeed did plagiarize Kenyon, Hagin is the real father of the Word-Faith movement.
- The distinctive theology of the Word-Faith movement is in many respects seriously unbiblical, and at least some of the movement's leading teachers espouse heresy. This heresy, however, is not accurately described in the literature critical of the Word-Faith movement.
- Sweeping generalizations about the Word-Faith movement as cultic or heretical fail to take sufficient stock of the diversity within the movement.
- The Word-Faith teachers' views on healing and prosperity are actually the least problematic aspects of their distinctive theology. In significant ways their views, while troublesome, are more moderate than those of their precursors in the faith-cure and early Pentecostal traditions.
- The popular characterization of the Word-Faith teaching as a "gospel of greed" hawked by religious con artists is generally an unfair caricature applying only to certain teachers on the fringe of the movement.

- While the errors of the Word-Faith movement are largely rooted in problematic elements of the Pentecostal tradition, a theologically sound form of Pentecostalism has emerged that rises above those weaknesses.

The last point bears amplification. I prefer to describe my views as *non*-charismatic but not *anti*charismatic. Ironically, most of the harshest critics of the Word-Faith movement are charismatics. It is, of course, understandable that charismatic critics of the movement would be anxious to distance themselves from it. This may explain why these critics favor the theory that the Word-Faith teaching is a metaphysical heresy imported into the Pentecostal and charismatic tradition. The reverse has not held true: that is, anticharismatics have *not* rejected the metaphysical connection or argued that the Word-Faith doctrine is generic Pentecostalism. Most of the anticharismatic critics of the movement have viewed it as a mix or synthesis of Pentecostal and metaphysical beliefs.

My own assessment, that the Word-Faith movement is a Pentecostal phenomenon that owes very little to metaphysical influences, might easily be misunderstood as an assault on all Pentecostalism. Such a misunderstanding would very much miss the point. I do think that there are weaknesses in classical Pentecostalism that have taken an especially radical and troubling form in the Word-Faith movement. But at the same time the Pentecostal tradition has matured, and many Pentecostal churches have overcome the weaknesses of their tradition at its worst and now represent that tradition at its best. Telling Pentecostals to dismiss the Word-Faith movement as a non-Pentecostal phenomenon is a serious mistake. Rather, I believe that Pentecostals need to be told that the Word-Faith movement is Pentecostalism at its (near) worst, so as to encourage them to pursue a rich, mature, biblically sound Pentecostalism at its best.

This book is the culmination of about fifteen years of research, study, and dialogue. In that time I have had the opportunity to work with several Christian discernment ministries engaged in research into the Word-Faith movement. These ministries include the Christian Research Institute (CRI), where I worked first under the late Walter Martin and then under his successor, Hank Hanegraaff; the Atlanta Christian Apologetics Project (ACAP), headed by Donald Dicks; and Watchman Fellowship, an organization of countercult ministries with branch offices in several states, headed by James Walker.

Comments, questions, corrections, and criticisms are welcome. I may be contacted via e-mail at acts17@hotmail.com or by regular mail at P.O. Box 60511, Pasadena, CA 91116.

Introduction

The War of the Words

Under the banner "Jesus is Lord," multitudes are being duped by a gospel of greed and are embracing doctrines straight from the metaphysical cults. . . . The Faith movement is every bit as cultic as the teachings of the Mormons, the Jehovah's Witnesses, and Christian Science.

Hank Hanegraaff[1]

The day is coming when those that attack us will drop dead. You say, "What did you say?" I speak this under the anointing of the Spirit. Can I tell you something? Don't touch God's servants; it's deadly. . . . Woe to you that touch God's servants. You're going to pay.

Benny Hinn[2]

A gentle answer turns away wrath,
But a harsh word stirs up anger.
The tongue of the wise makes knowledge acceptable,
But the mouth of fools spouts folly.

Proverbs 15:1–2

If any of us are to learn anything in this controversy, we must decide to stop fighting each other with words. By that I do *not* mean that we should not criticize one another's doctrines or actions when we are honestly convinced that they are wrong. I mean that we must deal honestly and calmly with the issues and avoid inflammatory and exaggerated statements about those with whom we disagree. Unfortunately the debate over the Word-Faith teaching has been characterized up to now largely by sensationalistic attacks from both sides. In order to make this point clear to both sides (since each is likely to view the other as by far the more guilty), I will review some of the rhetoric that has been used in this debate.

The Rhetoric of the Word-Faith Teachers

I begin with the Word-Faith teachers and their supporters. It is a simple fact that the Word-Faith teachers initiated the war of words. Based on their belief that their ministry is a "move of God" to restore critical spiritual truths and experiences, the Word-Faith teachers routinely attack traditional Christianity in a variety of ways. For example, Kenneth Hagin asserts that his view of the anointing of the Holy Spirit has "not been properly understood . . . because we have been religiously brainwashed."[3] Likewise, Kenneth Copeland claims that his understanding of what happened to Christ between his death and resurrection is "necessary for the life of the Christian" but is "almost nonexistent in the traditional church teaching," suggesting this is "because it's been covered up and hidden in tradition."[4]

The fact that the Word-Faith teachers started this war of words is not an excuse to fire back with excessively harsh and sensationalized accusations. However, it does show that Christian apologists are right to defend historic Christianity against the verbal attacks of the Word-Faith movement. And this is generally what they are trying to do—albeit frequently with overheated rhetoric and, worse still, trumped-up charges in addition to legitimate complaints.

James Spencer, who defends the Word-Faith teachers in his book *Heresy Hunters,* is therefore wrong when he accuses the apologists of starting the war. He writes, "If a man commits a crime, you can't accuse the defense attorney of starting a fight."[5] I think Spencer means that if a man *is accused of* committing a crime, the defense attorney cannot be blamed for starting a fight. Fair enough. But on the flip side, if there is good reason to believe that a man really has committed a crime, you can't fairly accuse the prosecuting attorney of picking a fight. If the Word-Faith teachers have unfairly attacked traditional, orthodox Christianity, "bringing them up on charges" is a legitimate thing to do.

If I May Shock You . . .

One of the ways in which the Word-Faith teachers most frequently set their teaching against traditional Christianity is by "warning" their listeners that what they are about to reveal to them will be "shocking." Charles Capps, for example, writes the following: "This book may come as a shock to the religious mind. Don't read it with your religious eyeglasses on, for this book will take you on a scriptural journey that will shock the average churchgoer."[6]

Sometimes the Word-Faith teacher professes that he himself was shocked when he learned some new truth. Hagin, for example, tells a story about a vision of Jesus in which the Lord did nothing about a demon and Hagin himself was forced to command the demon to leave. Hagin concludes the story as follows:

> Jesus looked at me and said, "If you hadn't done something about that, I couldn't have." That came as a real shock to me—it astounded me. I replied, "Lord, I know I didn't hear you right! You said You *wouldn't*, didn't you?" He replied, "No, if you hadn't done something about that, I *couldn't* have." I went through this four times with Him. He was emphatic about it, saying, "No, I didn't say I *would* not, I said I *could* not."[7]

The Word-Faith teachers seem to enjoy telling shocking stories like these as well as making shocking doctrinal statements. Indeed, it seems that to be a Word-Faith teacher one is practically required to make such statements! Here's one from Fred Price, making a point similar to that made by Hagin's story: "Now this is a shocker! But God has to be given *permission* to work in this earth realm on behalf of man."[8]

Perhaps the boldest such "shock" statements have come from Kenneth Copeland. For example:

> And I say this with all respect, so that it don't upset you too bad, but I say it anyway: When I read in the Bible where He says, "I AM," I just smile and say, "Yes, I AM too."[9]

> I was shocked when I found out who the biggest failure in the Bible actually is. . . . The biggest one in the whole Bible is God.[10]

Of course, such statements have to be understood in their contexts, and in some cases the Word-Faith teachers mean something not *quite* as bizarre as these "shockers" suggest. (I will attempt to explain such statements in their context later in this book.) But the point is that the Word-Faith teachers *intend* to shock Christians with their teaching. They do it on purpose, and they go out of their way to point out that their teachings will be shocking.

When Benny Hinn was an avowed advocate of the Word-Faith doctrine, he emulated this aspect of its teaching style perfectly in what may be his most notorious theological statement: "See, God the Father is a person, God the Son is a person, God the Holy Ghost is a person; but each one of them is a triune being by Himself. If I can shock you, and maybe I should, there's nine of 'em."[11]

It is true that Hinn later told *Christianity Today* that this statement was "very dumb,"[12] and that he admitted on other occasions to making erroneous statements. Unfortunately within a short period of time he would go out and make similarly "dumb" statements. In fact, a year later he was teaching the same doctrine of God as three separate individuals with three separate bodies—although avoiding the ridiculous "nine of 'em" conclusion.[13]

Still, I give credit where it is due: Hinn is the only televangelist that I know of who has made such humbling admissions. We have yet to hear Hagin, Copeland, or any of the other Word-Faith televangelists recant any of their "shocking" and unbiblical statements.

Dire Consequences

Shocking statements are not the only way in which the Word-Faith teachers have allowed their rhetoric to get out of hand. The Word-Faith teachers often warn of dire consequences to Christians who reject their message. Kenneth Hagin claims that God told him that people will sometimes die because they reject his message:

> The Lord said to me, "If you give a message for an individual, a church, or a pastor, and they don't accept it, you will not be responsible. They will be responsible. There will be ministers who don't accept it and will fall dead in the pulpit."
>
> I say this with reluctance, but this actually happened in one place where I preached. Two weeks from the day that I closed the meeting, the pastor fell dead in the pulpit. . . . Why? Because he didn't accept the message that God gave me to give him from the Holy Spirit.[14]

The verbal responses of Word-Faith teachers to their critics have also at times been extremely vindictive and even dangerous. Shortly after Hinn made his "nine of 'em" statement and, understandably, received some pointed criticism for it, he issued the following warning to his critic:

> Somebody's attacking me because of something I'm teaching. Let me tell you something, brother: You watch it! . . . You know, I've looked for one verse in the Bible—I just can't seem to find it—one verse that said, "If you don't like them, kill them." I really wish I could find it! . . . You stink, frankly—that's the way I think about it. . . . Sometimes I wish God will give me a Holy Ghost machine gun—I'll blow your head off![15]

What concerns me about Hinn's tirade here is that even though he said he couldn't find a verse to justify killing his enemies, one of his devoted followers might have found one. Again, Hinn later confessed that he had spoken out of turn here. The problem is that such statements are highly dangerous and should be corrected just as publicly as they are made. Moreover, Hinn did not learn from his mistake, because a year later he was at it again, this time at a large convention:

> The day is coming when those that attack us will drop dead. You say, "What did you say?" I speak this under the anointing of the Spirit. Can I tell you something? Don't touch God's servants; it's deadly. . . . Woe to you that touch God's servants. You're going to pay.[16]

A similar public outburst on international television came from Paul Crouch, president of TBN. He had this to say on one occasion about the critics of the Word-Faith teaching:

> I think they're damned and on their way to hell and I don't think there's any redemption for them. . . . I say, to hell with you! Get out of my life! Get out of the way! . . . And I want to say to all you scribes, Pharisees, heresy hunters— all of you that are going around picking little bits of doctrinal error out of everybody's eyes. . . . Get out of God's way; quit blocking God's bridges, or God's going to shoot you if I don't. . . . Get out of my life! I don't even want to talk to you or hear you! I don't want to see your ugly face! Get out of my face in Jesus' name.[17]

Since Crouch's statements on this occasion were made in the heat of anger, it is possible that they do not reflect his considered opinion. On other occasions he has referred to the "heresy hunters" as brothers in Christ. On the other hand, one might suppose that his angry outburst reflects his real, unguarded opinion. Either way, this sort of intemperate judgment ought to have been retracted just as publicly and forcefully as it was made. Better still, it ought never to have been spoken in the first place.

The Rhetoric of the Critics

I wish I could say that the critics of the Word-Faith teaching did nothing to warrant such outbursts from the Word-Faith teachers. Unfortunately the critics often have made such outlandish accusations against the Word-Faith teachers that I can understand their anger (though I do not excuse their acting improperly on it).

Most of the books that have been written about the Word-Faith movement have painted its errors in black-and-white terms. Daniel R. McConnell's book *A Different Gospel* (a title that makes his position clear) argues that the Word-Faith movement is both "cultic" and "heretical."[18] Dave Hunt views the Word-Faith movement, along with the New Age movement and other occult trends, as "part of the delusion that is preparing us" for the coming Antichrist.[19] Judith Matta argues that "the Word-Faith teaching is perhaps the most subtle, heretical system to emerge in our own times"[20] and describes the Word-Faith movement as a modern "Gnostic cult."[21] Albert James Dager describes aspects of the Word-Faith teaching as "unconscionably blasphemous" and "witchcraft."[22] Rod Rosenbladt, writing in the book *The Agony of Deceit*, warns, "Virtually all of the leading American TV ministers have drunk at the trough of the esoteric, Swedenborgian, theosophical speculations of the late E. W. Kenyon."[23] John MacArthur (who is usually more restrained) concludes, "Word Faith doctrine is a mongrel system, a blend of mysticism, dualism, and neo-gnosticism that borrows generously from the teachings of the metaphysical cults."[24]

One of the harshest critics of the Word-Faith teaching, Hank Hanegraaff, denounces the Word-Faith teachers in the strongest possible language. In his book *Christianity in Crisis* he warns that "the church is in horrifying danger" as "multitudes are being duped by a gospel of greed and are embracing doctrines straight from the metaphysical cults," throwing Christianity "into a crisis of unparalleled proportions."[25] (He then assures us that he is "no alarmist"!) He goes on to assert, "The Faith movement is *every bit as cultic* as the teachings of the Mormons, the Jehovah's Witnesses, and Christian Science" (emphasis added).[26] The Word-Faith teaching is "a monstrous lie," "frightening," "madness," and "blasphemous," and its teachers are "spiritual charlatans."[27] Although Hanegraaff claims "it is truly difficult to overstate the horrifying implications of this worldview,"[28] one suspects that in fact he has done just that.

Occasionally critics of the Word-Faith teaching do offer some moderate concessions to "balance" their condemning rhetoric. Hanegraaff, for example, states that *"there are many sincere, born-again believers within the movement"* (his emphasis).[29] Most of the critics of the Word-Faith movement would agree. Unfortunately such concessive statements produce confusion, not balance. If the Word-Faith movement is "every bit as cultic as the teachings of the Mormons, the Jehovah's Witnesses, and Christian Science," and if it is a blasphemous, monstrous lie, how can its members be Christians? Does Hanegraaff think that there are "many sincere, born-again believers" among the Jehovah's Witnesses and the Mormons?

Of all the critics of the Word-Faith teaching who regard it as heretical, John MacArthur seemed to labor the hardest at striking a balance in his book *Charismatic Chaos*, as the following quotation attests:

> I hesitate to label the Word Faith movement a cult only because its boundaries are as yet somewhat hazy. Many sincere believers hover around the periphery of Word Faith teaching, and some in the movement who adhere to the core of Word Faith teaching reject some of the most extreme teachings of the group. Nevertheless, all the elements that are common to the cults exist within the movement. . . . Without some exacting corrections in the movement's doctrinal foundations, the movement is well on its way to being established as a false cult in every sense of the term.[30]

MacArthur was more cautious here than Hanegraaff, while still forcefully issuing his judgment that the Word-Faith movement is on its way to being a cult, if it is not already there. Such careful use of language is to be commended, whether or not one agrees with his assessment.

My point, in other words, is not to censure the critics for labeling the Word-Faith movement as heretical or cultic. By no means am I saying that it is always inappropriate to label false teachings as heretical, cultic, or blasphemous. I have no trouble, for instance, labeling the Jehovah's Witnesses a cult, or the United Pentecostal Church a heretical sect, or the teachings of Sun Myung Moon and his Unification Church as blasphemous. Nor am I timid to label someone within the orthodox church community a heretic (ultraliberals like John Shelby Spong come immediately to mind). Still, I would never write or speak about even outright cultic religions or heretics in the church in the harsh, mean-spirited way that some Christians have written and spoken about the Word-Faith movement.

In addition, I have some serious qualms about labeling the Word-Faith movement as cultic without at least some very serious qualifications. I shall make my reasons for these qualms clear as we proceed. But no matter what our assessment of the Word-Faith movement, we ought to express our conclusions in a gracious, judicious manner.

If the truth about the Word-Faith movement is to be known, we must approach the subject in a more dispassionate manner than has frequently been the case. Certainly there are important issues here, and we may and must be concerned about them. There is a place for expressing emotionally the seriousness of the errors that we find in the Word-Faith movement or anywhere else. But that place comes only after a careful, objective, and fair-minded effort to understand and evaluate the Word-Faith teaching on the basis of Scripture and in the light of the historic Christian faith. Anything less would be folly (Prov. 18:13) and contrary to Christian love (Matt. 7:12).

One last point: Although my goal in this book is to model a biblical balance of tough-minded forthrightness about the Word-Faith teaching and tenderhearted concern and respect toward the people in the Word-Faith movement, I do not expect to do this perfectly. I myself have had to grow in this area over the years, and I anticipate that I have more growing ahead of me. If I make statements that are uncharitable or inflammatory, I hope they will be pointed out to me. If I misunderstand or misrepresent the Word-Faith teaching—either by making it sound worse than it is or by making it sound better than it is—I hope someone will point out my error to me. This is a complex subject, and there is room for reasonable differences of opinion on some aspects of the debate. On the other hand, there is no room for excessive dogmatism or vindictive rhetoric. Let's stop fighting in carnal fashion and let's start "speaking the truth in love" (Eph. 4:15).

PART 1

The Roots
of the
Word-Faith
Movement

1

Understanding
the Word-Faith Teaching

Once upon a time, long long ago, on a faraway planet, there lived a good God. . . . Because Jesus was re-created from a satanic being to an incarnation of God, you too can become an incarnation—as much an incarnation as was Jesus of Nazareth! And, as an incarnation of God, you can have unlimited health and unlimited wealth—a palace like the Taj Mahal with a Rolls Royce in your driveway. You are a little messiah running around on earth! All it takes is to recognize your own divinity.

> Hank Hanegraaff (summarizing the Word-Faith teaching)[1]

It seems our friends, the book writers, have invented an entirely new theology called the "born again Jesus" built upon a conglomeration of quotations taken from 6 or 7 ministers, pulled out of context, and combined as though we all believed identically the same thing or were even speaking about the same subject when quoted (which, in some cases, we were not). And the reader is told we all believe this "born again Jesus" theology, believe exactly alike about it, and we're all heretics. Yet I am diametrically opposed to some of the doctrines held by those who are quoted on the same page as me!

> Kenneth E. Hagin[2]

He who gives an answer before he hears,
It is folly and shame to him.

> Proverbs 18:13

If we are to evaluate the Word-Faith teaching, we first need to understand it. As Solomon counseled, "He who gives an answer before he hears, it is folly and shame to him" (Prov. 18:13). We need to grasp the Word-Faith theology as a whole and understand how it all fits together from the perspective of the Word-Faith teachers if we are to make an intelligent decision as to whether it is biblical. Moreover, we need to look at the movement from all sides and consider it from every relevant angle in order to make our assessment as complete and balanced as possible. In this chapter I will set forth an agenda for such a complete assessment and then explain the Word-Faith teaching in order to make its basic message understandable.

The Roots, Shoots, and Fruits

A complete evaluation of any movement's teachings requires that we look at three aspects of the teachings, which may be called the roots, shoots, and fruits of a doctrine.[3]

Exposing the Roots

The *roots* of a doctrine are the sources or origins of the teachings. Did the ideas come from the Bible? Did they come from the biblically based teaching of a sound Christian teacher? Did they come from a source that is clearly cultic or non-Christian? Or did they come from a mixture of all three types of sources? If certain ideas can be traced to non-Christian or cultic roots, how were these ideas transferred?

An examination of the "roots" of a teaching is never sufficient by itself, because non-Christians, after all, can express truths and can have genuine insights. It is perfectly fine for a Christian teacher to "plunder the Egyptians" by taking over ideas or formulations found in non-Christian thought and putting them into a soundly Christian context. So we must be careful not to argue that a particular doctrine is false *merely* because a cultist or other non-Christian advocated it. In logic this is called the *genetic fallacy*— attempting to dismiss an idea on the basis of its genesis, or origin.

William DeArteaga, in his book defending the Word-Faith movement, claims that Daniel R. McConnell's critique of the Word-Faith teaching commits the "genetic fallacy" by arguing that "Hagin derived his teachings from Kenyon, who in turn was associated with the Metaphysical movement."[4] DeArteaga calls this error "the pharisaical objection of origins," referring to his belief that the Pharisees erred by rejecting any workings of the Spirit that contradicted their theology or which they could not explain.[5] This is an odd theory: the Pharisees never criticized Jesus' teachings for supposedly deriving from a suspect source (say, that Jesus got his ideas from the pagan Greeks). They did accuse him of having a demon (Matt. 9:34; 12:24; John 7:20; 8:48, 52; 10:20), but this is a "genetic" argument of a very different sort! Setting aside this strange reference to the Pharisees, DeArteaga's criticism overlooks the fact that McConnell explicitly denies trying to discredit the Word-Faith teaching by a simple exposé of its origins:

> The historical origins of the Faith movement are not enough, however, to justify the charge of cultism. That would be an example of theological guilt by mere historical association. To prove cultism requires that it be demonstrated in no uncertain terms that the beliefs and practices of the contemporary Faith movement (not just those of Kenyon) are both cultic and heretical. . . . The Faith movement is cultic not just because of where it comes from, but also because of what it teaches.[6]

DeArteaga elsewhere shows that he does take the question of the origins of the Word-Faith teaching to be relevant. In answer to McConnell, he argues that Kenyon's doctrines of revelation-knowledge and of the Christian life are not really Gnostic at all but are instead rooted in the theology of the apostle Paul.[7]

If the genetic fallacy is to be avoided, then why examine the roots at all? There are two reasons for doing so. First, sometimes teachers will misrepresent the source of their teachings in order to exaggerate their own originality or because the true sources are a potential embarrassment to them. In some cases professing Christian teachers have been known to plagiarize whole sermons or books from various cultic or questionable sources. Obviously, if they pass off as new insights or revelations from God ideas that they actually lifted word for word from a non-Christian or cultic writer, this constitutes a serious problem. Exposing these teachers' lack of honesty in this area serves its own purpose independent of evaluating the teachings themselves.

Here again, DeArteaga argues that McConnell has criticized Kenneth Hagin unjustly by accusing him of plagiarism. According to DeArteaga, "McConnell also accuses Hagin of passing off his theology as pure 'revelation knowledge' without *any* credits to human sources" (emphasis added).

DeArteaga points to the preface of *The Name of Jesus* in which Hagin acknowledges drawing on Kenyon's *The Wonderful Name of Jesus* as proof that McConnell is wrong.[8] Yet McConnell himself quotes Hagin's preface and comments, "This is one of the few candid, direct acknowledgments of Kenyon to appear in any of Hagin's writings."[9] McConnell also observes that "Hagin demonstrates the ability to give credit where credit is due with regard to the sources that he drew on to develop a particular idea," *except* concerning those sources from which he plagiarized extensively.[10] His contention is simply that Hagin's repeated, massive plagiarism of the writings of Kenyon, along with those of John A. MacMillan, demonstrate that Hagin's claim to have learned the Word-Faith teaching directly from visitations and revelations from God is patently false. DeArteaga's criticisms of McConnell in this matter are not cogent.

Second, identifying the source of someone's questionable doctrines can aid us in pinpointing the real problems in those doctrines. If certain doctrinal errors have been taught before and have been answered by sound Christian teachers, then finding these antecedents can be very helpful in identifying and refuting the errors. Discovering the true roots of the Word-Faith teaching, once it is shown to be unbiblical and damaging to authentic Christian faith, will then aid us in getting to the core of the problem. It will also enable us to be better on guard against similar errors in the future.

Again, we do not expose the roots of a doctrine to prove it false. We examine the roots to help us diagnose the problems and prescribe a cure.

Examining the Shoots

The second aspect of any doctrine is the substance or idea of the doctrine itself. This is what for convenience I call the *shoots*, though it would be more precise to talk about the trunk and branches. More technically, the shoots of a doctrine are the doctrine itself *as* a doctrine—what the doctrine says in theory and the arguments or reasons given in its support.

Most of the time, we identify a tree by its shoots. That is, we can usually tell what sort of a tree it is simply by looking at its overall appearance as shaped primarily by its trunk and branches. A quick glance at the shoots of a fir tree is enough to determine that it is not an oak.

Examining doctrines is often not as easy, of course, because doctrines are not tangible entities that can be perceived with a single glance. What we purpose to do in examining a doctrine, though, is not merely to identify it but also to evaluate its soundness and strength. When examining a tree, for example, we would check various branches to see if they are strong and well connected to the trunk. If there was some doubt about the health of the tree, we might cut through the bark to examine the interior of the wood. When examining a doctrine, we would test its soundness and strength by examining the reasoning used to support the conclusion and seeing if that reasoning is firmly based on the Bible.

Examining the shoots, then, comes down to comparing the contemporary teachings with the teachings of the Bible. The Word-Faith teachers tend to resist this kind of critical examination, offering various reasons why their teachings should not be critiqued. I have evaluated these objections to doctrinal discernment in *Orthodoxy and Heresy*.[11] Here I will point out simply that this sort of study is strongly encouraged in the Bible itself (see Matt. 22:29; Acts 17:11; 2 Tim. 3:16). It is the basic method used by Christians throughout the centuries to test novel and controversial teachings as they have arisen in the church.

Looking at the Fruits

The third and final aspect of testing a doctrine is to look at its *fruit*. This test is perhaps the best known because of the words of Jesus regarding false prophets: "You will know them by their fruits" (Matt. 7:16, 20). Unfortunately these words are among the most abused words in Scripture. They are all too commonly cited to prove that testing someone's teachings by comparing them with Scripture is either unnecessary or illegitimate. Yet this claim is itself a doctrine that people try to prove by citing Scripture!

What Jesus says here is absolutely true: One can know a false prophet by his or her "fruits." We need to ask, though, what is included, and what is not, in these fruits. One thing Jesus makes very clear in the context is that prophetic utterances and miracles are *not* included (Matt. 7:22). This is important because Word-Faith teachers and those who support them often point to stories of healings, apparent supernatural revelations, and other amazing incidents as proof that God has blessed their ministry. But Jesus *specifically excludes such things* from the "fruits" by which we would be able to tell a false prophet from a true one.

On the other hand, Jesus does not discourage testing doctrines by comparing them with Scripture. Indeed, his focus is not on the truth or falsity of a particular doctrine but on the divine calling of a professed prophet. The purpose of the test is to tell apart true and false prophets, both of whom seem to speak in the name of the Lord (Matt. 7:21–22). The implication is that a true prophet must represent the Lord truly both in word *and* in action. Thus the point here is not that true prophets can say anything they want as long as their outward lives are good. Rather, it is that a prophet is false if his fruit is evil, no matter how good or true his words seem to be.

A short while later in the same passage, Jesus contrasts the wise person with the foolish person. The wise person acts on Jesus' *words*, while the foolish person fails to do so (Matt. 7:24–27). The implication is that one may and should compare people's actions to the words of Jesus to see whether their actions are wise or foolish.

One bad fruit that is always produced by false prophets is confusion and division. When false prophets come along and teach false doctrines or make false claims, it is their fault when confusion and division ensue. It is certainly not the fault of those who oppose their unbiblical teachings.

The sum of the matter is this. The test Jesus sets forth in Matthew 7 is intended to expose false prophets. It is not the only such test, but it is a valid and crucial test. It cannot be used to avoid responsibility to teach doctrine that is faithful to the same Bible in which this test appears. False and unsound doctrine always contradicts biblical doctrine and results in bad fruit.[12]

On Defining the Word-Faith Teaching

Before explaining the Word-Faith teaching, I need to say some things about the approach taken here. In discussing this subject with advocates of the Word-Faith teaching and with its critics, I have learned that how one approaches the discussion virtually determines whether communication and understanding will ever take place.

Is There a "Word-Faith Teaching"?

Some people object to any critique of the "Word-Faith teaching" on two grounds. First, it is sometimes said that the Word-Faith teachers are evangelists, healers, prophets, or pastors, not teachers or theologians, and that they should not be judged as if they were theologians. Second, it has been argued that the critics of the Word-Faith movement have created a strawman "Word-Faith teaching" from statements taken out of context or shoehorned into a theology that none of the Word-Faith teachers espouse. We are told that the Word-Faith teachers differ markedly on a number of doctrinal points, so that the doctrine attributed to them as a group is an artificial construct of the critics' own imagination.

It is, of course, true that none of the Word-Faith teachers is a systematic theologian or even a methodical teacher whose theological "system" is easily encapsulated from his writings. This does not mean, however, that the Word-Faith leaders are not teachers. Whatever they may see as their primary calling, when they regularly present teaching on matters of Christian belief, they make themselves teachers. It is silly to say that individuals who teach doctrine on television and radio, write books and magazine articles, and disseminate video and audiotapes of their messages on doctrinal topics are not teachers.

In any case, at least some of these men *do* claim to be teachers. Kenneth Hagin, who claims that his primary calling is to the ministry of a prophet, also claims to serve in the ministry of a teacher. Thus it is perfectly appropriate to hold the Word-Faith teachers to a higher standard of doctrinal accuracy than we do persons in ministry who do not presume to teach doctrine (James 3:1).[13]

As for the second objection, it simply is not true that the Word-Faith teachers have no theological system. The lack of a formal Word-Faith "systematic theology" does not mean that there is no structural or thematic unity in their teaching. If a Word-Faith teacher's teaching is at all coherent or consistent, it should be possible to systematize his teachings in order to bring out its coherence and essential ideas. If such systematization is not possible, it only goes to show that his teaching is chaotic and therefore that he is a poor teacher.

Kenneth Hagin has complained that the theology attributed to him and other Word-Faith teachers is an invention of the critics (see the quotation at the beginning of this chapter). Hagin's objection has some justice, but the legitimate point he is making should not be exaggerated. There is a core of doctrinal teaching that makes the Word-Faith movement distinctive and identifiable, a core of teaching to which the Word-Faith televangelists generally subscribe and that sets them apart from other Christian traditions. I agree that some of the critics of the Word-Faith teachers have erred in superimposing on the Word-Faith movement a greater degree of unity than is actually there. But the error of this extreme does not justify the opposite extreme of denying any distinctive doctrinal unity in the movement.

In this chapter, then, I will attempt to state that core theology of the Word-Faith movement. It may be that some Word-Faith advocates will disagree somewhat with the way their doctrine is presented here, but I believe that overall this presentation of the Word-Faith theology is accurate and representative of their teachings.

How Shall the Word-Faith Teaching Be Defined?

It is easy to make the Word-Faith doctrine sound silly or absurd. Indeed, one can do so by just stringing together a number of the more colorful statements that have been made by Word-Faith teachers. When critics of the movement do this and then fill in the gaps with their own interpretative embellishments, the result is a caricature.

This is the problem, as I see it, with the way in which the Word-Faith teaching is represented in the section titled "Once Upon a Time . . ." in

Hank Hanegraaff's *Christianity in Crisis*.[14] Hanegraaff himself makes the following admission in a prefatory note in very small print:

> The following tale is *a composite* of the erroneous teachings of individuals like Benny Hinn, Kenneth Copeland, Kenneth Hagin, Frederick Price, and many others. While not all the Faith teachers hold to every aspect of this tale, they have all made substantial contributions to both the production and the proliferation of these aberrations and heresies. (emphasis added)[15]

What Hanegraaff fails to acknowledge, unfortunately, is that *none* of the Word-Faith teachers "holds to every aspect of this tale." The "composite" fails to represent accurately the views of *any* of the Word-Faith teachers, because none of them holds to the whole thing. Moreover, some of the elements of this "composite" are not held by *any* of the Word-Faith teachers but are Hanegraaff's own imaginative and colorful additions. Hanegraaff describes the Word-Faith teachers' God as hoping to get "lucky." He describes the Jesus of the Word-Faith teaching as becoming "a satanic being" when he died. He claims that the Word-Faith teaching asserts that Christians can have "a palace like the Taj Mahal. . . . All it takes is to recognize your own divinity."[16] These descriptions, however, make the Word-Faith movement sound more akin to Eastern religions or the New Age movement than it really is. In truth *none of the Word-Faith teachers ever talk this way.*

This way of presenting the Word-Faith teaching, while it has shock value, unnecessarily offends those who embrace the Word-Faith teaching. Just as we would not want our beliefs to be misrepresented, we must be careful not to misrepresent the beliefs of those in the Word-Faith movement (Matt. 7:12). When they hear the views of their favorite televangelists being exaggerated or sensationalized, they use that to dismiss out of hand the many valid criticisms of the Word-Faith teaching that critics offer.

We must never lose sight of the fact that many persons do, after all, find in the Word-Faith doctrine a convincing and coherent message. I will therefore be presenting the teaching in such a form as I think a systematically minded advocate of the Word-Faith teaching might articulate it. What I have attempted to do here is to set forth the Word-Faith teaching in the *best* possible light, focusing on the most prominent and essential aspects of that teaching. This way, what is being refuted is not the *worst* possible representation of the teaching but the doctrine at its *best*.[17]

I hasten to add that the more colorful and extreme ideas that have been taught by Word-Faith teachers are certainly, in and of themselves, fair targets for criticism. I will be critiquing some of them in this book. But these more outlandish ideas need to be placed *fairly* in the context of the Word-Faith teaching.

In order to be as fair to the Word-Faith movement as possible, I will base my exposition of its teaching solely on the words of Kenneth Hagin and Kenneth Copeland. Since these two men are the undisputed leaders of the Word-Faith movement, any doctrine to which *both* of them subscribe may be safely regarded as part of the Word-Faith teaching. With one important exception, I have avoided mentioning in this summary any doctrine taught by only one, and not the other, of these two men. Persons who acknowledge Hagin or Copeland as teachers and who accept the general ideas of the Word-Faith teaching, even if they deviate in one or a few particulars, may also be regarded as part of the Word-Faith movement.

What follows, then, is a summary of the theology of the Word-Faith movement, including the doctrinal issues that will be explored later in this book.

Human Beings Are Spirits

Basic to the Word-Faith theology is a particular understanding of human nature as spirit, soul, and body. Spirit is more real than the physical, according to the Word-Faith teaching, and therefore the spirit is the real person. It is the spirit that is made in God's image, allowing the Word-Faith teachers to conclude that human beings are exact duplicates of God, or little gods.

Furthermore, it is the spirit to which God communicates (not the mind), and the spirit that is supposed to control the soul and especially the body. The problem with the human race is that we are allowing our bodies to control our lives, or our reason to dictate to our spirits, rather than having our spirits take control over our whole beings. This is fundamental for the Word-Faith teachers, since in their view we should disbelieve our senses when they tell us we are sick or poor, and disbelieve our reason when it tells us that the Word-Faith teaching is illogical or false (see chapter 6).

God and Humanity

According to the Word-Faith teachers, God is much more like a man than Christians generally have supposed. God is a God of faith; he created the world by faith and accomplishes all that he desires by believing in his heart and speaking the word of faith, thereby bringing things into existence (see chapter 7).

There is another respect in which Word-Faith teaching makes God more like a man than is traditionally thought. Although God is in essence a spirit, the Word-Faith teachers hold that God, like human beings, is spirit, soul, *and body*—albeit a "spirit body" (see chapter 8).

Likewise, the Word-Faith teachers insist that human beings are much more like God than Christians have usually believed. Our creation in God's image is interpreted to mean that we exist in God's "class" as the same kind of being as God, though on a smaller scale (as "little gods"). Moreover, the purpose of the coming of Jesus was to restore humanity to godhood by creating a new race of humans who, like Jesus, would be God incarnate (see chapter 9).

Humanity's potential as little gods was, according to the Word-Faith teaching, thwarted by the fall. Adam forfeited his status as the god of this world by obeying the devil and thereby making Satan the god of this world. In sinning, Adam gave Satan legal dominion over this world and passed Satan's nature of death, with its corresponding symptoms of sickness and poverty, down to the rest of humanity (see chapter 10).

Jesus Christ

To correct the situation arising from the fall, God, according to Word-Faith theology, implemented a strategy for reclaiming dominion from the devil. The centerpiece of this strategy was his becoming a man. Although Word-Faith teachers affirm that Jesus Christ was God incarnate, their understanding of what this incarnation meant is in some respects highly unusual.

First, all Word-Faith teachers argue that Christians are just as much "incarnations of God" as was Jesus Christ. This implies that "incarnation" in Word-Faith teaching does not mean the same thing it means in traditional Christian usage. Much of what the Word-Faith teachers say suggests that in their view anyone who is indwelled by the Spirit is an incarnation.

Second, Word-Faith teachers are not altogether clear as to whether it was the preexistent, eternal Son of God who became incarnate. Some Word-Faith teachers, such as Hagin, seem to assume this traditional, biblical view. Others, though, notably Kenneth Copeland and Charles Capps, teach that the Word that became incarnate was God's Word of promise that he would redeem humanity, and that this Word was "positively confessed" into personal existence by the Virgin Mary (see chapter 11).

The Word-Faith teachers also have a distinctive view of what Christ did to effect our salvation. In their view, what Jesus did that was unique was to die, not merely physically but spiritually as well (thus taking on himself Satan's nature), and go to hell. There, they say, he was "born again," rising from the dead with God's nature (which, it is sometimes implied, he had lost in dying spiritually). By doing so, the Word-Faith teachers argue, Jesus paved the way for us to be born again and exhibit God's nature in our lives (see chapter 12).

As has already been mentioned, the Word-Faith teachers tend to interpret the incarnation as the prototype of God's Spirit dwelling in a human being. In this sense, they insist, Christians are as much an incarnation of God as was Jesus Christ. This lends support, in their view, to the claim that all Christians ought to be able to overcome difficulties in their lives and perform miracles in just the same way Jesus did. In principle any of us can do anything that Jesus did on earth (see chapter 13).

Faith, Prayer, and Confession

The distinctive ideas about God and man in Word-Faith theology are the basis for its views on faith and prayer. Faith is not only believing what God says but also believing that we have whatever we say. Prayer is not only speaking to God but also speaking to things and circumstances and commanding them to do as we say. This is the basis for the concept of positive and negative confession, the idea that what we believe and say, whether good or bad, will happen for us (see chapter 14).

On the basis of a positive confession—itself based on faith that we are divine spirits created and redeemed to rule our circumstances by speaking words of faith—Word-Faith theology says we are to obtain health and wealth. Since Christ died to free us from the curse of the law, reason the Word-Faith teachers, this must mean that Christians need no longer accept sickness or poverty in their lives. Christians ought to live in divine health and wealth as testimony to the power of God and as evidence that they are children of God (see chapter 15).

This is the Word-Faith theology to be studied in this book. For the most part, my focus will not be on the personalities who promote these views but on the biblical teachings that are relevant to evaluating the Word-Faith theology. However, in order to understand the teachings fully, we need to consider how they arose and know something about their sources. The next four chapters will deal with just these questions.

2

The Man behind the Message

Most of the failures of the Metaphysical movement occurred, according to Kenyon, because of the rejection of revelation knowledge (the Bible). . . . To Kenyon, Christians can move mountains by faith and have not done so because we have not taken the Bible at its face value. It was as if he had been the first Christian to read the book of Acts and the epistles and take every word literally.

William DeArteaga[1]

The facade of orthodoxy created by Kenyon's biblical proof-texting and evangelical jargon make the cultic elements in the Faith movement even more dangerous than a blatantly heretical cult, which would have been detected by charismatics long ago.

D. R. McConnell[2]

The first to plead his case seems just,
Until another comes and examines him.

Proverbs 18:17

The Word-Faith teaching did not arise in a vacuum. But many disagree as to its true origins. The Word-Faith advocates themselves, if they acknowledge any human precedent to their teaching, almost always single out Kenneth E. Hagin, a televangelist commonly acknowledged as the "father" of the Word-Faith teaching. Hagin himself claims to have received the teaching directly from God. Critics of the teaching, on the other hand, have usually focused on just one source of Hagin's doctrine—a man named E. W. Kenyon.

As I shall attempt to demonstrate, the truth seems to be that a number of important figures were responsible for bringing about the Word-Faith movement and its theology. Among these individuals, though, the most important by far is indeed Kenyon. His importance is so great, in fact, that I shall have to devote this and the following two chapters to a discussion of Kenyon and his role in the origins of the Word-Faith movement.

E. W. Kenyon: Grandfather of the Word-Faith Movement

Essek William Kenyon (1867–1948) lived before the age of television and so was not a televangelist. He was, however, the closest thing: a radio evangelist. As an evangelist, pastor, and writer, Kenyon originated much of the doctrinal substance, and even the terminology and expressions, of the Word-Faith movement. His influence is so great that D. R. McConnell has called Kenyon "the true father of the modern faith movement."[3] Likewise Hank Hanegraaff asserts that Kenyon "is the real father of the modern-day Word-Faith movement and that 'Dad' Hagin merely popularized his material."[4] William DeArteaga, who views Kenyon positively, agrees: "The pioneer theologian and true father of the contemporary Word-Faith movement was E. W. Kenyon."[5] I think this might be a little too strong; I would prefer to call Kenyon the *grandfather* of the Word-Faith movement. But in any case these writers are right about the importance of Kenyon for the movement.

The essential facts of Kenyon's life are these.[6] Kenyon was a New Englander who lived in Boston during the early 1890s. During that time he was exposed to the teaching of various evangelical Christian and New Thought leaders. (New Thought was one branch of the metaphysical or "mind science" movement that included Christian Science and the Unity School of Christianity—and is clearly heretical.) In 1893 Kenyon became a Baptist pastor, and in 1898 he started a Bible school. Although Kenyon was a Baptist and rejected the distinctives of Pentecostal doctrine, his teaching was well received among Pentecostals. In the 1920s he was a popular speaker in the meetings of Aimee Semple McPherson and other Pentecostal evangelists. Kenyon was also one of the first radio evangelists, his most famous program being *Kenyon's Church of the Air* broadcast from Seattle in the 1930s.

Kenyon's exposure to New Thought and his connections with the Pentecostal movement raise an important question. To what extent was Kenyon's theology influenced by New Thought? Were his distinctive doctrinal ideas taken straight from the metaphysical cults, or was their origination more complex? Or, to look at the question from a different perspective, to what extent was Kenyon's teaching compatible with Pentecostalism? Was his teaching an alien, cultic intrusion into Pentecostalism, or did it fit fairly comfortably into that context?

These questions are now hotly debated. The matter is sufficiently complex that I will devote the entire next two chapters to it. Here we may begin rather modestly with this observation: However alien Kenyon's theology may have been in certain respects, his teaching was widely received within Pentecostalism, particularly by that segment of the movement especially concerned with faith healing.

Most of the core theological distinctives of the Word-Faith movement can be traced back from Kenneth Hagin directly to E. W. Kenyon. The following doctrines of the Word-Faith teaching either originated from Kenyon or received their distinctive formulation from him:

- Human nature is spirit, soul, and body, but is most fundamentally spirit.
- God created the world by speaking words of faith and does everything else by faith, and we are intended to exercise the same kind of faith.
- In the fall human beings took on Satan's nature and forfeited to Satan their divine dominion, making him the legal god of this world.
- Jesus died spiritually as well as physically, taking on Satan's nature and suffering in hell to redeem us, and then was born again.
- By our positive confession with the God kind of faith we may overcome sickness and poverty.

As McConnell has argued, and as shall be confirmed in subsequent chapters in this book, Hagin took over these doctrines from Kenyon not only in substance but also in language, going so far as to plagiarize from Kenyon's books. Clearly, then, much if not most of the distinctive Word-Faith teachings originate in their formulations from Kenyon.

There are, on the other hand, some aspects of the Word-Faith theology as taught by Hagin, Copeland, and most of the modern Word-Faith teachers that differ from the teaching of Kenyon. For one thing, Hagin has put the Word-Faith teaching into an *explicitly* Pentecostal or charismatic context. For Hagin and his disciples, the baptism of the Holy Spirit and speaking in tongues are essential to a fully developed Christian experience.[7]

The modern Word-Faith teaching also differs from Kenyon in more distinctive ways. For instance, Kenyon did not hold that God has a body. Also, while Kenyon did speak of created and redeemed humanity as sharing in some sense in God's "nature," he evidently did not speak of human beings as "gods," "little gods," "exact duplicates of God," or the like. In general, Kenyon attributed divine characteristics to human beings more carefully and cautiously than Hagin and (especially) Copeland do. Kenyon's views on prosperity were also more moderate than the views of most modern Word-Faith teachers (though Hagin's views on this subject do not go far beyond Kenyon's).

In short, Kenyon is the source of most, but not all, of the distinctive and controversial teachings of the Word-Faith movement. Moreover, on at least some important points the Word-Faith teachers have developed Kenyon's teaching beyond anything that he taught. This is the main reason why I call Kenyon the grandfather, not the father, of the Word-Faith movement. The other reason is that other individuals played an important role in the origins of the Word-Faith movement. I discuss the contribution of these men in chapter 5. But if some critics have focused a bit too exclusively on Kenyon as the father of the movement, those who completely deny his involvement or who ignore or minimize it are guilty of a far greater error.

Two Views of Origins

Kenyon's role as the grandfather of the movement raises the question of the roots of the Word-Faith teaching—an issue that has been fiercely debated.

One school of thought sees the Word-Faith movement as simply an extension—if a more radical or extreme one—of the larger Pentecostal/ charismatic movement. On this view the Word-Faith theology is an essentially Pentecostal one. This is the accepted view among adherents and friends of the Word-Faith movement. The Word-Faith teachers themselves view their teaching and movement as the latest "move of God" within the Pentecostal and charismatic tradition. Friendly observers who express criti-

cisms of varying severity of the Word-Faith teaching all view it as authentically Pentecostal. These would include William DeArteaga,[8] a charismatic
whose criticisms are fairly mild, and Charles Farah,[9] a charismatic whose
criticisms have been slightly sharper. In his 1987 book *The Health and Wealth
Gospel*, Bruce Barron took a similar view, criticizing the movement's extremes but arguing that with some "fine-tuning" its teachings could have
great value.[10] In a book review Barron more recently expressed a harsher
view of the Word-Faith movement but did not indicate whether his view
of the movement's origins had changed.[11]

On the other side, most if not all of the critics of the Word-Faith teaching have so far denied that Kenyon's distinctive theology originated from
Pentecostalism or any other stream of orthodox Christian belief. Instead,
they trace Kenyon's Word-Faith theology to the metaphysical or mind-
science cults, specifically the New Thought teaching to which Kenyon was
exposed in Boston during the 1890s. This theory of the origins of Kenyon's
teaching was introduced by various writers around 1980,[12] was popularized by Dave Hunt in the mid-1980s,[13] and is defended by Hank Hanegraaff.[14] McConnell's book *A Different Gospel*, based on his 1982 master's
thesis at Oral Roberts University,[15] is devoted entirely to defending the New
Thought theory, arguing that Hagin's theology derived directly from
Kenyon's and Kenyon's in turn derived from New Thought.[16] Other critics of the Word-Faith teaching have also characterized Kenyon's theology
as metaphysical. According to Curtis Crenshaw, the Word-Faith movement
and the mind-science cults alike "have repeated the errors of gnosticism,
adopting as their theology the ideas of the metaphysical cults that arose
from 1830 to 1860 in New England and became very popular in the latter
part of the 1800s."[17]

Complex Roots?

Although most of the polemical writings on the subject argue that the
Word-Faith theology is rooted in *either* the metaphysical cults *or* the Pentecostal and charismatic tradition, it is possible that a more complex situation is the historical reality. One writer who suggested this idea was Robert
Jackson, a British author who noted that while Kenyon was not a Pentecostal, the modern Word-Faith movement is. Jackson followed McConnell
in characterizing Kenyon as having developed "a 'Christianized' metaphysical cult,"[18] yet he sees Word-Faith practice as more Pentecostal. He
concludes, "Thus, while the doctrines are undoubtedly those of Kenyon,
very often the practices are those of the charismatic Pentecostals."[19]

Another writer who also seems to recognize a more complex situation
is John MacArthur. In his systematic critique of charismatic Christianity,

MacArthur regularly cites Hagin, Copeland, and other Word-Faith tel-evangelists and writers as evidence of the errors to which he argues that charismatic religion is prone.[20] At the beginning of his chapter on the Word-Faith movement, MacArthur says that it was "spawned" by "the charismatic movement" and that it "is a subdivision of the charismatic movement."[21] At the end of the same chapter MacArthur writes:

> Why is that [Hagin's plagiarism of Kenyon] significant? Because McConnell also reveals that Kenyon's roots were in the metaphysical cults. He was a faith-healer, not in the Pentecostal tradition, but in the tradition of Mary Baker Eddy and Christian Science. . . . In short, McConnell's book . . . demonstrates irrefutably that Word Faith teachers owe their ancestry to groups like Christian Science, Swedenborgianism, Theosophy, Science of Mind, and New Thought—not to classical Pentecostalism.[22]

Less than a page later MacArthur returns to his earlier statement that the Word-Faith movement "has grown out of the charismatic movement."[23] In his conclusion he again refers to the Word-Faith teaching as having been "bred by the charismatic movement" and expresses his conviction that the errors of the Word-Faith teaching, though rejected by many charismatic Christians, "are inherent in the very doctrines that distinguish the charismatic position."[24]

As it stands MacArthur's position appears contradictory. Is the Word-Faith movement a part of the charismatic tradition, spawned, bred, and grown there, with its errors rooted in the distinctive beliefs of charismatic Christianity? Or is it a metaphysical movement rooted not in classical Pentecostalism but in the cultic doctrines of groups like Christian Science and New Thought?

While MacArthur's position as stated is contradictory, it is also suggestive. Perhaps the origins of the Word-Faith movement are more complex than drawing a straight line to either Pentecostalism or the metaphysical movement. Perhaps both traditions contributed significantly to the Word-Faith teaching.

A more sophisticated analysis of the roots of Kenyon's thought is presented by Dale Simmons in a recently published revision of his doctoral dissertation. According to Simmons, the studies critical of Kenyon have failed to take into account his roots in the evangelical "Higher Life" and faith-cure traditions of the late nineteenth century. Simmons maintains that "a thorough investigation of Kenyon's writings makes it clear that both the teachings of the Higher Christian Life movement and New Thought played a central role in the development of his own thought."[25] More specifically, Simmons regards Kenyon as belonging within the Higher Life tradition, though stressing certain ideas in a way more characteristic of New

Thought. Ironically, Simmons argues that these two religious traditions were not nearly as far apart then as they seem to be now.[26]

Taking a Fresh Look

Settling the question of the roots of the Word-Faith teaching is certainly not all-determinative. It is just possible, even if its distinctive ideas originated from a cultic, metaphysical source, that the ideas are nevertheless biblically acceptable. On the other hand, even if the ideas of the Word-Faith teaching originate primarily within a Christian religious context, they might be authentically Christian or they might be unbiblical and heretical deviations or perversions of Christian ideas.

My point is that we should not allow our desire either to condemn the Word-Faith teaching or to defend it to prejudice our thinking on its origins. We should, instead, try to examine the overall evidence as fairly as we can. Only after examining the origins of the doctrine and comparing it with Scripture should any judgments be formed about its alleged Christian or cultic character.

The method I will use here is as follows: In chapter 3 we will consider the historical and theological relationship between Kenyon and New Thought. Next, in chapter 4 we will consider the relationship between Kenyon and the Pentecostal and related healing movements. Finally, in chapter 5 we will note the contributions that others besides Kenyon have made to the rise of the modern Word-Faith teaching. We will conclude our study of the roots of the Word-Faith movement by attempting to integrate these three lines of study and draw some conclusions that do justice to all of the evidence.

3

A Metaphysical Mind-Set?

Although it seems to be a harsh charge to call the Positive Confession movement a charismatic form of Christian Science, which in turn is an Ameri-
canized version of Hinduism, that charge has been made by many and can
be substantiated by simply comparing the similarities in their common beliefs.

Dave Hunt[1]

Hunt never stops to consider whether what Kenyon said was biblically valid
and, therefore, a positive and useful influence on Kenneth Hagin. He only
reveals that Kenyon was a New Thought writer so whatever Kenyon said
must be heretical.

William DeArteaga[2]

See to it that no one takes you captive through philosophy and empty deception, according to the tradition of men, according to the elementary principles of the world, rather than according to Christ.

Colossians 2:8

Two factors must be considered in determining the relationship of
Kenyon's thought to that of the metaphysical movement in general and
New Thought in particular: (1) Kenyon's associations with and attitudes

43

toward metaphysical thought, and (2) the parallels between Kenyon's teachings and those of metaphysical thought. We shall examine both of these in turn.

Metaphysical Connections

There is no doubt that Kenyon studied metaphysical thought and exposed himself to the teaching of various persons espousing New Thought or other variations of metaphysical religion. During the 1890s Kenyon lived in Boston and heard the preaching and teaching of various Unitarian, Transcendentalist, and New Thought leaders. He attended Emerson College, where Transcendentalism and New Thought dominated the curriculum, at the same time as the famed New Thought writer Ralph Waldo Trine. McConnell documents that Kenyon had an extensive library of metaphysical literature and read such works with interest.

None of this is in dispute. Kenyon's staunchest defender, William DeArteaga, agrees that "at Emerson he was surrounded by New Thought influence."[3] The issue is not whether Kenyon sustained considerable exposure to metaphysical ideas but how he responded to them. Is it true, as John MacArthur asserted, that "he imported and adapted into his system most of the essential ideas these cults propagated"?[4] Or might he have studied the metaphysical religions in order to learn what good he could take from them while rejecting their heretical teachings?

This leads us to Kenyon's own testimony and that of those who knew him. What do they have to say about the impact of New Thought on his thinking? McConnell admits that "we do not have any *written* confession by Kenyon in which he admits to having formed his theology from cultic sources."[5] What we do have, continues McConnell, are reports from persons who say that Kenyon admitted *orally* to having drawn from metaphysical sources. Unfortunately, this evidence is hearsay and comes from just two men, both of whom were critical of Kenyon.[6]

The fact is that Kenyon did make some statements in writing that bear on this subject, even if they are not "written confessions" of cultism. Consider, for instance, the following passage:

> We cannot ignore the amazing growth of Christian Science, Unity, New Thought, and Spiritism. . . .
>
> We cannot close our eyes to the fact that in many of our cities on the Pacific Coast, Mrs. Eddy has a stronger following today and a larger attendance at her churches than have the old line denominations; and the largest percentage of her followers have at one time been worshippers in the denomi-

nations—they have left them because they believe they are receiving more help from Mrs. Eddy's teaching than from the preachers.

They will tell you how they were healed and how they were helped in their spiritual life by this strange cult.

This is a libel upon the modern Church—it is not only a libel but a challenge.[7]

McConnell quotes this passage to document Kenyon's familiarity with the metaphysical cults, a fact certainly not to be disputed.[8] Yet, as McConnell concedes, the point Kenyon was making in context was that people were turning to Christian Science because they wanted a miraculous Christianity. Thus, Kenyon continues, "Christian Science could not have grown to the place where it is dominating many of our large cities unless there had been a demand in the heart of the people for a supernatural religion."[9] Whatever one thinks of his theology, Kenyon's observation was indisputably correct. Moreover, it is clear from this passage that Kenyon saw Christian Science and the related cults as false systems and viewed his own efforts as directed at producing a biblically faithful Christianity that answered the metaphysical cults' challenge. Kenyon was convinced that these cults, though false religions, were exploiting truths that the church had been ignoring, especially truths about faith and healing.

McConnell quotes another passage in his thesis: "Natural man can develop his spirit until it becomes a force in him. We see this in Christian Science, Unity, Spiritualism and other psychological religions."[10] For McConnell this passage is evidence that Kenyon had too high a view of the metaphysical religions. But what McConnell does not quote are Kenyon's next sentences, which put Kenyon's statement in a different light:

> This is the natural, unregenerated human spirit being cultivated. The human spirit is naturally very religious, because it is God-hungry. It is the mother of all human religions. Christianity is God's answer to the hunger of the human spirit. Every human religion attempts to answer this hunger and fails.[11]

Kenyon, then, saw the metaphysical religions as producing some results on a natural, human level but as ultimately failing to answer the need of the human spirit. What he therefore wanted to do was to develop "a new type of Christianity" without falling into the errors of "a new philosophy or a new metaphysical concept of Christ."[12] Thus, he did not see his teaching as rooted in the metaphysical movement but instead as presenting an alternative to it. The question that needs to be asked is whether in trying to develop such an alternative Kenyon inadvertently made unbiblical concessions to the metaphysical approach.

Metaphysical Comparisons

This leads us to the second factor to be considered, namely, the actual parallels between Kenyon and the metaphysical teachings. The usual method is to search through the metaphysical writings for statements that have verbal and conceptual parallels to Kenyon's writings. From these parallels it is then concluded that Kenyon was heavily influenced by New Thought.

The problem with this methodology is that it fails to compare Kenyon's teachings with New Thought teachings in a systemic fashion. Instead of comparing the whole of Kenyon's system with the whole of the New Thought system, it compares parts of one with parts of the other. The result is that the comparison is inevitably biased toward finding New Thought influence in Kenyon.

A New Approach

The approach I follow is to compare whole with whole rather than parts with parts. In the following table the basic tenets of the New Thought movement are set forth in the far left column. To avoid bias, I have not constructed my own list but instead have drawn these tenets from three overlapping lists of New Thought beliefs found in standard works on the subject.[13] Now, since the metaphysical or mind-science movement has been rather diverse, I have also listed Christian Science, arguably the most conservative sect within that movement, and noted with an X those points on which it is in essential agreement with New Thought. Finally, I have listed Kenyon on the far right, noting those points with an X on which Kenyon agreed substantially with New Thought. Where there is some legitimate debate about whether the views of Christian Science or Kenyon are genuinely similar to those of New Thought, I have placed the X in parentheses.

The results are quite instructive. Kenyon's system appears to have little resemblance overall to New Thought. By contrast, it is more like Christian Science than it is like New Thought. Yet the similarities between Christian Science and Kenyonism are largely positive from an orthodox Christian perspective. For example, both Christian Science and Kenyon agree that Christians should offer prayers of petition, or requests, to God. Both agree that there is a legitimate role for religious authorities. Both view Christianity as the only true religion. In these and other respects Kenyon, like Christian Science, is actually closer to orthodox Christianity than is New Thought or other segments of the metaphysical religious movement. And, in fact, Kenyon appears from this list to be far closer to orthodoxy than is Christian Science.

New Thought Compared
with Christian Science and Kenyon

New Thought	Christian Science	E. W. Kenyon
1. Absolute rejection of creeds, creedal theology	X	
2. Essential divinity of man	X	(X)
3. Impersonal view of God as Principle	(X)	
4. Monistic or pantheistic view of God	X	
5. Jesus as way-shower, Christ as Principle	X	
6. Rejection of sin, grace, atonement	X	
7. Sin and sickness as unreal or mental error	X	
8. Pragmatic test of truth		
9. Salvation as self-realization or knowledge		
10. Experiential orientation	X	
11. Psychologistic view of reality		
12. Optimistic view of human goodness	X	
13. Emphasis on success, prosperity		(X)
14. Esoteric interpretation of the Bible	X	
15. Healing primarily through the mind or spirit	X	X
16. Spiritual/mental causes as primary	X	X
17. Humans as basically spiritual beings	X	X
18. Uselessness of petitionary prayer		
19. Heaven and hell as mental states	X	
20. Validity of much non-Christian religion		
21. Rejection of all human religious authority		
22. Universal salvation of all humanity	X	
23. Viewing Christianity as a science	X	(X)

The point here is not to deny some influence on Kenyon from New Thought or Christian Science. No one denies that Kenyon studied metaphysical teachings and attempted to incorporate at least some aspects of them into his own. The point I am making is that Kenyon's theology was not a simple recycling of New Thought, "a 'baptized' version of metaphysics," as McConnell (and others) have put it.[14] Kenyon's doctrine is actually more unlike New Thought than like it. Even McConnell says that "it must be admitted that Kenyon did not approve of much of the cults' doctrine."[15] But I would go further: Kenyon differed radically from all of the metaphysical cults on a number of *essential* theological and philosophical matters. Thus, we cannot classify his teaching as belonging in the metaphysical tradition. The *most* that could be said is that Kenyon was significantly influenced by metaphysical teachings.

Since it is commonly said that D. R. McConnell's book documented beyond doubt the metaphysical context of Kenyon's teaching, it is necessary to review his arguments. McConnell identifies five doctrinal matters on which he argues that Kenyon's doctrine is a cultic heresy rooted in the metaphysical tradition. These five doctrines are (1) revelation knowledge, the idea of a higher knowledge that contradicts the senses; (2) identification, the idea that humans are or become divine; (3) faith as a spiritual law or force used by God himself; (4) healing exclusively through spiritual means; and (5) material prosperity as a divine right.[16]

I shall discuss all of these doctrines in detail in the course of this book. Here I wish to argue that Kenyon's views on these subjects, while in some cases sharing points of contact with metaphysical thought, are fundamentally different from the views of the metaphysical writers quoted by McConnell.[17] Please note that I am *not* defending Kenyon's views on these matters (all of which I reject). I am simply arguing that these views are not metaphysical doctrines.

It should also be noted that the focus here is entirely on the views of Kenyon, since the metaphysical influence on the modern Word-Faith movement was supposedly mediated exclusively through him. One of the problems with McConnell's argument is that he quotes from Hagin, Copeland, and other modern Word-Faith teachers to fill in the gaps of his picture of Kenyon's theology. Other critics of the Word-Faith teaching go further, drawing most or all of their evidence for metaphysical parallels to the Word-Faith teaching from the writings of Hagin rather than Kenyon.[18] This methodology is faulty, though, because (as everyone agrees) Hagin had no significant contact with the metaphysical cults, and any influence they had on him had to have come through Kenyon's writings. So, if there is a metaphysical basis to the Word-Faith teaching, it should be documentable in Kenyon's writings themselves. For this reason, we shall deliberately postpone examination of the contemporary Word-Faith teachers until after the question of the origins of Kenyon's theology has been settled.

Revelation Knowledge

According to McConnell, Kenyon's idea of "revelation knowledge" as opposed to "sense knowledge" comes from the metaphysical cults. He observes that both Kenyon and the metaphysicians adhere to a "radical dualism" between knowledge from the sensory realm and knowledge from a higher realm, that of spirit. He finds Kenyon's view to be "almost exactly the same" as that of Mary Baker Eddy.[19]

McConnell's comparison here is odd, to say the least. As McConnell himself points out, Eddy taught that the sensory realm was illusory and the physical world unreal.[20] Eddy flatly rejected the biblical teaching that God created the material world and placed us into it as material beings.[21] By contrast, Kenyon believed that the material world was real enough and that it was created by God. "Man's soul and body fit him for his life upon this material universe which has been created for him. . . . There exists, according to the Scriptures, a spiritual realm *as well as* a physical" (emphasis added).[22] For Kenyon, then, we are essentially spirits, but the bodies in which we are living are quite real and created by God. For Eddy, we are essentially spirits, and the material bodies we think we inhabit are not real.

Thus, the "dualism" in Christian Science is really rooted in a *monism*— a doctrine of all reality as of one essence or nature, that of spirit. The "dualism" in Christian Science is between the real and the unreal, whereas in Kenyon it is between the natural and the supernatural. In Christian Science the real is divine, spiritual, and good, while the unreal is earthly, material, and evil. This dualism is akin to Gnosticism, a religious movement in the early centuries of Christianity that was staunchly resisted by the orthodox church. Kenyon's theology was not (as is commonly asserted) Gnostic, because he viewed the material world as neither unreal nor evil.[23]

An idea related to these "dualisms" is the notion that the knowledge of the senses must be denied. It is true that both Kenyon and Mary Baker Eddy said this,[24] but the rationale and meaning of their statements differed. For Eddy all of the sensory "knowledge" we have is fundamentally misleading because the belief in the sensory realm is itself an error. Eddy takes this so far that anything in the Bible that contradicts this premise is regarded as error. For Kenyon, on the other hand, sensory knowledge is in error only insofar as it contradicts what God has said in the Bible. Since our sense knowledge cannot rise to the knowledge of the spiritual realm, it stands in contradiction to that higher knowledge, a knowledge that can only come by "revelation" from God.[25]

A similar difference pertains to the parallel notions of perfect knowledge of God taught by Kenyon and Ralph Waldo Trine. Kenyon's view is that God's revelation in the Bible gives us "perfect knowledge" of God's will so that we have no excuse for living "in weakness and failure and in ignorance of the Father's will."[26] Trine's view is that we all have an innate spiritual sense that has perfect knowledge by virtue of our inherent oneness with the divine Spirit, Principle, or Power immanent in all reality. McConnell quotes Trine as speaking of "an inner spiritual sense through which man is opened to the direct revelation and knowledge of God" and that is "unerring, *absolutely unerring*, in its guidance."[27] What McConnell does not make clear is that Trine sees this "inner spiritual sense" as an "intuition" we possess by virtue of our essential oneness with the Infinite Life he calls God. For Trine this intuition is a "revelation" from within our own divine selves, not from a transcendent God in the Bible:

> Intuition . . . is an inner spiritual sense through which man is opened to the direct revelation and knowledge of God, the secrets of nature and life, and through which he is brought into conscious unity and fellowship with God, and made to realize his own deific nature and supremacy of being as the son

of God. . . . In the degree that we come into the recognition of our own *true* selves, into the realization of the oneness of our own life with the Infinite Life, and in the degree that we open ourselves to this divine inflow, does this voice of intuition, this voice of the soul, this voice of God, speak clearly; and in the degree that we recognize, listen to and obey it, does it speak ever more clearly; until by and by there comes the time when it is unerring, *absolutely unerring*, in its guidance.[28]

The importance of this point must not be missed. As even McConnell acknowledges, Kenyon, unlike the metaphysical cults, viewed the Bible as "the only legitimate source of revelation knowledge."[29] This puts a check on the unbiblical flights of fancy one finds in New Thought or Christian Science. Kenyon's idea of revelation knowledge may be problematical, but it differs in essential ways from the view of knowledge found in the metaphysical cults.

Identification

The doctrine of "identification" consists of four related ideas in Kenyon's theology that McConnell traces to the metaphysical cults. The first is the teaching that man's nature is fundamentally spiritual.[30] Kenyon's teaching that "man's spirit is the real man"[31] is compared to Eddy's doctrine that "man is not material; he is spiritual"[32] as well as Trine's view of man as a spiritual being.[33] As I have already pointed out, for Kenyon man is a spirit inhabiting a real material body, whereas for Eddy the spirit is all that there is. Kenyon's view likewise differs from that of Trine, for whom the spirit in man is the universal spirit or higher self of all reality, so that Trine's view is essentially pantheistic.

The second aspect of the doctrine of identification is the idea of the God-likeness of man. Kenyon's view that man "is in God's class of being"[34] is compared with Trine's assertion that *"in essence the life of God and the life of man are identically the same, and so are one."*[35] Here again McConnell's analysis fails to come to grips with the different worldviews of Kenyon and Trine. Kenyon thinks of human beings as created "in God's class," while Trine thinks of human beings as particular manifestations of the one God that is Infinite Principle. Thus Kenyon's view is fundamentally monotheistic, while Trine's is, once again, fundamentally pantheistic.

The third aspect of identification that McConnell identifies as cultic is Kenyon's denial that Jesus' physical death did not redeem us from our sins. McConnell cites Mary Baker Eddy as an example of a metaphysical teacher who flatly denied that "the material blood of Jesus" could "cleanse from sin."[36] But the difference between Kenyon's view and the view of Eddy and the other metaphysical cults is vast. For Kenyon, sin is real, the need for a substitute to die to free man from sin is real, physical death is real, Jesus' death on the cross was real, and Jesus' physical death was a necessary part of his redemptive work. On the other hand, for Eddy sin is not real, the idea of a substitute dying for the sins of others is false, death is not real, the cross was not real, Jesus did not die, and therefore the supposed physical death of Jesus is irrelevant to Christian Science. For Kenyon, the important and distinctive point is that Jesus had to die spiritually *as well as* physically; for Eddy, the important and distinctive point is that Jesus did not have to die *at all*.

Likewise the New Thought teachers, while generally allowing that in some sense Jesus (though not the "Christ" Principle) did die, roundly and utterly reject the ideas of sin and substitutionary atonement. For Kenyon, the physical death of Jesus was not *sufficient* to accomplish redemption; for New Thought, no redemption is needed and the physical death of Jesus is therefore irrelevant.

The fourth aspect of identification is Kenyon's teaching that in the new birth Christians receive once again "the nature and life of God in one's spirit."[37] McConnell compares this teaching to Trine's statement, "In the degree that we open ourselves to this divine inflow we are changed from mere men into God men."[38] McConnell adds, "Like the Faith teachers, Trine taught that believers needed to realize their true 'identity' as God men."[39] But McConnell has smoothed over the differences between Trine and Kenyon. Trine did not hold that *believers* become "God men" by virtue of a supernatural new birth, as Kenyon held. Rather, Trine taught that *all* human beings were *already* God men by virtue of their inherent oneness with God, and just need to realize that oneness in order to live as God men:

> They [most people] have never as yet come into a knowledge of the real identity of their true selves.
>
> Mankind has not yet realized that the real self is one with the life of God. Through its ignorance it has never yet opened itself to the divine inflow, and so has never made itself a channel through which the infinite powers and forces can manifest. When we know ourselves merely as men, we live accordingly, and have merely the powers of men. When we come into the realization of the fact that we are God men, then again we live accordingly, and have the powers of God men. *In the degree that we open ourselves to this divine inflow we are changed from mere men into God men.*[40]

Once again, there is a fundamental difference between the pantheism of the metaphysical cults and the basic monotheism of Kenyon. McConnell, however, tries to show that Kenyon's theology has a view of God similar to that of the metaphysical movement. He does this in his chapter on the doctrine of faith.

Faith and the Nature of God

McConnell accurately describes the metaphysical view of God:

> The god in which the metaphysical cults believe is not a personal god who sovereignly governs the universe. Their god is an impersonal force: "the Infinite Power," "the Spirit of Infinite Life," and "the Infinite Intelligence." This infinite, but impersonal, force rules the universe indirectly through "immutable laws" rather than directly through his presence and wisdom. Historically, this concept of God could be categorized as a spiritualized form of "deism" so prevalent in the late 19th century.[41]

The only thing I would add to McConnell's description is that the metaphysical concept of God, while it did develop historically from deism, ended up more akin to pantheism than to deism. *Deism* regards God as a personal being who is distinct from the world he created and who governs the world by unchanging natural laws that even he never violates (so that miracles do not occur). *Pantheism* regards God as an impersonal or semipersonal being immanent in the world and more or less identical to the unchanging laws governing reality.[42]

Now, what is striking is that McConnell provides very little evidence for viewing Kenyon's doctrine of God as anything close to the metaphysical doctrine. He points out that Kenyon believed God created the world using "faith-filled words" and that there are "great spiritual laws that govern the unseen forces of life."[43] Somehow from these statements (mixed with more extensive quotations from Hagin) McConnell infers that Kenyon believed in "a universe governed by spiritual laws, instead of by God," and that Kenyon's God "must do the bidding of the spiritual laws that govern the universe" and is even "controlled" by these laws.[44] But Kenyon does not say that God is subject to these spiritual laws or that God is "controlled" by them. Nor is there anything in Kenyon's writings to suggest that God is impersonal "Infinite Power" as in metaphysical theology.

Even McConnell acknowledges that "the Faith theology in principle teaches a personal God." He immediately goes on, though, to assert that "in practice the Faith god differs little from the god of the metaphysical cults."[45] Hank Hanegraaff repeats these statements almost verbatim: "In fact, the Faith teachers present a personal God in principle, but in practice they teach a metaphysical God."[46] Notice that whereas McConnell's statement is qualified to avoid equating the metaphysical concept of God *directly* with the Word-Faith concept ("differs little from . . ."), Hanegraaff drops this qualification. In any case, whether the Word-Faith view of God is said "in practice" to be the same as or little different from the metaphysical view of God, the meager evidence that McConnell and Hanegraaff present from

Kenyon's writings is insufficient to substantiate this serious charge. There is a wide gap between the belief in spiritual laws set in place by a personal God and the belief in an impersonal Divine Power that can be tapped by observing the spiritual laws, which describe how that Power operates. Kenyon's view of spiritual law may justly be criticized as unbiblical—even as inconsistent with the confession of God as personal—but it cannot be made the basis of the charge that Kenyon believed in practice in an impersonal, pantheistic concept of God. Hanegraaff himself rather inconsistently acknowledges this point several pages after equating Kenyon's concept with the metaphysical concept:

> Next, it is important to draw a clear distinction between the concept of divinity taught by metaphysical cults . . . and the doctrine of deification taught by the Faith movement. . . . The Faith movement and the metaphysical cults are similar in that they both proclaim the divinity of man. They are distinct in that the Faith teachers reject the concept of an impersonal God permeating creation.[47]

Health and Wealth

Here I am combining McConnell's fourth and fifth doctrinal issues in which he finds Kenyon's doctrine to be rooted in the metaphysical cults. To a large extent McConnell is on solid ground in claiming some affinity between Kenyon and New Thought on the subject of sickness and health. He points out that Kenyon's view that "sickness is a spiritual condition manifested in the physical body"[48] is akin to the metaphysical notion that all sickness has spiritual causes.[49] Likewise, both Kenyon and New Thought taught that while the physical realm is real and sickness does exist, the proper response is to ignore the symptoms and refuse to acknowledge or affirm the sickness verbally.[50] On the other hand, McConnell has virtually no basis for connecting Kenyon's doctrine of prosperity to the metaphysical cults. He quotes Kenyon's statement that "it is abnormal for believers to be in bondage to poverty so that they have to go to the world for help."[51] But it is a long way from this sentiment to the New Thought claim that prosperity is a divine right that can be attained by following impersonal cosmic laws.

Rethinking the "Kenyon Connection"

McConnell has drawn attention to some genuine points of contact or affinity between New Thought and Kenyon. Both taught that man was fundamentally a spirit inhabiting a material body so that the body was subject to the control of the spirit. Both believed in spiritual laws in addition to physical laws and believed that by knowing and observing spiritual laws one could attain a quality of life beyond what human beings usually experience. Both taught that sickness was caused by spiritual factors and should be dealt with in a spiritual manner by refusing to acknowledge the sickness and speaking instead about one's divine right to health.

These commonalities do reasonably support the conclusion that Kenyon was influenced by the metaphysical religions. But there is not enough evidence to support the conclusion that Kenyon's theology is *essentially* metaphysical. Kenyon's teaching is actually more unlike New Thought than like it. Unlike New Thought teachers, Kenyon assumed the absolute reliability of the Bible and interpreted it without recourse to esoteric, metaphysical explanations.[52] He therefore self-consciously rejected the metaphysical cults on doctrinal grounds:

> Christian Science, Unity, and the other Metaphysical and philosophical teachers of today do not believe that God is a person.
>
> They will tell you that He is perfect mind, but He has no location.
>
> It is just a great universal mind which finds its home in every individual. He has no headquarters. . . .
>
> They do not believe in sin as Paul taught it in the Revelation given to him.
>
> They do not believe that Jesus died for our sins, but that He died as a martyr.
>
> They do not believe that He had a literal Resurrection, a physical Resurrection, but put it as, "a metaphysical resurrection" (whatever that means).
>
> If God is not a person and Jesus did not put sin away, then who is Jesus and what is the value of our faith in Him?[53]

Kenyon, then, held that God was personal, not impersonal or semipersonal, as in New Thought. He accepted the doctrine of the Trinity,[54] believed in a literal devil and both good and bad angels, and viewed humankind as fallen into sin and in need of redemption. He held to the literal, physical resurrection of Jesus from the dead, which New Thought did not.

Moreover, Kenyon made his doctrinal orientation and commitment clear by teaching exclusively in Christian circles, mostly in Baptist and Pentecostal settings, and not in New Thought circles. The argument here is not that Kenyon could not be a metaphysical teacher merely because he taught in Baptist and Pentecostal churches. The argument is that his orientation as nonmetaphysical is *confirmed* by *both* his complete rejection and noninvolvement in metaphysical circles *and* his sustained acceptance and involvement in Baptist and Pentecostal circles.

Thus, however strongly we may disagree with Kenyon's theology, it is simply not right to classify it with the metaphysical theologies of New

Thought, Christian Science, or other similar cults. This does not mean that one cannot conclude that Kenyon's theology was seriously defective or even heretical. It does mean that Kenyon's theology cannot be understood wholly or even principally in terms of New Thought.

In the next chapter, we will consider the other stream of religious belief with which Kenyon had significant contact—that of the late nineteenth-century faith-cure movement and the early twentieth-century Pentecostal movement.

4

Kenyon's "Pentecostal" Context

Healing and the supernatual [sic] were very much alive in the nineteenth-century Faith-Cure movement led by Charles Cullis and spread by William Boardman, Andrew Murray, Adoniram Gordon, Carrie Judd Montgomery, and A. B. Simpson. Any of these pioneers in the American divine healing movement could have served nobly as a theological foundation for Kenyon's healing ministry. . . . He could have easily drawn upon Pentecostal or Faith-Cure sources for his theology, but he chose not to do so.

D. R. McConnell[1]

As for Kenyon himself, it would appear that he is best placed within the Keswickean/Higher Christian Life tradition. Indeed, even after his death, Kenyon's daughter continued to include articles by R. A. Torrey, H. W. Webb-Peploe, A. J. Gordon, George Müller, Andrew Murray, and A. B. Simpson in the columns of the ministry's newsletter.

Dale H. Simmons[2]

Do not judge according to appearance, but judge with righteous judgment.

John 7:24

We saw in the previous chapter that the metaphysical cults, while exerting significant influence on the thought of E. W. Kenyon, were not the primary religious context of his teaching. In this chapter we turn to early Pentecostalism and the pre-Pentecostal movements emphasizing a "higher life" and healing. I shall argue that these Pentecostal and pre-Pentecostal traditions indeed provide the theological and religious context in which Kenyon's teaching must be placed.

I first presented the argument advanced in this and the preceding chapter at the annual conference of the Evangelical Ministries to New Religions in Philadelphia in 1994. Since then I have had the opportunity to read Dale H. Simmons's study titled *E. W. Kenyon and the Postbellum Pursuit of Peace, Power, and Plenty*, published in 1997. This book, based on Simmons's 1990 doctoral dissertation,[3] also contends that Kenyon belongs in the evangelical faith-cure and "higher life" traditions. I have found much in his research and analysis to be helpful, and I refer to some of his findings here.

However, Simmons also argues that New Thought was not as different from the evangelical Higher Life movement as is commonly supposed. He concludes that "on a practical level, New Thought and the Higher Christian Life movement were birds of a feather emerging from the same Gilded Age. This is not to say that the two groups were of the same species, but it is to recognize that they were certainly of the same genus."[4] Throughout his work Simmons makes it increasingly clear that he is critical of both movements. William DeArteaga, after reading Simmons's dissertation, agreed in general with his analysis of Kenyon's roots while arguing for a positive assessment both of the Higher Christian Life movement and of Kenyon.[5]

The present work takes a somewhat different approach from either Simmons or DeArteaga. While I agree that there are important similarities between New Thought and the Higher Life movement, I consider the differences to be far more fundamental. New Thought is thoroughly heretical; the Higher Christian Life movement, while deservedly subject in my opinion to some theological criticisms, is an orthodox Christian tradition.

What Do We Mean by "Pentecostal"?

In popular and even some scholarly writings a sharp division is often made or implied between Pentecostal and non-Pentecostal individuals, teachings, and movements. Such a sharp distinction is difficult to maintain consistently. The distinction is usually based on one issue, namely, speaking in tongues. Thus, early twentieth-century Christians who believed in speaking in tongues are labeled "Pentecostals" and all other Christians are regarded as non-Pentecostals. This terminological division is useful as far as it goes. However, the distinction has its problems. Some pre-Pentecostals in the nineteenth century believed and even practiced speaking in tongues.

Some people restrict the Pentecostal label to those who believe that *all* Spirit-filled Christians will speak in tongues; on that definition many members of classic Pentecostal churches would be excluded. Since about 1950 there has been an explosion of religious teaching and experience that includes speaking in tongues but is generally classified as charismatic rather than Pentecostal. Moreover, on a great many other issues the boundary between Pentecostals and non-Pentecostals was blurred. These issues included the meaning of faith, the question of supernatural healing, the nature of the believer, and other questions of importance to our discussion of the origins of the Word-Faith teaching.

Pentecostalism did not spring into existence overnight out of thin air. Rather, it was a movement with roots in earlier teachings, events, and personalities. Likewise, Pentecostalism does not exist in neat isolation from other movements and traditions. Rather, a wide range of churches, teachings, and individuals are more or less associated with Pentecostalism in some way. These include, of course, the classic Pentecostal denominations such as the Assemblies of God, the Church of God in Christ, and the International Church of the Foursquare Gospel. Also included, however, are the numerous independent charismatic churches and ministries, as well as the charismatic renewal movements within the mainline denominations (Roman Catholic, Episcopal, Presbyterian, Baptist, Methodist, and many others).

Recent scholarship tends with some justification, then, to classify various pre-Pentecostal movements, Pentecostalism, and modern quasi-Pentecostal movements as belonging broadly in the same tradition. E. W. Kenyon belongs firmly in this larger tradition. Specifically, I maintain that Kenyon's teaching was rooted in the pre-Pentecostal "Higher Life" and healing or "faith-cure" movements that paved the way for Pentecostalism, and that the mature Kenyon felt more at home in Pentecostal circles than anywhere else.

Before Pentecostalism

In the last half of the nineteenth century various efforts were under way to bring renewal to the church that prepared the way for the development of Pentecostalism. Two related movements deserve our attention here.[6]

The Holiness Movement

The first is the Holiness movement, of which two streams can be distinguished: the "Wesleyan" and the "Keswick" (pronounced KESS-ick) branches. In the nineteenth century, the Wesleyan revivalists Charles G. Finney and Phoebe Palmer promoted the idea that true faith claims the blessings promised in the New Testament, particularly holiness or "perfection," as present and immediate possessions. Palmer and other revivalists popularized the idea of the "baptism of the Holy Spirit" as a second experience producing an empowered Christian life.[7] For some of these teachers, healing was to be included in the supernatural experience of the Spirit-baptized Christian.

Developing largely out of the Wesleyan tradition, but attracting interest and support outside of that tradition, was the "deeper life" or "higher life" renewal movement, often known as the "Keswick" or "Oxford" movement. The Keswick movement included such still-popular writers as Hannah Whitehall Smith (1832–1911) and Andrew Murray (1828–1917).[8] In contrast to the Wesleyanism of Finney, Palmer, and others, the Keswick tradition emphasized the progressive character of Christian experience. Higher Life teaching called on Christians to experience a supernatural life by yielding to Christ's indwelling life, allowing Christ to live his life through the believer. This higher life was to be characterized by an absolute dependence on Christ for personal holiness, for one's material needs, and—as many increasingly came to think—for one's physical health and well-being.

The Healing Movements

Associated in turn with both the Wesleyan and Keswick traditions, though again not exclusively confined to them, was the healing movement, also known as the "faith-healing" or "faith-cure" movement. Arguably we should speak here of "movements," so widespread and diverse were the efforts to bring divine healing into the Christian experience. But the common thread in all of these efforts was the belief that healing could and even should be sought as a supernatural blessing from God through faith.

For our purposes the most important segment of the healing movement or movements was the one that found its impetus in the work of Charles Cullis. Paul Chappell, a specialist in the history of the faith-cure movement, observes that Cullis, "a medical doctor in Boston, did more than any other person to propagate faith healing and to draw the attention of the American Church to the doctrine. He was the single most important figure in the development of the divine healing movement in America."[9] During the 1870s and 1880s, Cullis, an Episcopalian, popularized the idea that salvation or redemption was intended for the body as well as the soul or spirit. He also brought to America the practice of establishing "faith works," ministries that eschewed soliciting funds and relied instead entirely on God to

supply their needs through faith and prayer. Cullis found his models for
such a ministry in various European faith works that ministered to the sick
and the homeless, including the famous orphanage of George Müller
(1805–1898) in Bristol, England. Cullis had read Müller's autobiography[10]
and had visited the Bristol orphanage, and he consciously modeled his faith
work after Müller's. Cullis's healing conference center in Old Orchard
Beach, Maine, was a kind of American evangelical Lourdes.[11]

Among the teachers of divine healing inspired by the teaching and example of Cullis were A. J. Gordon and A. B. Simpson. Adoniram Judson Gordon (1836–1895)[12] was the pastor of a Baptist church in Boston, the founder
of Gordon College, and an associate of Cullis. In 1882 Gordon authored
The Ministry of Healing as an apologetic for the faith-healing movement,
arguing that the testimony of both Scripture and church history supported
the practice of seeking supernatural healing in prayer.[13]

Albert Benjamin Simpson (1844–1919), a Presbyterian pastor in New
York who experienced healing at one of Cullis's "faith conventions," went
on to establish the Christian and Missionary Alliance. More radical than
Cullis or Gordon (though not critical of them), Simpson taught that divine
healing through prayer was the *only* appropriate means of healing for the
obedient Christian. Pentecostals and charismatics today customarily credit
Simpson with having brought the "healing message" to the American
church. Ironically, Simpson's own radical views on healing are not generally accepted today within the Christian and Missionary Alliance
denomination.

Another wing of the American healing tradition that deserves our attention might be described as the proto-Pentecostal movement. The central
American figure in this movement was John Alexander Dowie (1847–
1907). Dowie was heavily influenced by Edward Irving (1792–1834),
founder of the Catholic Apostolic Church in Britain. Irving had called for
a restoration of New Testament Christian experience, including the "five-
fold ministry" of apostles, prophets, evangelists, pastors, and teachers, as
well as the charismatic gifts, including speaking in tongues, prophesying,
and healing. In the 1890s Dowie started an evangelistic healing ministry
near Chicago that blossomed into the Christian Catholic Church (note the
similarity of the name to Irving's church). Like Simpson, Dowie took a radical view of faith healing as incompatible with the use of medicines or the
help of physicians. Dowie, however, was sharply critical of Simpson and
other healing evangelists in the tradition of Charles Cullis. In the early
1900s Dowie founded Zion City as a community modeling faith, holiness,
and the restoration of New Testament Christianity in preparation for the
second coming of Christ. Dowie presented himself as the latter-day Elijah
and founding apostle of the restored, end-times church.[14]

When Dowie died in 1907, he had fallen from favor in Zion City and elsewhere in the faith-healing movement due to his extreme views, his sharp criticisms of other faith-healing proponents, and his exalted claims for himself. But Dowie's ministry and work had a lasting impact. While Dowie himself was not a Pentecostal, his restorationist message and his emphasis on healing as a crucial part of a supernatural Christian experience set the stage for the new Pentecostal movement. Shortly before Dowie died, Charles Parham, "the father of the twentieth-century Pentecostal movement," came to Zion City in 1906 and helped to make that city "the second most significant center in the world for the spreading of the new Pentecostal message."[15]

Three of the most important Pentecostal evangelists to emerge from Zion City were F. F. Bosworth, John G. Lake, and Gordon Lindsay. Fred Francis Bosworth (1877–1958)[16] was converted to Pentecostalism in Zion City through Parham's ministry and became a leader in the early years of the Assemblies of God (now the largest Pentecostal denomination in the world). When the Assemblies adopted the hard-line view that speaking in tongues was the sole "initial evidence" of the baptism of the Holy Spirit, Bosworth was forced to withdraw, moving eventually into A. B. Simpson's Christian and Missionary Alliance.

John G. Lake (1870–1935) was also a Zion City–based advocate of faith healing, converted to Pentecostal beliefs in the early years of that movement. After serving as a missionary in Africa for five years, Lake moved back to the United States and established evangelistic healing ministries in Spokane, Washington, and Portland, Oregon.

Gordon Lindsay (1906–1973) was born in Zion City and later became a Pentecostal in Portland, Oregon, through the preaching of Charles Parham. He became associated with John G. Lake and later became a pastor. In the late 1940s Bosworth and Lindsay were both involved in the healing ministry of William Branham, which ushered in the postwar faith-healing era.

In introducing Parham, Bosworth, Lake, and Lindsay, we have crossed the line from the pre-Pentecostal healing movement over to Pentecostalism. But the historical and ministerial transition between the two movements is virtually seamless. We now need to back up a bit and say something about the origins of Pentecostalism.

Parham and Pentecostalism

As has already been mentioned, the father of Pentecostalism was Charles Fox Parham (1873–1929).[17] Before he went to Zion City, Parham had originated the Pentecostal movement through his teaching ministry in Topeka,

Kansas. There he had led his students to the conclusion, based on the apostles' experience at Pentecost in Acts 2, that speaking in tongues (that is, he believed, in human foreign languages unknown to the speaker) was the initial evidence of the baptism of the Holy Spirit. In 1901 Parham and many of his students began speaking in tongues, and for the next few years Parham struggled to bring his Pentecostal message to the world. In 1906 William J. Seymour, a black Holiness student who briefly attended a Parham training course in Texas, took the Pentecostal experience and message to Los Angeles, where it sparked the famous Azusa Street revival that launched Pentecostalism as a worldwide movement. Meanwhile Parham briefly ministered in Zion City, where, despite his inability to gain control of the city, his teaching succeeded in making Zion City a prominent center of Pentecostalism. After leaving Zion City he was enmeshed in scandal, after which his influence waned even further.

Despite the obscurity into which Parham's name fell, he was truly the founder of Pentecostalism. One historian of Pentecostalism comments:

> The following generation of Pentecostal preachers ignored him, never mentioned him, and secretly regarded him as a sectarian, even though the Pentecostal movement as it is at the present day would never have come into being without the "sectarianism" of its leaders.[18]

It was Parham who originated the classic Pentecostal formulation that speaking in tongues is the initial evidence of the baptism of the Holy Spirit. It was also Parham who developed the standard Pentecostal view of church history. According to this view, the original apostolic church experienced the "former rain" of the Holy Spirit, after which the church fell into a dry spell of apostasy, or falling away, from the fullness of Christian experience. This falling away was gradually reversed through a series of restorations: justification by faith (through Martin Luther); sanctification (through Wesley); healing (especially through Simpson); and the Pentecostal baptism in the Holy Spirit, through himself, of course.[19]

Parham's views on healing were aligned with the views of the radical healing evangelists such as Simpson and Dowie. At one time he contemplated becoming a doctor, but he reported having repented of that desire: "'The devil,' he later said, 'tried to make me believe I could be a physician and a Christian too.'"[20] Parham, like Dowie, also taught the doctrine of a modern-day restoration of apostles and prophets.[21]

Unfortunately, Parham held some other views that helped to marginalize him in the burgeoning Pentecostal movement he had started. For instance, probably under the influence of Quakers, he rejected the orthodox doctrine of eternal punishment in favor of annihilationism.[22] For several years he also rejected water baptism, though he later returned to the practice.[23] Parham also held to a version of Anglo-Israelite doctrine, according to which his own English forebears and those of select other races were identified as the true Israelites.[24] With opinions like these, it is no surprise that Pentecostals of more traditional doctrinal orientations refused to support Parham or acknowledge his importance in their movement.

Kenyon: "Pentecostal" Connections

As we have seen, in the nineteenth century a movement arose that is usually described as the evangelical healing or faith-cure movement. Much of the impetus for this movement came from the Holiness tradition in both its Wesleyan and Keswick branches, both of which also fed into the early Pentecostal movement. More broadly, though, the healing movement cut across the theological spectrum to include Episcopalians, Methodists, Baptists, Presbyterians, and various other denominations. Kenyon, then, cannot be excluded from the faith-cure tradition simply by noting that his theology was not squarely in the Wesleyan tradition, as D. R. McConnell suggested.[25]

McConnell's quick dismissal of the idea that Kenyon should be placed in the non-Pentecostal evangelical healing tradition is perhaps the greatest weakness of his book. Somehow he concludes that Kenyon's theology was closer to the metaphysical cults than to the Wesleyan-Holiness tradition because Kenyon did not adhere to the doctrines of second blessing and entire sanctification. Yet he places Kenyon in the metaphysical tradition despite his many fundamental differences with them. Furthermore, Kenyon's views on sanctification were very similar to those of the Keswick movement, which rejected second-blessing theology and advocated a model of progressive growth in sanctification.

Having provided some historical background on the Holiness, faith-healing, and early Pentecostal movements, we are now in a position to see whether and to what extent Kenyon's teaching and ministry fit into the context of these related movements. We shall proceed as we did in the previous chapter on Kenyon and New Thought. First, we will consider Kenyon's associations with the movements in question and his attitudes toward them. Second, we will examine the teachings of some of the healing and Pentecostal leaders and compare them with those of Kenyon.

Kenyon's connections with the Holiness, faith-healing, and Pentecostal movements throughout his ministry years were many and varied. His first ordination and ministry experience was in the Methodist church (the main denomination deriving from the ministry of Wesley). This suggests at least some early exposure to Wesleyan views of the Christian life.

In the early and middle 1890s Kenyon lived in Boston, where for a brief period he attended Emerson College of Oratory, a fact that McConnell emphasizes to establish a metaphysical connection. One difficulty with making so much of this aspect of Kenyon's Boston experience is that Boston arguably was *the* American intellectual and cultural center of Kenyon's day. Thus, besides being exposed there to metaphysical thought, Kenyon was exposed to a wide variety of religious traditions.

Among these traditions was the growing evangelical faith-cure movement. The founder of Emerson College of Oratory, Charles Wesley Emerson, had strong links to the evangelical faith-cure movement. The dominant American figure in that movement was Charles Cullis, whose Boston-based healing ministry has already been mentioned. Emerson had served without pay on the faculty of Cullis's Faith Training College in Boston from 1876 to 1877 and was apparently comfortable theologically and practically with the movement represented by Cullis.[26]

Kenyon's exposure to the evangelical faith-cure movement soon became personal experience. In 1893 Kenyon, at this time something of an agnostic, attended A. J. Gordon's church and recommitted his life to Christ. Gordon, as we noted earlier, was a Baptist pastor in Boston and a leading defender of the evangelical faith-cure teaching. Within a few months Kenyon had decided to become a Baptist pastor.[27]

In 1900 Kenyon founded the Bethel Bible Institute in Spencer, Massachusetts, about fifty miles west of Boston.[28] As McConnell reports, "Kenyon patterned Bethel after the 'faith works' of George Müller's orphanages and Charles Cullis's hospices."[29] Kenyon had read Cullis's biography[30] and Müller's autobiography,[31] and he sought to operate his school as a faith work.

The Pentecostal movement began in 1901, and within a few years Kenyon was beginning to forge ties with various Pentecostal leaders, particularly during his visits to Chicago. During this period, Kenyon met John Alexander Dowie, whose Zion City healing ministry in the Chicago area made a positive impression on Kenyon. In 1907 Kenyon met with William H. Durham, also in Zion City. Durham (1873–1912) is credited with introducing the concept of "the finished work of Christ" into Pentecostalism. This is the belief that the fullness of the Spirit's power for holiness and service is already secured for every Christian in Christ's atonement, so that a "second work of grace" (as in the usual Wesleyan and Holiness position) is not needed. It turns out, though, that Kenyon was apparently responsible for introducing this idea to Durham. Around the same time Kenyon met F. F. Bosworth, the healing evangelist. In his book *Christ the Healer,* Bosworth credited Kenyon with some of his most significant material.[32] In 1910 Kenyon published an article in his newsletter about

Aimee Semple McPherson's experience of healing, reprinted from Durham's *Pentecostal Testimony*.[33] Durham had ordained Aimee and her husband, Robert Semple (who died of malaria in 1910), in 1909, and they had gone that year with Durham on his evangelistic travels.[34]

Although Kenyon was generally critical of Pentecostalism during its early years, he enjoyed good relations with most Pentecostals and his own views were often warmly received. His views on Pentecostalism were similar to those of other quasi-Pentecostals during this period: He acknowledged the validity of speaking in tongues but rejected the "initial evidence" doctrine and expressed concerns about various other aspects of the movement. Kenyon also enjoyed good relations with Christian leaders in the Higher Life movement, though again he was an independent thinker and did not agree with some aspects of that tradition. So, for example, Kenyon was invited to preach at the Clarendon Street Baptist Church, where he had been brought into association with the faith-cure wing of the Higher Life movement through the preaching of A. J. Gordon. He was also invited to preach at an Easter service at A. B. Simpson's church, Gospel Tabernacle, in New York.[35]

In 1924 Kenyon resigned from Bethel and moved to California. According to McConnell, in California Kenyon's "ministry was interdenominational in scope, although he often frequented Pentecostal circles. Aimee Semple McPherson invited him to speak in her Angelus Temple on several occasions."[36] In 1931 Kenyon moved to Seattle, Washington, where his ministry as a radio evangelist began and where he lived out the rest of his life.

Despite the misgivings Kenyon had expressed about Pentecostalism in its earliest years, by the time he began ministering in California he had, as McConnell aptly puts it, "made his peace with the Pentecostals."[37] Thus, although Kenyon was a Baptist and non-Pentecostal in certain key respects, he felt comfortable ministering to Pentecostals and his ministry was well received by them. If he accused Pentecostals generally of "extravagances and fanaticism,"[38] well, so did some Pentecostals themselves.

If we review this trail of evidence from Kenyon's entire life, it becomes evident that he had positive associations with all three of the evangelical movements discussed in this chapter—the Holiness, healing, and Pentecostal movements. These associations, in the case of the healing and Pentecostal movements, were not simply informal relationships or brief forays into their religious institutions, but they were sustained participation characterized by a mutual give-and-take. Kenyon never ministered in metaphysical contexts, never modeled his ministry institutions on metaphysical ones, and was never received by the metaphysical community. By contrast, all three of these things are true of Kenyon's connections with the evangelical faith-cure and early Pentecostal movements. If one considers just his historical and institutional connections, one would have to conclude that Kenyon's deepest ties were to these evangelical movements.

"Pentecostal" Comparisons

Fruitful comparisons on various levels can be drawn between the teachings of Kenyon and those of the healing and Pentecostal evangelists of his day.

Kenyon's Basic Theology

First of all, the general and rudimentary theological assumptions and beliefs of Kenyon were the same as those of the various evangelical traditions with which he associated. All of these persons were evangelical Protestants. They assumed a "literal" interpretation of the Bible and accorded it infallible authority for Christian doctrine and practice. They accepted at face value the biblical accounts of God's supernatural dealings with Israel in the Old Testament, his divine incarnation in Jesus of Nazareth in the Gospels, and his miraculous establishment of the church through the ministries of the apostles in the rest of the New Testament. They affirmed the virgin birth of Christ, his sinless life, his physical death on the cross as a substitutionary atonement for sins, his personal, physical resurrection from the dead, and his personal future return to the earth in glory. They preached a gospel of salvation by grace through faith in Christ alone. In all of these respects Kenyon was generically evangelical and Protestant, just as were the faith-healing and Pentecostal leaders.

Given this evangelical Protestant context, Kenyon's distinctive positions place him unmistakably in the same broad tradition as the faith-cure movement. Kenyon summoned Christians to a supernatural Christianity characterized by holiness and health. This supernatural experience was to be taken as a present possession by the same faith that received forgiveness of sins and eternal life by simply resting on God's promises in Scripture. As we saw earlier, this view of faith as receiving God's promises as present possessions is characteristic of the Keswick tradition. Kenyon grounded the promise of health on the significance of the atonement, which he believed brought salvation or health to the body as well as to the soul, just as A. B. Simpson and most if not all of the other late nineteenth-century evangelical faith-curists believed. Theologically, then, there really can be no doubting that Kenyon belonged in the faith-cure tradition.

The Name of Jesus

The deeper we go, the more the evidence mounts for placing Kenyon in the faith-cure tradition. One of the distinctive features of the religious expressions of the Holiness and healing traditions was their emphasis on Jesus.[39] In their hymns, in their devotional literature, and in their teaching, an almost exclusive emphasis was placed on Jesus. The doctrine of the Trinity was not denied, but it was generally ignored. Neglect of the Trinity was reinforced by a general attitude of *anticreedalism*—the belief that adherence to complicated, man-made creeds was both unnecessary and incompatible with a simple faith in Christ and the Bible. It is true, as Simmons points out, that both New Thought and the evangelical faith-cure movement were anticreedal.[40] However, while New Thought was thoroughly anticreedal *in substance*—rejecting most of the distinctive Christian affirmations of the early creeds—evangelical faith-curists were not. Instead, they were anticreedal *in principle*—they accepted most if not necessarily all of what the creeds said, but they deplored the way in which the creeds said it and the tendency in traditional churches to give a high priority to doctrinal orthodoxy. Thus, while evangelical faith-curists were not antitrinitarian, they tended to give little if any attention to the doctrine. The result was a pietistic "Jesus-centrism" that emphasized the *name* of Jesus.

This Jesus-centrism goes back to John and Charles Wesley (one thinks of Charles Wesley's many hymns, such as "Gentle Jesus, Meek and Mild" and "Jesus, Lover of My Soul") and becomes fairly explicit in late nineteenth-century American revivalism. A. B. Simpson is a good example. His hymns are characteristically centered on Jesus, as in "I Have Seen Jesus," "Jesus Is Mine," "Look to Jesus," "Glory to the Name of Jesus," "The Power of His Name," and even "Jesus Only."[41] His classic formulation of the gospel was the "fourfold" message of Jesus as Savior, Sanctifier, Healer, and Coming King (a formulation adopted almost without change by Aimee Semple McPherson, founder of the International Church of the *Foursquare* Gospel).

Kenyon stood solidly in this tradition, as can be seen throughout his writings but especially in his popular book *The Wonderful Name of Jesus*. According to Kenyon, the whole of the Christian message and experience may be summed up in the idea that we have been given the name of Jesus.[42] The following statement out of the many that could be quoted is representative: "All He was, is in that Name; all He is today, is in that Name—and that Name is ours. Jesus was given that Name, that He might give it to us."[43] So centered on Jesus was Kenyon's teaching in this book that it was widely read and appreciated by Oneness Pentecostals—a branch of Pentecostalism that explicitly rejects the Trinity in favor of the view that Jesus is the name of the Father, Son, and Holy Spirit.[44]

Lest I be misunderstood, my point is not that there is something wrong with an emphasis on and devotion to Jesus, although in some extreme quarters I would say it is imbalanced. My point is that Kenyon's emphasis on Jesus and his name is characteristic of the evangelical faith-cure and early Pentecostal traditions. Indeed, modern Pentecostals and charismatics take the centrality of Jesus and the power of his name so for granted that it generally would not even occur to them to see this emphasis as in any way distinctive.

Controversial Teachings

So far we have not considered parallels in the faith-cure and Pentecostal movements to Kenyon's more controversial teachings—his disputed views on faith, healing, confession, spiritual laws, the human spirit, the nature of the believer, and the like. There is actually a wealth of material that could be used to document parallels between Kenyon and the healing and Pentecostal movements.

In my own research I have noted such parallels to be particularly abundant in the writings of A. B. Simpson and John G. Lake. I have already mentioned that Simpson invited Kenyon to preach at his church. I have no historical evidence to show that Kenyon would have been familiar with Lake or vice versa, though it is possible: Lake was winding down his career in the 1920s and died in Spokane, Washington, just four years after Kenyon had moved from Los Angeles to Seattle in 1931.

In what follows, then, I will be quoting most frequently from Simpson and Lake but occasionally from other sources in the faith-cure and early Pentecostal traditions. What I will be attempting to document is not *direct influence* from Lake or Simpson to Kenyon. Rather, my more modest aim is to show that Kenyon's controversial teachings have significant antecedents in the teachings of the faith-healing teachers (e.g., Simpson) and parallels in the early Pentecostal evangelists (e.g., Lake). We have already established that Kenyon's ministry activities, associations, and basic theological views were in those traditions. If many of his controversial views have parallels in those traditions as well, we will have to conclude that Kenyon's teachings represent a development within the evangelical faith-cure and Pentecostal movements.

Faith

We have already mentioned one aspect of Kenyon's teaching on faith, namely, his view that faith is a present-tense taking or living in what we already have in Christ. Faith "is bringing into the present tense things which were in the future for us."[45] Similarly, A. B. Simpson wrote, "Sometimes in those that are not healed there is an expectation and hope rather than an immediate and present tense faith. Real faith takes and acts now."[46]

Another even more controversial aspect of Kenyon's view of faith was his teaching that what Jesus was saying in Mark 11:22 was not, "Have faith in God," but rather, "Have the faith of God." For Kenyon this means that "we have God's faith produced in us by His living Word, by His nature that is imparted to us."[47] Where this way of construing Mark 11:22 originated I do not know, but it evidently goes back at least to Simpson. Note the following passages:

> It is just having "The Faith of God" (Mark 11:22, margin). "And the faith I now live in the flesh, I live," not by faith *on* the Son of God, but "by the faith *of* the Son of God" (Gal. 2:20). That is it. It is not *your* faith. You have no faith in you, any more than you have life or anything else in you. . . . You have to take His faith as well as His life and healing, and have simply to say, "I live by the faith of the Son of God."[48]

> Yes, we can speak that word of faith, and lo, the flesh withers and dies. We can speak it again, and lo, the poison tree of sickness is withered. . . . The secret of all is this: "Have the faith of God." The faith *of* God is as different from faith *in* God as Christ's faith is from that of the disciples who were laboring with the demoniac boy.[49]

There is a difference here: For Kenyon it is God's nature given to us that enables us to have God's faith, whereas for Simpson it is not God's nature but God himself in us that exhibits this faith. The difference, though, is subtle, and there is no reason to think that Kenyon was consciously differing from Simpson or disagreeing with him (if he was even aware of these specific passages in Simpson's writings). The point is, the idea that Mark 11:22 means that in some sense God has faith and we can have his faith does not originate with Kenyon but has precedents in the evangelical faith-healing movement.

Similarly, John G. Lake understood Hebrews 11:3 to be attributing faith to God in his activity of creation:

> Now Jesus was a faith worker. The Father was a faith worker before him. Our Heavenly Father has done everything He has done by faith. When He wanted the earth, He said, "Let there be." *"Through faith we understand that the worlds were framed by the word of God, so that things which are seen were not made of things that appear"* (Hebrews 11:3).[50]

Divine Life

To prove that Kenyon's theology was cultic, McConnell quotes statements from his writings that attribute to humanity God's nature. For example, Kenyon taught that we were created "in God's class of being" and in the new birth receive "the nature and life of God in one's spirit."[51] However, Kenyon's ideas here and even his way of expressing those ideas are much closer to the healing and Pentecostal traditions than to the metaphysical cults.

A. B. Simpson, for example, wrote that God "gave divine strength to Abraham and Sarah, something that was a part of God Himself, because He wanted it to be of a higher order."[52] Simpson's idea here is no different from the standard Keswick teaching that the believer's strength is never his or her own but is rather God's strength experienced as God himself fills and empowers the believer.

R. A. Torrey, a Higher Life advocate, described the new birth in language identical to that used by Kenyon. According to Torrey, "The new birth is simply the impartation of a new nature, the impartation of God's nature."[53]

John G. Lake's teaching is arguably even more radical than that of Kenyon. He taught, in terms very much like that of Simpson, that "divine life is that union of the soul by which the recipient becomes the partaker of His life."[54] But Lake took this so far as to say that people were gods and created to be part of God: "Man is not a separate creation detached from God, he is part of God Himself. . . . God intends us to be gods. The inner man was the real governor, the true man that Jesus said was a god."[55] Likewise, Lake articulated a doctrine of incarnation that sounds identical to that of Kenyon:

> God was in Christ, wasn't He? An incarnation. God is in you, an incarnation, if you are born again. You are incarnate. God is in you. . . . Friends, you are a son of God. You are a partaker of the divine nature. That is incarnation. Plus that, you have the Holy Spirit dwelling in you. You have the nature of God in you. . . . That puts a man in God's class. Can you see what the incarnation means? It is not something to reason and talk about. It is life.[56]

That Kenyon's doctrine here belongs in the evangelical Higher-Life and faith-cure tradition may be especially proven from the fact that in one of his most important writings Kenyon quotes from A. J. Gordon in support of his teaching: "The new birth therefore is not a change of nature as it is sometimes defined; it is rather the communication of the Divine nature."[57]

Spiritual Forces and Spiritual Laws

One of the major criticisms of the Word-Faith teaching is that it tends to depersonalize God by speaking of spiritual "forces" (a term used especially by Copeland with reference to faith) and of "spiritual laws" governing the universe, including mankind. Whatever one may think about such ideas and expressions, Kenyon did not bring them into the Pentecostal movement. Such ideas were taught by both Simpson and Lake. Simpson, for example, wrote about "the laws of the Holy Ghost" and "the great law of faith":

> Now, get to work and study the laws of the Holy Ghost; find out all the modes of His operation, the things that help to bring Him, and then adjust yourself to Him, and you will find out that the Spirit of God will fit into your life as perfectly as the power fits into our machinery.[58]

> "Believe ye?" He asks, and then utters the great law of faith which determines for every one of us the measure of our blessings, "According to your faith be it unto you." . . . And there is a secret which opens heaven—commands all the forces and resources of the throne. It is not agonizing prayer; it is not much labor; it is simply this: "According to your faith be it unto you."[59]

Note that Simpson not only talks about the laws of the Spirit and the law of faith but also compares the working of the Spirit in our lives to "power" in "our machinery." Now, Simpson clearly and emphatically taught a personal view of God, but here he speaks of God in quite "impersonal" terms. This sort of metaphor was common in the Higher Life tradition. For example, Hannah Whitall Smith described the surrender of the Christian to God as being "like making the junction between the machinery and the steam-engine: the machinery is yielded up to the power of the engine, and the engine works it, and it goes easily and without effort because of the mighty power that is behind it."[60]

John G. Lake stated that "Jesus Christ came to reveal the laws of the Spirit and to apply them."[61] Lake also described in graphic terms the healing presence of the Spirit in the believer as a force:

> The Spirit of God is just as tangible as electricity is. You handle it, you minister it to another, you receive it from God through faith and prayer, your person becomes supercharged with it. . . . It is one of the most difficult things in all the world for people who are not familiar with the ministry of healing to comprehend that the Spirit of God is tangible, actual, a living quantity, just as real as electricity, just as real as any other native force. Yea and a great deal more. The life principle that stands behind all manifestations of life everywhere.[62]

Man as a Spirit

Related to the idea of spiritual forces is the idea that man himself is fundamentally a spirit. The idea pervades Kenyon's writings; but it is also found in the writings of such men as John G. Lake. Note this passage:

> Your spirit is the life quality of you, the life principle that gives you action. Not just your mind, but the in-breathed Spirit of God, the breath that God breathed into man. That is eternal. Take this outward man and bury him in the ground, and the worms will eat him. But they will not eat the real man— the one that lives within. So few have any conception of giving that inner man his proper place, or recognizing his divine right to rule and govern the whole being.[63]

What is striking here is the statement, so common in Kenyon and the Word-Faith teachers, that "the real man" is the inner one, the spirit. Moreover, this idea appears linked in Lake's teaching to the idea that the inner man or spirit is meant to rule "the whole being," that is, that the spirit is supposed to rule the mind and body. This is a crucial assumption in Kenyon's teaching, and we find it in an early Pentecostal faith healer.

Positive Confession

The idea of "positive confession"—that what we believe and say is what we get—has parallels in the healing and Pentecostal traditions as well as in the metaphysical cults. But the understanding of positive confession in Kenyon's thought is rooted directly in evangelical Higher Life thought. The idea was developed in the Keswick movement as a way of encouraging people to experience the fullness of the Spirit in their Christian lives. Specifically, the Keswick teachers rejected the idea that some manifestation or evidence of the "baptism" or "fullness" of the Spirit was needed before one could be confident of its possession. Instead they urged Christians to "confess" that they had that blessing as soon as they had fulfilled the biblical conditions for receiving it. The model for this confession in the absence of palpable evidence was the evangelical doctrine of justification by faith. We can believe that God forgives us, reckons us as righteous, and has reconciled us to himself solely on the basis of his promise to do so if we believe. If we can believe God for justification, the Keswick teachers argued, we can and should also believe that God gives us the fullness of the Spirit and perfect holiness simply because he has promised to do so if we repent and believe.[64]

This line of reasoning was sometimes applied to healing in ways similar to the teaching of Kenyon. A. B. Simpson frequently focused on what

Kenyon would later call "negative confession," bringing trouble on yourself by verbalizing fears or worries:

> Do not ever let the devil know that he has hurt you. Do not ever let him hear you say, "It is hard." If he feels that he does hurt you he will stay and try harder, but if he thinks he does not hurt you he will not waste his time on you. Do not for the world let people tell you about your troubles; do not let them sympathize with you. Always rejoice, always be cheerful. . . . When we are looking for trouble we get trouble. When we are in the complaining mood we shall get something to complain about.[65]

> *How should I act if I should break my arm?*
> Ask the Lord to keep it from breaking. Then do not calculate on breaking it, or you may according to your faith. . . . For yourself, trust God in the present moment, and do not have any supposes, else you may have Job's experience, "I feared a fear and it came upon me."[66]

> It is a serious matter to complain, for it may bring the thing we fear, or worse. "For the thing which I greatly feared has come upon me."[67]

Also like Kenyon, Simpson taught that to receive blessings from God (particularly healing), one must verbalize one's faith and not merely think or feel it: "We must confess Him as our Guardian and Deliverer. 'I will say of the Lord, He is my refuge and my fortress.' We must say it as well as feel it."[68] He also quoted Romans 4:17, "Faith must always first 'call the things that are not as though they were,'" to support his contention that we must believe we have healing before our body exhibits healthy symptoms. He then addressed the following question:

> *But have we a right to call that real which is not real?*
> If God calls it so, we can echo His declaration. And faith must always first reckon and then receive.[69]

John G. Lake also taught a form of the positive confession doctrine:

> I cannot imagine that when Adam wanted the cows or the sheep he went out with a dog or a club to get them. Living as he did in the place of God where God had the fullness of access to his nature, he had a better control of the cows and the sheep than that. I believe that when he spoke to the cows they came home; that when he wanted the birds he said "Come," and they came.[70]

Lake is not merely speculating about what Adam was able to accomplish before the fall. He is arguing that when God has "the fullness of access" to our nature, we will be able to command creatures with our words as well. And, of course, Lake thinks we should be able in some measure to begin seeing this kind of power in our lives now.

Lake also articulates the standard Word-Faith teaching that faith and fear are opposites and that positive thinking is therefore essential to faith and healing:

> Faith is the very opposite of fear. Faith has the opposite effect in spirit, and soul, and body. Faith causes the spirit of man to become confident. It causes the mind of man to become restful, and positive. A positive mind repels disease. Consequently, the emanation of the Spirit destroys disease germs.[71]

Like Simpson, then, Lake urges Christians not to be "negative," warning that one's negativity can adversely affect others as well as oneself: "Job's comforters were of the negative kind. Let us not be a gloom pot or a tar brush. If you are my friend, and you come to me, you are going to say something with faith in God in it."[72]

Again, I am not claiming that Kenyon's teaching was identical to these other men's views or that they anticipated his doctrine of positive confession in every respect. I am saying, though, that Kenyon's teaching represents a fairly natural development within the larger tradition of the healing and Pentecostal movements.

Disease and Healing

The basic presupposition of Kenyon's doctrine of healing is the belief known as "healing in the atonement." As has already been explained, this idea originated in the nineteenth-century evangelical healing movement and is often associated with A. B. Simpson (though he did not originate it). The following passage from Simpson sums up the core theological rationale for the doctrine:

> The Lord is a God of infinite benevolence and goodness and "in him is no darkness at all" [1 John 1:5]. Sickness and pain are as foreign to His nature and beneficent will as sin and death. The original creation He made "very good," [Gen. 1:31] and the ravages of disease are wholly due to the presence and power of Satan. Christ has come to destroy the works of the devil, and His blessed Gospel includes the healing of our diseases as truly as the forgiveness of our sins. Only a prejudiced and faithless theology could restrict the blessings of His great salvation to mere spiritual blessings and rob a suffering world of the touch of His healing wings.[73]

That healing is just as much a part of Christ's atoning work—and therefore just as much a part of the gospel—as forgiveness of sins is standard Pentecostal doctrine. The official statement of faith of the Assemblies of God, the largest Pentecostal denomination, states: "Deliverance from sickness is provided for in the atonement, and is the privilege of all believers (Isa. 53:4–5; Matt. 8:16–17)."[74] Walter Hollenweger, the historian of Pentecostalism, observes that "it must not be forgotten that the healing evangelists do not represent any more extreme a view than what was known until a short time ago in the Assemblies of God as 'the full gospel'"—a fact sometimes indeed forgotten by critics of the Word-Faith theology.[75]

Some of the other most often criticized aspects of Kenyon's teaching on healing were already being taught in faith-cure circles. For example, Kenyon and the Word-Faith teachers are (rightly) criticized for teaching that those who would have faith for healing from God must ignore their symptoms. Kenyon, for instance, wrote:

> I make the confession that "by His stripes I am healed"; the disease and its symptoms may not leave my body at once, but I hold fast to my confession. . . . I know that I am healed because He said I was healed, and it makes no difference what the symptoms may be in my body.[76]

Yet this teaching was common fare in the faith-healing movement and in the Pentecostalism of Kenyon's day. Simpson, for instance, told Christians, "Keep your eyes off your symptoms and on Christ."[77]

> Not to show your faith, or display your courage, but because of your faith, begin to act as one that is healed. . . . And then, when you do go forth to act your faith, be careful not to begin to watch the result or look at the symptoms, or see if you stand. You must ignore all symptoms, and see only Him there before you, almighty to sustain you and save you from falling. . . . Do not look always for the immediate removal of the symptoms. Do not think of them. Simply ignore them and press forward, claiming the reality back of all symptoms.[78]

Another aspect of the healing doctrine of both Kenyon and the Word-Faith televangelists that is highly controversial is their claim that the faithful Christian should not die of any disease but simply pass quietly into death when God calls us home. Kenyon put it this way: "I believe that it is the plan of the Father that no believer should ever be sick, that he should live his full length of time and actually wear out and fall asleep."[79] Simpson, though, says exactly the same thing, even using the expression "wear out" to describe the body's passage from life to death:

He has not provided that there shall be no disease, but that disease should it come shall be overcome. . . . There is no need that we should die of disease. The system might just wear out and pass away as naturally as the apple ripens and falls in autumn, or the wheat matures and dies in June. It has simply fulfilled its natural period. . . . The promise of healing is not physical immortality, but health until our life work is done.[80]

Prayer and God's Will

One of the aspects of the Word-Faith doctrine that many of its critics have regarded as most outrageous is the assertion that it is wrong to offer petitions to God for healing or finances with the qualification "Thy will be done" or "if it be thy will." Fred Price's assertion on national television in 1990 that such a prayer is "really stupidity" and implies that God is "a fool" is typically quoted in this connection.[81] While Kenyon did not use such inflammatory language, he did teach that such qualifications were inappropriate inasmuch as we already know from Scripture what God's will is in such matters:

> You say, "Mr. Kenyon, when Jesus prayed in the garden He said, not my will but thine be done." I know. . . . We know that saving lost men is His will. We know that carrying the Gospel to the world is His will. We know that teaching and building up the believer is His will. We know one hundred things that are His will. It is His will that our bills should be paid, that we should be strong and vigorous in our walk, that we should have a testimony that would make people strong to trust Him.[82]

What has been overlooked is the fact that this teaching is part and parcel of the "healing in the atonement" doctrine taught by faith-curists and Pentecostals throughout Kenyon's lifetime. Consider, for example, the teaching of Dr. Lilian B. Yeomans. By her testimony she was healed through the ministry of John A. Dowie in 1898. She became a Pentecostal healing evangelist and taught at L.I.F.E. Bible College (founded by Aimee Semple McPherson). Dr. Yeomans wrote: "Many of us have been taught to pray, 'If it be Thy will, heal me.' That wasn't the way David prayed." After citing Psalm 6:2–9, she commented, "There were no ifs, no buts in that prayer. . . ."[83] And her opinion was hardly new or unique. A. B. Simpson taught the same thing:

> The prayer for healing, "if it be His will," carries with it no claim for which Satan will quit his hold. This is a matter about which we ought to know His will before we ask, and then will and claim it because it is His will. . . . If the Lord Jesus has purchased it for us in His redemption, it must be God's will

for us to have it, for Christ's whole redeeming work was simply the executing of the Father's will. . . . No one thinks of asking for forgiveness "if the Lord will." Nor should we throw any stronger doubt on His promise of physical redemption.[84]

John G. Lake taught precisely the same thing:

> The Church at large has taught that healing is dependent on the exercise of the Will of God, and that the proper attitude for the Christian to assume is, "If it be thy will." . . . We believe that this attitude of mind and this character of reasoning is due to the ignorance of the plain Word and Will of God, as revealed through Jesus Christ. We contend that God is always the Healer. We contend further that it is not necessary for God to will the healing or the non-healing of any individual. In His desire to bless mankind, He willed once and for all and forever that man should be blessed and healed.[85]

The Metaphysical Cults as Counterfeits

We could go on and on documenting parallels between the teachings of Kenyon and the faith-healing and Pentecostal teachings. However, there is one other comparison that is critical to make. If Kenyon found it necessary to assure his listeners and readers that he was not teaching metaphysical thought, the same was true of the evangelical faith-curists and early Pentecostals.

McConnell in particular has drawn attention to the fact that the Word-Faith teachers have felt it necessary to disavow any relationship with the metaphysical cults. He cites, for example, Kenneth Hagin's admission, "When I preach on the mind, it frightens some congregations. They immediately think of Christian Science."[86] Likewise, McConnell argues that Kenyon protested too much, as it were, that his teaching was not metaphysical:

> In all his various denunciations of the cults, it is significant to note that Kenyon criticizes only a certain type of cult: those that derived from Quimby's metaphysical writings. . . . Kenyon was in the habit, as are many in the Faith movement, of issuing disclaimers as to the obvious similarities between his teaching and the cults. The typical pattern in such instances is to disclaim any similarities with cultic teaching on a particular topic and then proceed to teach exactly what the cults teach.[87]

McConnell then cites such disclaimers from Kenyon as these: "We are not dealing with mysticism, philosophy or metaphysics," or, "This is not a new metaphysics or philosophy." Following these disclaimers, Kenyon would assert doctrines that McConnell identifies as cultic, such as that there are "great spiritual laws that govern the unseen forces of life," or that God imparts "His own nature to the human spirit."[88]

Three observations about McConnell's argument need to be made. First, most or all of these doctrines are not "exactly what the cults teach" but differ from the cults in important ways. For example, Kenyon's teaching that God imparts his nature to our spirits in the new birth bears little resemblance to the metaphysical view, according to which God is the impersonal divine reality in which the entire cosmos and all life participates and of which all human spirits are a part whether they realize or believe it or not.

Second, most or all of these doctrines taught by Kenyon have antecedents in the healing/Pentecostal tradition, as we have seen. Again, Kenyon's teaching that God imparts his nature to the believer is standard Keswick holiness doctrine, was taught by Simpson and other evangelical faith-curists, and was standard fare in early Pentecostalism as well.

Third, as might be expected, the faith-curists and Pentecostals also found it necessary to give the metaphysical cults, especially Christian Science, special attention and to distinguish their teachings from those of such cults. Consider, for example, this statement from Simpson:

> Now you cannot stop being careful for everything just by mere negation, as the folly of Christian Science teaches. That will not do. I cannot say there is nothing the matter with me when there is. I may say there is no trouble. But there is trouble. I cannot cancel my debts by saying there are no debts. But I can hand them over to another.[89]

Simpson went on to urge Christians to hand over their troubles to God in prayer. Elsewhere he admitted, "The same results as are claimed for faith in the healing of disease are also said to follow the practices of Spiritualism, animal magnetism, clairvoyance, etc."[90] He even complained, "Many persons strangely confound this strange anti-Christian error with divine healing."[91]

John G. Lake found it necessary to make similar statements. For example, in a letter written to the newspaper responding to a sermon critical of the faith-cure movement, Lake wrote:

> This must not be construed as a defense of Christian Science. . . . The dying world is stretching out her hands for help. The Church on account of her laxness in this matter opens the doors for the existence of Christian Science and all the thousand and one worn out philosophies that follow in her train. . . . All the abstract criticism in the world is powerless to stop the drift from the churches to Christian Science so long as Christian Science heals the sick and the Church does not.[92]

Examples could be multiplied from the faith-healing evangelists. For instance, John Alexander Dowie in 1902 wrote that "Divine Healing is opposed by diabolical counterfeits (Christian Science, Mind Healing etc.)."[93] Charles Fox Parham, the father of Pentecostalism, went even further. He admitted that the metaphysical cults do exhibit some power but contended that they were the counterfeit of which Pentecostalism is the real:

> When we heard and studied the pretended claims of Medical, Mental, and Christian Sciences, hypnotism, etc., we said: God has the real of which these sorceries are the counterfeit. We found him who bare our sicknesses (Matt. 8:17) and was lifted up for us even as Moses lifted up the serpent in the wilderness (John 3:14). When beholding the power of spiritualism, for though 99 per cent of it is slight [sic] of hand it does contain certain forces, as the possession of mediums, speaking under the control of evil spirits, etc. We said, God has the real of this: and, lo, when the power of Pentecost came we found the real, and everyone who has received the Baptism of the Holy Spirit has again spoken in tongues.[94]

A Pentecostal historian, Edith Blumhofer, has recently made the following observations:

> The perception of Christian Science as an arch enemy suggests how close evangelical teaching on healing and Christian Science teaching were. When early Pentecostals listed their enemies, Christian Science usually led the list. Early Pentecostal periodicals contain many articles exposing the errors of Christian Science, suggesting that they felt especially threatened by it. Preoccupation with Christian Science waned in the 1920s, when Christian Science came to be perceived simply as one of a long list of unorthodox groups.[95]

When Blumhofer says that evangelical and Christian Science teachings on healing were "close," she does not mean that they were based on similar theologies. Rather, she is simply pointing out that because both spoke of obtaining healing through faith instead of medicine, the evangelical faith-curists saw Christian Science as a clever counterfeit. Blumhofer concludes that

> evangelical considerations of physical healing [toward the end of the nineteenth century] can be understood as a partial response to Christian Science, Unity, and other mind cure movements. Evangelicals concluded that such movements thrived precisely because Christianity failed to offer hope for physical renewal.[96]

What Blumhofer says about the evangelical faith-curists and Pentecostals applies equally to E. W. Kenyon. He saw his own work as a response, not an adaptation, of the metaphysical cults. In this regard his perspective was no different from that of men like A. B. Simpson, J. A. Dowie, or Charles Parham.

Crosscurrents

In this and the preceding chapter I have argued that Kenyon's thought belongs in the evangelical faith-cure and proto-Pentecostal traditions, not in the category of the metaphysical cults. However, though it is valid to stress the dissimilarities between these two religious contexts, some similarities and crosscurrents between the two should be acknowledged.

We have already noted a relevant focal point of such crosscurrents in Emerson College of Oratory, where Kenyon briefly attended. Charles Wesley Emerson was associated with the faith-cure movement even as he was developing an increasingly metaphysical philosophy. One of the more interesting guest speakers ever to appear at Emerson was Henry Drummond, an evolutionist who was involved in mesmerism and other metaphysical interests. Drummond had been a popular preacher in evangelical circles and was even a close associate of Dwight L. Moody, a towering figure in the evangelical Higher Christian Life movement.

The crosscurrents between New Thought and the Higher Life movement were to a great extent currents swirling throughout late nineteenth-century society. Both evangelicals, notably some of those in the Keswick movement, and New Thought teachers drew inspiration from earlier Christian mystics such as Fénelon and Madame Guyon. Of course, the two movements derived significantly different ideas from those Christian mystics.

Ironically, even as interest in miracles and mysticism was increasing, the general culture was highly enamored of science, and virtually all religious traditions were trying to express themselves in scientific terms. Newtonian science viewed the world as operating according to immutable and universal laws, and Christians sought to show that Christianity viewed the world in the same way. Nearly everyone from revivalist Charles Finney to the New Thought writer Ralph Waldo Trine spoke of immutable spiritual laws. The language has survived and even has a central place in what may be the most widely used tract of the twentieth century: Bill Bright's *The Four Spiritual Laws*. "Just as there are physical laws that govern the physical universe, so also there are spiritual laws that govern our relationship to God."

The point is that both New Thought and the evangelical Higher Life and Pentecostal traditions reflected various cultural and philosophical trends of the period. The same was true of Kenyon. It may not be possible to iden-

tify the direct source for each and every idea in Kenyon's system of doctrine. What is clear enough is that his interests and formulations show evidence of contact with New Thought and other metaphysical beliefs but that
the substance of his doctrine is essentially evangelical in origin and in general outlook.

Conclusion

I have argued at considerable length in this chapter that E. W. Kenyon's
theology should properly be regarded as a development within the broad
tradition that included the evangelical faith-cure movement and early Pentecostal movements. This interpretation of Kenyon will no doubt be viewed
by those in the modern Word-Faith movement as vindicating their position, since they are only too glad to see themselves in that tradition. Critics of Word-Faith teaching, on the other hand, especially the many critics
who are themselves Pentecostals or charismatics, may look on the interpretation of Kenyon presented here with some consternation, if not outrage. They may conclude that I am letting the Word-Faith teaching off the
hook by conceding its claim to be rooted in an orthodox Christian tradition. In concluding this chapter I would like to explain why I think both
of these predictable reactions may be misplaced.

First of all, I have *not* argued here that Kenyon's teaching is identical to
the teachings of the healing-evangelicals and Pentecostals of his day. Rather,
I have argued that his teaching can be seen as a *development* within that tradition. Furthermore, in my judgment the development is in several respects
an *unhealthy* one, as, hopefully, subsequent chapters will demonstrate.

Second, it must be remembered that I have not claimed that Kenyon
was *uninfluenced* by the metaphysical concepts he studied in Boston. Rather,
I have argued that Kenyon, despite whatever influence metaphysical
thought had on his teachings, remained essentially outside that movement.
One might still conclude that Kenyon was *unduly* influenced by the metaphysical cults and that this influence contributed to some serious doctrinal
errors in his teaching.

Third, the possibility exists that the evangelical faith-cure movement
and early Pentecostalism were also influenced in some respects by metaphysical thought. This is a question left relatively unexplored in this book.
I simply note Blumhofer's opinion, cited earlier, that these Christian movements were at least in part taking up a challenge posed to the church by
the metaphysical cults. Many of the ideas and expressions one finds in all
of these movements, Christian and non-Christian, seem to have been "in
the air" in late nineteenth-century American culture. It may be somewhat

beside the point, then, to worry too much about exactly who influenced whom in what ways.

Fourth, if various aspects of the Word-Faith teaching are unbiblical and even spiritually harmful, and if these aspects are part and parcel of "classic" Pentecostal doctrine, then, frankly, so much the worse for classic Pentecostal doctrine. In my discussions with Pentecostals and charismatics in various parts of the country, I have found many who believed that certain doctrinal and practical weaknesses were inherent in classic Pentecostalism and should be abandoned by contemporary Spirit-filled Christians. For example, many Pentecostals disavow the doctrine that speaking in tongues is the only "initial evidence" of baptism in the Spirit. To disallow as "anticharismatic" all criticisms of the Word-Faith teaching that also implicate other Pentecostal or charismatic streams of belief and practice would be obscuring the truth.

Moreover, it is a strategic mistake not to admit that some aspects of the Word-Faith teaching that often come under fire (say, healing in the atonement) are indeed authentically Pentecostal. If we attack the Word-Faith teaching as if it were a wholly alien intrusion into Pentecostalism, knowledgeable advocates of Word-Faith teaching will rightly reject our critique.

We paint ourselves into a corner if we attack the Word-Faith doctrine as a metaphysical Trojan horse within the Pentecostal and charismatic camp. This is well illustrated by two books written by Hank Hanegraaff. In the first, *Christianity in Crisis,* Hanegraaff insists that "the Faith movement is not charismatic; it is cultic." The Faith teachers, he complains, "have been able to cleverly disguise themselves as charismatics, thereby tarnishing the reputation of a legitimate movement within Christianity." Hanegraaff criticizes those noncharismatics who "have attempted to use the Faith teachers to prove that the charismatic movement is in chaos" (a not-so-subtle reference to John MacArthur's book *Charismatic Chaos*).[97]

In his second book, *Counterfeit Revival,* Hanegraaff takes on the "Toronto Blessing" and related revivalist developments in recent years. He rightly notes the close connection of the Toronto revival to the Word-Faith movement, specifically the support given to it by Hagin, Copeland, and Hinn.[98] Yet, in the course of his critique of this "Counterfeit Revival," Hanegraaff traces its historical precedents to the likes of A. A. Allen, William Branham, Jack Coe, David du Plessis, Kathryn Kuhlman, Aimee Semple McPherson, Charles Parham, Smith Wigglesworth, and Maria B. Woodworth-Etter.[99] It would be extremely difficult to dissociate all of these men and women from the Pentecostal and charismatic tradition. Significantly, in *Counterfeit Revival* Hanegraaff makes no effort to characterize the revival as a cultic transplant. Undoubtedly the Toronto Blessing has its roots in the Pentecostal and charismatic tradition. Yet, as we have seen, the ministry of E. W.

Kenyon also has its roots in the proto-Pentecostal and early Pentecostal context.

Again, my point here is not to condemn all Pentecostalism. It is evident, as Hanegraaff himself points out, that there are many mature, biblically sound Pentecostal and charismatic churches and individuals. But insofar as this is the case, it is the result of Pentecostal and charismatic Christians outgrowing the tradition's immaturity and leaving behind the dubious aspects of its origins. My Pentecostal and charismatic friends would be among the first to agree that there is a great deal of "chaos" in the charismatic movement. Better to acknowledge this reality and deal with it candidly than to shift the blame to the metaphysical cults.

Fifth, one should not overlook the fact that just as Kenyon's views represented a development within the faith-cure tradition and were not identical to it, the Word-Faith teaching of Kenneth Hagin is not identical to that of Kenyon in all respects. In turn, the teachings of Hagin's disciples, notably those of Kenneth Copeland and Charles Capps, are in some respects more radical than Hagin's own teaching. Thus, how one categorizes Kenyon's teaching does not settle definitively how one should view the teaching of Hagin and his disciples.

This leads us to the question of the transition from Kenyon's teaching in the period between the two World Wars to the teaching of Hagin on health and wealth since the 1950s. Answering that question will complete our study of the roots of the Word-Faith teaching and will be the subject of the next chapter.

Fathers of the Word-Faith Movement

There is no denying that much of Faith theology is derived directly from metaphysics. Some of the substance, style, and scams endemic to the movement, however, can be traced to teachings and practices expressed primarily by certain post-World-War-II faith healers and revivalists operating within Pentecostal circles.

Hank Hanegraaff[1]

Hanegraaff's attack on the Word-Faith ministers and theology violates the historian's mandate of fair representation and [William] James' (and [Jonathan] Edwards') understanding that religious movements generate both the extreme and the moderate examples.

William DeArteaga[2]

Likewise urge the young men to be sensible; in all things show yourself to be an example of good deeds, with purity in doctrine, dignified, sound in speech which is beyond reproach, so that the opponent will be put to shame, having nothing bad to say about us.

Titus 2:6–8

In the preceding three chapters I have focused on the teachings of E. W. Kenyon. We have seen that he formulated many of the distinctive ideas of the modern Word-Faith movement. And we have also seen that while he was influenced to some extent by the metaphysical cults, overall his ministry and teachings were developed in the context of the evangelical faith-healing tradition and the early Pentecostal movement. Kenyon was not, however, a Pentecostal, and in some important respects his teachings differed from those of most Pentecostals.

Today, however, the Word-Faith teaching is an explicitly Pentecostal or charismatic teaching. That is, it is advocated primarily, if not exclusively, by persons who view spiritual gifts—especially speaking in tongues but also prophecy, healing, and other supernatural manifestations—as integral aspects of the Christian life. Its appeal is limited almost entirely to Christians in the Pentecostal and independent charismatic churches. The question that remains is how the Word-Faith movement came to take the form it has today.

As I see it, a number of important figures contributed to the origins of the televangelist Word-Faith movement and its theology, among whom four stand out. The first of these, E. W. Kenyon, has been considered at length already. In this chapter, then, I will examine the role of three other men in the rise of the Word-Faith movement: William Branham, Oral Roberts, and Kenneth Hagin. These individuals, along with Kenyon, are the men I would call the four "fathers" of the Word-Faith movement.

William Branham and the Latter-Rain Movement

The Word-Faith teaching in its core concepts about faith does go back to E. W. Kenyon. But this doctrine was filtered through a particular strain of Pentecostalism known as the Latter-Rain movement of 1948. This movement was sparked by the teaching and ministry of William Branham, the second "father" of the modern Word-Faith movement.[3]

The term "latter rain" has been used throughout the twentieth century by Pentecostals to refer to a final outpouring of the Holy Spirit to occur shortly before Christ's return, generally accompanied by specific supernatural manifestations. Originally it was used simply of the Pentecostal movement itself, and some Pentecostals still use the term in that sense.[4] However, many independent charismatics have for some time used the term "latter rain" to refer not to the restoration of the charismatic gifts but to a subsequent restoration of other "lost truths."

Specifically, the term "latter rain" is often used to refer to a movement that arose within Pentecostalism in the late 1940s. This movement originated in revival meetings held in 1948 by the Sharon Orphanage and Schools in North Battleford, Saskatchewan, Canada, under the leadership of Herrick Holt and George and Ern Hawtin. This revivalist movement soon spread throughout the Assemblies of God in the United States, as well as the Canadian counterpart, the Pentecostal Assemblies of Canada. By late 1949 the Assemblies of God found it necessary in its General Council to denounce the New Order of the Latter Rain, as it had come to be known.[5] In order to distinguish this usage from the classic Pentecostal usage, I will refer to the 1940s movement as the "Latter-Rain" movement.

The initial impetus of the Latter-Rain movement was the "fasting message" of Franklin Hall, who came into prominence in 1946 with his book *Atomic Power with God through Fasting and Prayer*. Hall encouraged long fasts, with one disciple fasting for a reported eighty-three days. Through such marathon sessions of fasting and praying, one could obtain God's power to perform miracles, especially miracles of healing. This "fasting message" was picked up by a number of now famous Pentecostal evangelists.

Hall also made a number of claims that were not generally accepted and that put him increasingly on the fringes of the movement he helped begin. For example, he taught that the Holy Spirit could keep people from exuding body odor. Hall dabbled in the "Christian astrology" that was popularized by Joseph A. Seiss and E. W. Bullinger in the late nineteenth century. He also taught that redeemed man should be able to achieve weightlessness and fly to outer space. One of the most important emphases of his teaching was the pursuit of immortality, believing that God intended his people to attain immortality before Christ's return. He suggested various ways this could be achieved, including the application of biblical formulas.[6]

As unacceptable as such speculations were to most Pentecostals, Hall's teaching inspired a number of Pentecostal evangelists to embark on healing crusades empowered by prayer and fasting. One such faith healer was William Branham.

William Branham

William Marrion Branham (1909–1965),[7] who was also influenced by Hall, is generally credited by Pentecostal historians with leading the way, along with Oral Roberts, in bringing the "healing message" into prominence in modern Pentecostalism. Hall's influence on Branham can be seen especially in two respects. First, Branham accepted Hall's "fasting message" and helped to spread that message through his healing crusades. Second, Branham, like Hall, dabbled in so-called Christian astrology.

Branham was also evidently influenced by Kenyon and helped to spread his message. Two of Branham's associates unquestionably taught doctrines of faith, confession, and healing learned from Kenyon. One of these was F. F. Bosworth, who came out of retirement to join Branham's healing crusades in 1948. Bosworth, though, had developed his thinking on faith with significant influence from Kenyon, as discussed in the previous chapter. In turn, Hagin knew Bosworth and was influenced by him directly. Bosworth's famous book *Christ the Healer* was at one time assigned to all students at Hagin's Rhema Bible Training Center.[8]

The other evangelist associated with Branham was T. L. Osborn, who joined Branham and Bosworth in their healing crusade in Flint, Michigan. He had been introduced to Kenyon's books shortly before Kenyon died and quickly began spreading Kenyon's word—quite literally. Osborn openly preached on many occasions directly from Kenyon's books, even reading a chapter of Kenyon in place of a sermon. Osborn's ministry has for years been based in Tulsa and continues to be very popular among Pentecostals and charismatics.[9]

Another interesting similarity between Branham and Kenyon was that Branham was also an independent Baptist minister who was most comfortable among Pentecostals. Branham began preaching as a tent revivalist in Indiana in 1933, and his emphasis on healing quickly caught the attention of Pentecostals, especially Oneness Pentecostals. Later Branham was to blame the death of his wife and baby in 1937 on his failure to preach in Oneness churches. In 1946 Branham claimed that an angel had visited him; that same year he began his healing crusades—the spark that ignited the Latter-Rain movement. He was joined in 1947 by Gordon Lindsay and other rising Pentecostal leaders, who brought Branham's healing message to the world.

Something of a maverick, Branham did not fit the classic mold of a Pentecostal in all of his doctrines. But his overall position was broadly Pentecostal, and he was widely accepted in Pentecostal circles. Branham taught a variation of the Oneness doctrine (that Jesus was the Father and the Son), though he avoided the terms "Oneness" and "Jesus only." Here again, some affinity with Kenyon may be detected, though to my knowledge there is no evidence of influence by Kenyon at this point. Branham, in fact, adamantly condemned the Trinity as of the devil. He also taught the doctrine of the "serpent's seed"—that Eve's sin in Eden was having sex with the serpent, resulting in a race of people living to this day whose biological father is Satan. Branham also claimed to be the Prophet to the "Laodicean" age, the supposed final period of church history. Branham's influence extended widely through his endorsement by the Full Gospel Business Men's Fellowship International, a Pentecostal ministry that, though not overtly Latter-Rain, has often promoted Latter-Rain teachers.

The Latter-Rain Movement

The Pentecostals at Sharon Orphanage and Schools, having read Hall's *Atomic Power* and attended Branham's healing crusades, were convinced that through these men they had learned of truths that God was restoring to the church in their day. Through the Sharon revivals, Branham's teachings quickly spread and took root in a number of ministries in North America. Some of Branham's more embarrassing or peculiar theories—the "serpent's seed" theory, his astrological speculations, etc.—were weeded out, and most of the Latter-Rain Pentecostals retained their belief in the Trinity (though a segment of the Latter-Rain was and is either Oneness or leans in that direction). However, the basic theological system of Latter-Rain teaching was developed directly from the distinctive ministry and teachings of Branham.

It is interesting to note that the Latter-Rain movement, along with its brightest light, William Branham, is generally not defended today by most Pentecostals and charismatics. Like E. W. Kenyon, Branham is a *persona non grata* as far as most charismatics are concerned. The extent to which Branham has been marginalized by his own tradition is illustrated by the entries on him and on the Latter-Rain movement in the *Dictionary of Pentecostal and Charismatic Movements,* which make no efforts to defend his extreme views, unlike most of the articles on various controversial figures.[10]

Still, whether most followers of the Word-Faith teaching realize it or not, the Word-Faith televangelists are heavily indebted to the Latter-Rain movement and especially to Branham. Their dependence on this movement can be seen not only in their doctrinal and practical similarities, which are many, but also in occasional admissions by the televangelists themselves. Kenneth Hagin, for example, has acknowledged Branham as a "prophet."[11] Branham is justly viewed, then, as the second father of the Word-Faith movement.

Oral Roberts and Pentecostal Televangelism

The third "father" of the Word-Faith movement is Oral Roberts. Including Roberts in this group does not mean that he belongs to the same school of thought as Kenyon or that he holds to the same Word-Faith theology as Hagin, Copeland, and the other Word-Faith televangelists. A movement is more than just its doctrine; one must also consider the practices of the movement and the forms it uses to communicate its message and increase its numbers. Despite somewhat different views on faith, Roberts made critical contributions to the rise of Pentecostal health-and-wealth televangelism.[12]

Born in Oklahoma in 1918, as a teenager Roberts was healed of tuberculosis and stuttering. Shortly afterward he was ordained in the Pentecostal Holiness church. In 1947 he began a healing ministry, first in Enid, Oklahoma;[13] then later that year he established his headquarters in Tulsa, where he began radio broadcasting the same year. Roberts was not part of the Latter-Rain movement, but he quickly established friendly relations with Branham and other Latter-Rain leaders. In 1951 he participated in establishing the Full Gospel Business Men's Fellowship, a Pentecostal association that promoted William Branham as well as other healing evangelists. In 1948 he began an itinerant tent healing crusade, and in 1955 he began his television broadcasts. In 1969 Roberts began televising programs emphasizing healing that aired during prime time. Roberts really pioneered what is now known as televangelism.[14]

Roberts is also well known for his building projects. In 1965 he opened Oral Roberts University (ORU), and in 1981 he opened his 250-million-dollar City of Faith Medical and Research Center. Sharing the platform at the dedication of the City of Faith were most of the modern Word-Faith televangelists, including Kenneth Hagin and Kenneth Copeland.[15] The City of Faith has turned out since to be a financial disaster for the Roberts empire.

As was mentioned previously, in some respects Roberts differs theologically from the Word-Faith teachers. Despite that fact, Roberts both prepared the way for much of their teaching and has supported them in their ministries. Branham's healing crusades may have been more spectacular, but Roberts brought Pentecostal healing ministries to uncountable millions through television. He has lent direct support and encouragement to the Word-Faith teachers and even given them platforms to speak at ORU, over the objections of several professors there.

Roberts also developed much of the thinking about faith and healing that is taken by the Word-Faith televangelists perhaps even further than Roberts himself would go. It was Roberts who coined such clichéd expressions as "God is a good God" (taken to mean that God will allow only good things to happen to those who have faith), "Expect a miracle" (meaning that even if it is true that a miracle won't *necessarily* happen, we should still *expect* one), and the term "seed-faith," denoting Roberts's teaching that we should give, expecting to get more back in return. Roberts also introduced to many people the standard holiness and faith-cure concept that faith is focused on the present—the "now"—as well as the idea that Christians should "release" or "loose" their faith and then wait for the miraculous results.

Roberts has also popularized the idea that Jesus appears to certain special individuals today. He claims that Jesus appeared to him in 1980 as a nine hundred-foot-tall man and that Jesus has appeared to him at other times as well.

During the first half or so of his ministry, Roberts taught in a fairly straightforward manner the classic Pentecostal view that healing was always God's will, that anyone could be healed if he or she had faith. During the latter half of his ministry, he has softened this position, making much more room for God's sovereign right to delay or withhold answers to prayer for his good purposes. Indeed, Roberts has been the leading proponent of the view that Christians should expect healing while not abandoning medicine. In this regard, too, his influence on the Word-Faith movement is significant, because all of the major Word-Faith teachers are careful to say that Christians should not discontinue medical treatment unless they are sure of their healing. Even if one is highly critical of Roberts (as I am), he may be credited with having done more than anyone else to convince Pentecostals to back away from the hard-line view of divine healing that had been taught by A. B. Simpson, John A. Dowie, Charles Parham, John G. Lake, and so many others in his tradition in the first half of the twentieth century.

Another relevant aspect of the ministry of Oral Roberts is his devaluation of doctrine in the interests of unity with all professing Christians. To Roberts, the only thing that matters is whether a person "knows Jesus," and within that stricture he is prepared to recognize people of widely differing doctrinal positions. Roberts took this so far that in 1968 he joined the United Methodist Church, one of the most liberal mainline denominations in America, precisely because of their tolerance for diverse expressions of Christianity. (The UMC, like all mainline denominations, has many fine evangelical Christian churches in it, but institutionally it has been dominated by liberalism for decades.) On one occasion Roberts defended the presence of a Mormon group on the campus at ORU by comparing their doctrinal differences to those between Catholics and Baptists (which, according to Roberts, are relatively inconsequential). His devaluation of doctrine has been repeated with intensity by all of the Word-Faith televangelists.

Oral Roberts, then, is one of the four "fathers" of the modern Word-Faith movement in several respects, both doctrinally and institutionally. He is without question *the* father of Pentecostal healing-revivalist televangelism. As such, through his own ministry and his encouragement and support of the ministries of others, Roberts made the phenomenon of health-and-wealth televangelism possible.

Kenneth Hagin's Word of Faith

Having examined in some detail the contributions of Kenyon, Branham, and Roberts to the modern Word-Faith movement, we are in a position to understand the teachings of Kenneth Hagin and the rest of today's Word-Faith televangelists in their historical, religious context. All agree that the man responsible for developing the teachings of E. W. Kenyon in light of the healing revivals of Branham and Roberts was Kenneth E. Hagin (born 1917). Hagin is the fourth "father" of the Word-Faith movement, the man who put it all together and has led the Word-Faith movement for a generation. The following account of Hagin's life is based on his own account, except as noted otherwise.

Hagin was a weak child with heart problems. His father left his family when he was six.[16] He was raised by his mother and then by her parents as a Southern Baptist,[17] but he considers himself not to have been a Christian during his childhood. For sixteen months during his teen years (1933–1934), he was bedridden with a terminal illness apparently related to his heart problems. (Hagin never says exactly what his illness was; as McConnell points out, apparently "no formal diagnosis was ever made."[18] This complicates the task of determining just how miraculous Hagin's healing was.) On the first evening of his illness Hagin had three nightmarish visions of hell and was converted.[19] Soon after, he began reading through the New Testament and came to Mark 11:24, "Therefore I say unto you, What things soever ye desire, when ye pray, believe that ye receive them, and ye shall have them" (KJV). After several months of wrestling with the import of this text, Hagin became convinced that he should simply accept as fact that he was healed and get out of his sickbed, despite the apparent symptoms.[20] (In another account, Hagin claims that it was Acts 10:38 that convinced him to do this.[21])

Hagin claims that since August 1933 he has never had a headache. This claim should probably be taken with a grain of salt (or perhaps an aspirin!), since Hagin has admitted that if he had a headache he "wouldn't tell anybody."[22] Furthermore, he does admit on one occasion that his "head started hurting" but claims that by telling the devil, "In the name of Jesus . . . I do not have a headache," the pain went away.[23] Evidently, then, when Hagin says he has not had a headache, he means he has never *admitted* to having one. The same goes for the following statement: "I have not had one sick day in 45 years. I did not say that the devil hadn't attacked me. But before the day is out, I am healed."[24]

The young Hagin remained a Southern Baptist and began preaching divine healing. At the same time he associated with Pentecostals, from whom he learned about speaking in tongues. In 1937 Hagin reports that he claimed the "baptism of the Holy Ghost" with speaking in tongues by faith, just as he had claimed healing, rather than "tarrying" for the baptism as Pentecostals had been urging him.[25] From 1939 to 1949 Hagin pastored several Assemblies of God churches. He focused almost exclusively on preaching until 1943, when, Hagin reports, while walking into his kitchen for a drink of water, a teaching gift "dropped down on me and inside me. It just clicked down on the inside of me like a coin drops inside a pay phone."[26]

In 1949 Hagin left the pastorate to begin an itinerant ministry to teach healing by faith. His embarking on this ministry at this time was no coincidence; he was one of dozens of such itinerant faith healers that emerged after the Branham crusades had sparked an enormous interest in such ministries. In fact, Hagin was active in the Voice of Healing conventions associated with Gordon Lindsay's *Voice of Healing* magazine, the official organ of the healing revival movement. Hagin makes the interesting claim that God had revealed to him two years before it happened that a minister "at the forefront of the Healing Revival" would die because he had strayed from his calling by trying to teach. Although he does not name the unfortunate minister, it is fairly obvious that he is referring to Branham.[27] Elsewhere Hagin, who considers himself a Bible teacher as well as a prophet of healing, is at pains to separate himself doctrinally from most of the Latter-Rain healing revivalists. "They made some of the most stupid statements concerning the Bible you ever heard in your life."[28] For all that, Hagin may himself be regarded as a Latter-Rain healer and teacher.

In 1950, Hagin reports, God told him to apply the same faith he had exercised for healing to finances, and Hagin began preaching prosperity. At this time God also supposedly revealed to Hagin the idea that Adam was originally the god of this world and that his sin was an act of high treason against God, which gave legal dominion over the world to Satan.[29] Hagin claims that these revelations came directly to him from God; but this was the same year that Hagin admits to having first read Kenyon's books, in which the same ideas are expressed.[30] In fact, Hagin has plagiarized Kenyon's books extensively, which D. R. McConnell has well documented.[31] In any case, Hagin leaves us in no doubt as to how highly he esteems Kenyon's writings, especially *The Wonderful Name of Jesus:* "It is a marvelous book. It is revelation knowledge. It is the Word of God. . . . And he [Kenyon] did preach faith and healing just like I do."[32]

In 1966 Hagin moved his ministry to Tulsa, and in 1974 he founded Rhema Bible Training Center. In 1979 Hagin and several other televangelists founded the International Convention of Faith Churches and Ministers (headquartered in Tulsa), which functions as a virtual denomination for the Word-Faith movement.

Hagin claims to have had several visitations by Jesus—an experience that seems to be a virtual requirement for a Word-Faith televangelist. The first occurred in 1950, the same year in which he became acquainted with Kenyon's teachings and began preaching prosperity. McConnell has given a good analysis of the typical pattern of the visions:

> (1) Jesus appears to Hagin, usually at some point of considerable need in his life; (2) Jesus imparts some new doctrine to Hagin; (3) skeptical at first, Hagin argues with Jesus about the new doctrine and demands proof from the Bible; (4) Jesus provides the proof from the Bible and Hagin is convinced; and (5) Jesus commands Hagin to teach the new doctrine to the church.[33]

On the basis of these visions, Hagin claims to be both teacher and prophet to the church for the last revival before the second coming of Christ.[34] He is accepted as such by the entire Word-Faith movement and its leaders, who commonly refer to him as "Dad Hagin." While it is true that he plagiarized Kenyon and took most of the defining beliefs of the Word-Faith teaching from Kenyon and others, he did synthesize Kenyon's teachings with Latter-Rain Pentecostalism and has led in the creation of the modern Word-Faith movement and several of its institutions. These facts make Hagin the undisputed living patriarch, if not original father, of the Word-Faith movement.

As Hagin presents it, the Word-Faith doctrine is an explicitly Pentecostal teaching. Admittedly Kenyon, Branham, and Roberts have all been to some extent on the fringes of Pentecostalism. Hagin, by contrast, was an Assemblies of God minister who went on to found a new Pentecostal movement, complete with a church association, ministerial training schools, publishing houses, and radio and television broadcasts. The Word-Faith teaching presupposes the necessity of receiving the Pentecostal "baptism of the Holy Spirit" and the importance of speaking in tongues and other charismatic gifts. Both institutionally and theologically, then, the Word-Faith movement is a segment of the Pentecostal/charismatic tradition.

The question that must be answered still is whether the Word-Faith movement represents Pentecostalism at its best and fullest expression, as the Word-Faith teachers themselves claim, or Pentecostalism at its worst. The only way to answer this question is to examine its teachings and see how they measure up to the teachings of the Bible and the historic beliefs of orthodox Christianity. In posing this question we leave the matter of the "roots" of the Word-Faith teaching and move on to examine its "shoots."

PART 2

The Shoots
of the Word-Faith
Teaching

6

Real Men Don't Use Reason

We cannot know God through our human knowledge, through our mind. God is only revealed to man through his spirit. It is the spirit of man that contacts God, for God is a Spirit. . . . We don't understand the Bible with our mind, it is spiritually understood. We understand it with our spirit, or our heart. . . . As we meditate in this Word, our assurance becomes deeper. This assurance in our spirit is independent of our human reasoning or of human knowledge. It may even contradict human reasoning or physical evidence.

Kenneth Hagin[1]

The trichotomous view of man appears to be a contributing factor in the denigration of the place of the intellect in the Christian life and in a de-emphasis on the importance of sound doctrine—although the degree of these degradations vary with the degree of emphasis placed, without balance, on the trichotomous view. If this view is held in an unqualified manner, the results clearly could be cultic.

Brian A. Onken[2]

And He said to him, "'You shall love the Lord your God with all your heart, and with all your soul, and with all your mind.' This is the great and foremost commandment."

Matthew 22:37–38

The Word-Faith teaching claims to be founded on revelatory insights into the Bible given to divinely anointed Pentecostal prophets, especially Kenneth Hagin. In fact, that teaching is based on the writings of the evangelical faith-healing teacher E. W. Kenyon, from whom Hagin borrowed and even plagiarized extensively. What remains to be seen is whether the theology built on that foundation is itself biblical.

One might begin examining the theological system of the Word-Faith teaching at various places. However, one doctrine stands out as the most basic theological presupposition of the entire Word-Faith teaching. That doctrine is the view that human beings are constituted in three parts—body, soul, and spirit—and that of these three parts it is the spirit that is the real human being, not the body or soul. This doctrine, commonly called *trichotomy,* is absolutely fundamental to the Word-Faith teaching. Only if trichotomy is true can human beings be said to exist in God's class, as the same kind of being as God. Only if trichotomy is true can it be claimed that the reasoning of the intellect (which is located in the soul, on this theory) and the feelings of the body are unreliable guides to what is really true. Only if the spirit is the real person would it make any sense to say that health and wealth come from the spirit realm into material existence through faith, as indeed the Word-Faith teachers all say. Thus, if the doctrine of trichotomy is false, the entire structure of Word-Faith theology is false.

I hasten to point out that the reverse is not true. If trichotomy were true, that would not of itself make the Word-Faith teaching true as well. It would leave the matter open. Many Christians who accept the trichotomous view do not accept any of the other doctrinal distinctives of the Word-Faith movement. But again, if trichotomy is false, the Word-Faith teaching *must* be false.

The Word-Faith Doctrine

The Word-Faith teaching on this matter is clear and reasonably uniform. Human beings are spirits, they have or possess a soul, and they have or live in a body.[3] "Your body is not you," as Copeland puts it.[4] The spirit is the "real man."[5] Because God and human beings are spirits, they "belong to the same class of being."[6]

Our spirits are intended to rule over our bodies through our souls, which include our reasoning faculties. When the body rules a person's reason, or when a person's reason rules his or her spirit, disaster is the result. The human spirit, when it is "reborn," as Copeland puts it, is competent to rule the soul and body. We should learn to listen to and obey our spirits, because if we are born again, they cannot fail us.[7] Our spirits are also the point of contact of communication with God. Faith is therefore a function of the spirit, not of the intellect.[8] As Hagin infers, we cannot expect to understand the Bible with our reason. Indeed, God's Word may contradict our reason and even the physical evidence.[9]

Capps teaches essentially the same doctrine of trichotomy as Hagin and Copeland, but he draws some significant comparisons between human trichotomy and the divine Trinity or triunity of God. According to Capps, because "man was made in God's image, then he is a triune being like God: the Father, the Son, and the Holy Ghost." Our triunity consists, though, of spirit, soul, and body. "Since man was created an exact duplication of God's kind, he has to be a triune being in order to qualify for the likeness of God."[10]

This kind of comparison between human nature as trichotomous and God's being as triune is not original with the Word-Faith teachers. However, it is theologically necessary in the Word-Faith teaching in a way that it is not in other traditions, because the Word-Faith teachers maintain, as Capps does, that human beings are "exact duplicates" of God. As we shall see in more detail as we progress, this leads the Word-Faith teachers to some conclusions that are patently sub-Christian if not outright heretical.

What should be noted here is that the comparison Capps makes assumes a defective view of the Trinity. In his explanation the three Persons of the Trinity are much more like modes of existence or ways in which God is known than like the three distinct Persons of orthodox trinitarianism. In fact, the explanation of the Trinity given here by Capps is fully compatible with the Oneness Pentecostal doctrine of God—the view espoused, with some variation, by William Branham, and with which even E. W. Kenyon's theology had some affinity. This is no accident, and we shall find as we proceed that Capps is not the only Word-Faith teacher who leans toward a Oneness-type view of the Godhead.

Evaluating the Doctrine of Trichotomy

We must keep in mind that trichotomy does not originate with the Word-Faith movement and that not everyone understands trichotomy in the same way. However, there are general tendencies in the theological traditions holding to trichotomy that do differentiate them from those traditions holding to dichotomy.

The dichotomy view is generally preferred by those in the Augustinian and Reformed traditions. The doctrine of trichotomy is more generally associated with the Alexandrian tradition in the early church and with the Wesleyan and Pentecostal traditions in the modern church. But there are exceptions on both sides.

Actually, there are three views to be considered. The third view is monism—the view that man is an indivisible unity, that the soul and/or spirit are inseparable from the body. This view is generally associated with liberals (who adopt the view sometimes without much regard for the biblical teaching on the subject) and with Adventism and Adventist-type sects such as Jehovah's Witnesses and Armstrongism (which argue that a literal reading of the Bible supports monism).

The Biblical Case for Monism

The biblical case for monism is stronger than evangelicals usually admit. Monists can point out that in Genesis 2:7 man becomes a "living soul" by having the "breath of life" placed into his body. Here man seems to be simply a physical organism, created by God, and called a "soul." Human beings are frequently called "souls" in both the Old Testament (e.g., Exod. 1:5) and the New (e.g., Acts 2:41). The Bible says very little about the soul or spirit existing beyond death apart from the body, and the meaning of what it does say is debated. Moreover, in the New Testament death is seen as unnatural, and the hope of the believer is not the immortality of the soul but the future resurrection of the body as an immortal human being (e.g., 1 Corinthians 15).

I do not say that monism is correct. Much in the Bible rules out a strict monism (as I shall show next). But there is enough to it that evangelical theologians more and more are affirming that human nature is a holistic unity, even if in some sense it is also composite.

The Biblical Case for Dualism or Dichotomy

It is no accident that the majority viewpoint of Christian theologians throughout church history has been *dichotomy,* or dualism. The Bible, particularly the New Testament, uses a variety of terms to describe man as having both a material aspect and an immaterial aspect:

• body and soul (Matt. 10:28)
• body and mind (Rom. 12:1–2)

- body and spirit (1 Cor. 7:34; James 2:26)
- flesh and spirit (1 Cor. 5:5; 2 Cor. 7:1)
- flesh and heart (Rom. 2:28–29)
- outer man and inner man (2 Cor. 4:16)

Sometimes more than one term is used for each of these two aspects. For example, in Romans 7 Paul uses the terms *body* and *flesh* interchangeably for that aspect of him that wants to sin (vv. 18, 23–25) and uses the terms *inner man* and *mind* interchangeably for that aspect of him that wants to obey God (vv. 22–23, 25). In Luke 1:46–47 it is apparent that the words *soul* and *spirit* are synonymous. In 1 Peter 3:4, "the hidden person of the heart" and "the spirit" are evidently synonymous.

There are other reasons for holding to the dichotomy view. Created realities are sometimes divided into two kinds, the visible and the invisible (Col. 1:16). Human beings, though they were created to live in the physical world, are capable of existing as persons in the spiritual realm as disembodied souls or spirits (Heb. 12:23; Rev. 6:9–11). All these points support dichotomy and count against both monism and trichotomy.

The Biblical Case for Trichotomy

The trichotomy view is based primarily on two or three passages. First Thessalonians 5:23 is the only verse that speaks of spirit, soul, and body together in a way that seems to distinguish them. The usual dichotomist response is to cite a text like Mark 12:30, that speaks of heart, soul, mind, and strength, but certainly does not distinguish them as separable or distinct parts or faculties. This response is not persuasive to trichotomists, though, since dichotomists admit that the body is distinct from the spirit and soul, so that Mark 12:30 seems not to be a fair parallel.

The second main text is Hebrews 4:12, which speaks of the Word of God penetrating "as far as the division of soul and spirit, of both joints and marrow, and able to judge the thoughts and intentions of the heart." One difficulty with reading this as supporting trichotomy is the question of how to relate "soul and spirit" to "the thoughts and intentions of the heart." Is "heart" here synonymous with the soul, the spirit, or does it include both? It is clear from other passages that the writer of Hebrews uses "heart" and "mind" interchangeably (8:10; 10:16).[11] But what he means by "soul and spirit" is uncertain. It may be that the word *division* here is not meant to imply a division *between* soul and spirit at all. It seems more likely that "soul and spirit" are being spoken of here as the innermost aspect of a person, "divided" or distinguished from the outer, surface aspect. The expression "soul and spirit" would then be using the two terms synonymously. Similarly, the last part of verse 12 is not saying that the Word of God discriminates between "thoughts" and "intentions," but that the Word of God discriminates or judges godly thoughts and intentions from ungodly ones; "thoughts and intentions" are synonymous. Thus Hebrews 4:12 does not really support trichotomy either.

A third text, not as often used, is 1 Corinthians 14:14–15, where Paul seems to distinguish between his spirit (with which he speaks in tongues) and his mind (with which he prays in an intelligible language). This is actually the best support of the three. However, while such language might be used to speak of two separable parts or aspects, there are some good reasons to doubt that this is meant here.

First, earlier in 1 Corinthians Paul seems to use "spirit" and "mind" synonymously (2:10–16; compare Eph. 4:23).

Second, Paul often, if not always, uses the term *mind* to mean "understanding" as a capacity—the cognitive function of his inner being—rather than as a part or distinguishable aspect of his inner being (1 Cor. 1:10; Phil. 2:5). As we have seen, when Paul does contrast the mind with some other aspect of human nature, it is always with the material aspect, the body or flesh (Rom. 7:22–25; 12:1–2).

For these reasons, I suggest that what Paul in 1 Corinthians 14:14–15 is saying is something like the following, keeping in mind the context of concern for edification of others: "For if I pray in a tongue, I am praying utilizing my capacity to act empowered by the Spirit, but my capacity to understand what I am praying [and thus edify others] is not being utilized. What, then? I shall pray empowered by the Spirit, and I shall also pray intelligently."

Are Human Beings Monistic, Dualistic, or Trichotomous?

In my judgment the dualistic view, or dichotomous, has the most to commend it. Man is fundamentally a twofold being, with immaterial and material aspects. But this dichotomy is holistic—it is a unity. That is the truth in monism. Moreover, in man's inner being (his immaterial aspect) there are natural and supernatural dimensions. The natural dimension has to do with our capacity for understanding and feeling—the mind or heart, as we often say. The supernatural dimension has to do with our capacity for relating to God. This is the truth in trichotomy. But these two dimensions are inseparable perspectives or functions of the inner being.

Thus, in my opinion dualism is basically correct, but there are things to be learned from trichotomy. And there is not enough to go on to be dogmatic about the matter or to regard either dualism or trichotomism as aberrant or heretical.

Trichotomy in Word-Faith Theology

What, then, shall we say about the trichotomy in the Word-Faith teaching? There are four points to be made here.

First, since the weight of biblical evidence favors dichotomy over trichotomy, the biblical evidence does not support the entire Word-Faith doctrine. Remember, trichotomy *must* be true or the Word-Faith theology cannot be true at all. In light of the biblical evidence discussed above, the Word-Faith doctrine is based on a very weak position. In addition, there are some specific problems with the Word-Faith theology's *interpretation* of trichotomy that should be recognized.

Second, saying that I am a "spirit" and that my spirit is the "real me" is problematical. I was not created as a spirit and then placed into a body (as the Mormons believe). Moreover, if the spirit is the "real man," then why does the Bible usually refer to the spirit as something *possessed by* the man (see 1 Cor. 14:14; Rom. 1:9)? In one sense I am a spirit, but in another sense—one much more frequently found in the Bible—I *have* a spirit. On the other hand, the Bible also frequently speaks of human beings as souls. Thus, depending on what passages we were using, we could say that I am a soul, I have a spirit, and I also have a body. Thus, the Word-Faith dictum that I *am* a spirit, I *have* a soul, and I *live in* a body, and that these three relations must not be confused, is simply false, based as it is on an overly rigid distinction of terms. Unfortunately this faulty idea spawns additional false and destructive conclusions. For example, the idea that in essence we are gods because, like God, we are essentially spirits is both false and spiritually dangerous.

Third, the doctrine that the human spirit is supposed to be in control of the body and soul, and that the basic problem in man is that his spirit is not in control, has no biblical basis. Texts that speak of being "led by the Spirit" are speaking of the Holy Spirit, not of the human spirit (see Rom. 8:14; Gal. 5:18). Proverbs 16:32 even speaks of the need for human beings to rule their spirits! The idea that the spirit is supposed to control the body is, ironically, a doctrine straight out of Platonism. What we need is not to get our spirit in control of the rest of us but to get our whole being under the control of God's Spirit. The Platonist doctrine implies that what is wrong with man is some metaphysical defect—man's system is out of whack—rather than simply a moral failure, a rebellion. It implies that body and soul just naturally go awry if the spirit loses control.

Fourth, perhaps the worst consequence of the Word-Faith understanding of trichotomy is the claim that God cannot communicate with the body or soul but only with the spirit. From this premise a radical anti-intellectualism follows. God does not, in this view, speak to our minds—he does not ask us to think logically or rationally—but rather speaks only to our spirits (whatever that would mean). This is a pietistic conclusion accepted by many other segments of the church that hold to trichotomy, and it is disastrous.[12] It opens the way for Christians to accept teachings that are irrational, contrary to the facts, and based on unsound interpretations of the Bible. Once a belief is accepted, all objections to it can be dismissed out of hand on the ground that they issue from the mind instead of the spirit.

7

Does God Have Faith?

God is a faith God. God released His faith in Words. . . . God created the universe by the methods which you have just put into motion by the words of your mouth. *God released His faith in words.* Man is created in the image of God, therefore man releases his faith in words.

Charles Capps[1]

Jesus was not conferring godhood upon men who have faith. He was exhorting men to have faith in God, that is, in his person, his character, and his saving deeds. This is yet another example of the disturbing tendency of Faith theology to reduce faith to an abstract human concept, such as PMA [positive mental attitude] or positive confession, thereby divorcing it from God.

D. R. McConnell[2]

Indeed, we had the sentence of death within ourselves so that we would not trust in ourselves, but in God who raises the dead.

2 Corinthians 1:9

The most important aspect of any theology is its view of God. Since God is the object of our faith, a proper understanding of the nature and character of God is absolutely essential for a sound faith. It is here that the error of the Word-Faith theology begins to loom large.

Several aspects of the Word-Faith doctrine of God could be examined. However, one stands out. The Word-Faith teachers claim that God does all of his works by faith and must speak words of faith to accomplish his will. This is the major premise on which they base their conclusion that, like God, we can speak "words of faith" by which we can get *our* will accomplished.

What the Word-Faith Teachers Say

The assertion that God has faith, and that indeed God must do everything by speaking words of faith, is surprising to many people. Yet this is a central and essential doctrine of the Word-Faith movement.

E. W. Kenyon, for example, wrote, "Faith is the creative force in man. Faith is the creative force in the Creator. God simply said, 'Let there be.'"[3]

Likewise, Kenneth Hagin asserts, "The God kind of faith . . . is the kind of faith that spoke the world into existence. . . . God created the universe with words. Words filled with faith are the most powerful things in all the world."[4]

According to Kenneth Copeland, "God is a faith being. . . . God does not do anything outside of faith."[5]

> Spiritual law gave birth to physical law. The world and the physical forces governing it were created by the power of faith—a spiritual force. God, a Spirit, created all matter and he created it with the force of faith. . . . Faith is a spiritual force, a spiritual energy, a spiritual power. It is this force of faith which makes the laws of the spirit world function.[6]

Charles Capps teaches the same doctrine: "*God is a faith God. God released His faith in Words. . . . God released His faith in words.* Man is created in the image of God, therefore man releases his faith in words."[7]

After asserting (as do all of the Word-Faith teachers) that Mark 11:22 means, "Have the God kind of faith," Fred Price comments, "Why distinguish the God kind of faith? Because there are two kinds of faith in existence in the world. 1. Natural human faith. 2. Spiritual faith. Or, the God kind of faith."[8] Price also argues that Hebrews 11:3

> is not just saying that by an exercise of our faith we believe that God spoke the worlds into existence. It is saying that, but it's also saying much more. It's telling us how God did it! By using His faith! . . . God believed in His heart that what He said with His mouth would come to pass, and He dared to say it. . . . If our Father is a faith God, then we must be faith children of a faith God.[9]

In order to evaluate this doctrine of God as "a faith God," we need to answer three questions: (1) Does Mark 11:22 really mean that we are to have the same kind of faith that God has? (2) Does Hebrews 11:3 really teach that God used his faith to create the universe? (3) Does the Bible teach that God must literally speak words to accomplish his will?

Mark 11:22—The God Kind of Faith?

In Mark 11:22 Jesus urges his disciples, "Have faith in God." From this translation no one would ever imagine that the verse might be saying that God has faith. However, there is a grammatical aspect of the sentence that has been misunderstood by the Word-Faith teachers to mean that the verse is really saying something like, "Have the kind of faith God has," or, as Hagin and his followers have put it, "Have the God kind of faith." Here I must go into some details about the grammar, but the matter is not so complex as it might seem, as I shall shortly explain.

The Grammatical Question

The Greek words here are *echete pistin theou,* which, if one were translating word for word and disregarding English grammar, could be translated "Have faith of God." The grammatical feature of the text in question here is the word translated "of God," *theou,* which is in a form known in grammar as the genitive case. (In Greek, nouns have different "cases," or functions in their sentences, indicated by different endings; thus, the Greek word for God can be spelled *theos, theou, theō,* or *theon* depending on its case.)

In Greek the genitive case can serve any one of several functions, and which one is operating in any one instance must be determined by usage and context. (We will get to usage and context a little later.) One of these functions is what is usually called the *subjective* use of the genitive. If "God" in Mark 11:22 were a subjective genitive, that would mean that God is the *subject* of faith—the one who has or possesses faith. Jesus' statement might then be translated, "Have God's faith," or something similar. This is the grammatical basis for the Word-Faith teachers' claim that Jesus was telling his disciples to have the kind of faith God has.

However, this is certainly a mistaken interpretation of Jesus' statement. As all translators and commentators have recognized, the genitive "God" here is not a subjective genitive but an *objective* genitive—that is, a genitive used to designate the *object,* not the subject, of the preceding noun. So in this case, "faith of God" means not "faith that God has" (subjective genitive) but "faith that has God as its object." In English the way we show that God is the object of the faith, not the one who possesses the faith, is to say that the faith is *"in* God." That is why all English translations render Mark 11:22 "Have faith in God" or some equivalent.

Where, then, did Hagin get the expression "the God kind of faith," which Word-Faith followers use to paraphrase Mark 11:22? I believe the source is almost certainly a comment by A. T. Robertson, the famed Baptist scholar of New Testament Greek, in his massive textbook on Greek grammar. His statement there is that "in Mark 11:22 *echete pistin theou* we rightly translate 'have faith in God,' though the genitive does not mean 'in,' but only the God kind of faith."[10]

There are three reasons why Robertson is likely to be the source. First, the phrase "the God kind of faith" is so distinctive that its use with reference to the same verse makes some connection highly probable. Second, the relative dates are right: Robertson's grammar appeared in 1934, and Hagin's Word-Faith theology was developed in the 1940s and 1950s. Third, Robertson was a Southern Baptist, his work has always been appreciated especially by Baptists, and Hagin was raised as a Southern Baptist. While these three factors do not prove conclusively that Robertson was the source of the expression "the God kind of faith," they do show it to be highly probable.

Now, what is significant about tracing Hagin's use of this phrase to Robertson is that Hagin certainly misunderstood him. By "the God kind of faith" Robertson did not mean "the kind of faith that God has" but rather "the kind of faith that has God as its object." We know this for two reasons. First, in the passage in question, Robertson is citing Mark 11:22 as an example of the *objective* genitive. Second, in the very sentence in which he uses this phrase he says that "we rightly translate 'have faith in God,'" showing that he agrees with the usual interpretation. When he says that "the genitive does not mean 'in,'" he is not saying that this is an incorrect translation but rather asserting that this is a good idiomatic way of expressing in English the idea of the Greek words in their context. Thus, in the previous sentence he states, "The resultant idea is due to the context and one must not suppose that the Greek genitive means all the different English prepositions used to translate the resultant idea."[11]

Usage and Context

As I said earlier, the genitive can be taken to signal different functions, and one must tell from usage and context which function is appropriate. Here usage and context leave no doubt as to the correct translation. To begin with usage, when the word "faith" *(pistis)* is followed by a noun in the genitive in New Testament Greek, that genitive usually if not always is objective. Typical examples include "faith in His name" (literally, "the faith of his name," Acts 3:16); "faith in the truth" (literally, "faith of truth," 2 Thess. 2:13); and "the faith of the gospel" (which surely means faith that believes in the gospel; Phil. 1:27). As for the word "God," when it is used in the genitive it is always quite clear whether it is subjective or objective. It is used in the objective sense in various passages, such as 1 Peter 2:19, "conscience toward God" (literally, "of God"); Luke 6:12, "prayer to God" (literally, "of God"); and Romans 3:18, "fear of God." (It would obviously be strange and obtuse to cite Romans 3:18 as proving that God has fear!)

What is really determinative, however, is context. The objective genitive must be correct in Mark 11:22, because in context Jesus is exhorting his disciples to have faith *when they pray* (v. 24). In other words, he is encouraging them to believe that God can answer their prayers—that he can and will give them what they ask him for in prayer. Jesus says nothing even hinting at the idea that God himself has faith.

We must conclude, then, that Mark 11:22 means what Christians have always understood it to mean, that our faith—our trust, our confidence—is to be directed toward God as its object. It does not mean that we are to imitate the kind of faith that God supposedly has and exercises in doing his will.

Hebrews 11:3—Did God Create the World by Faith?

As with Mark 11:22, no one reading Hebrews 11:3 in any English translation and not looking for the idea would ever imagine it was saying God created the universe by using his faith: "By faith we understand that the worlds were prepared by the word of God . . ." (NASB; other translations are similar). The usual way this verse has been read is that it is by faith that we have this understanding about the creation of the universe. But Kenyon and the Word-Faith teachers after him take the verse to be saying that we understand God to have created the world by speaking his word in faith.

The difference between these two interpretations grammatically comes down simply to *syntax,* or word order. From the usual view the statement should be read, "*By faith* we understand that the worlds were prepared by the word of God." From the Word-Faith theology view it should be read, "We understand that the worlds were prepared *by faith* by the word of God." In favor of this way of reading the text it can be argued that Greek word order often varies with little or no change in meaning, and that in any case Greek word order typically does not correspond to English word order. For those who find it helpful, the two ways of reading the sentence would be diagrammed as follows:

Hebrews 11:3a—Traditional Reading

that
we | understand \ the worlds | were prepared
        \ *by faith*   \ by the word of God

Hebrews 11:3a—Word-Faith Theology Reading

that
we | understand \ the worlds | were prepared
                         \ by faith   \ by the word of God

One thing this exercise in sentence diagramming helps make clear is that Fred Price's attempt to have it both ways will not work. Recall his assertion that Hebrews 11:3 "is not just saying that by an exercise of our faith we believe that God spoke the worlds into existence. It is saying that, but it's also saying much more. It's telling us how God did it! By using his faith!"[12] Price cannot have it both ways. Either "by faith" connects with "understand" or it connects with "were prepared." Both cannot be true, and a choice must be made.

While the Word-Faith teachers' interpretation cannot be absolutely disproved by simple grammar alone, the word order does strongly support the usual reading. Although word order in Greek is somewhat flexible, it is not meaningless. In Greek the statement reads as follows:

Pistei nooumen katērtisthai tous aiōnas rhēmati theou
(By) faith we understand were made the worlds (by) word of God

Here it is quite natural to connect "by faith" with "we understand" and quite unnatural to connect it with "were made." Had the author wanted to say what Kenyon and the Word-Faith teachers think he said, he could have made this clear by placing *nooumen* ("we understand") at the end of the clause or by moving *pistei* ("by faith") toward the end of the clause. As it stands, however, the traditional reading is automatic.

Besides the word order, there are at least four other reasons to reject the Word-Faith teachers' interpretation of this verse.

First, the whole chapter is talking about the faith exercised in God by human beings: "By faith Abel . . . By faith Enoch . . . By faith Noah . . . By faith Abraham . . . By faith even Sarah . . . ," and so forth. All told, the word *pistei*, "by faith," appears nineteen times in this chapter, always at the beginning of a sentence and always (unless verse 3 is excepted) with reference to human beings' faith in God (Heb. 11:3–5, 7–9, 11, 17, 20–24, 27–31, 33). The whole point of *faith* is believing that God exists and that he rewards those who seek him (11:6). It is therefore all too obvious from the context that the faith spoken of in verse 3 is also human faith in God as Creator, not God's faith that enabled him to be the Creator.

Second, just two sentences earlier we are told that "faith is the assurance of things hoped for" (Heb. 11:1). From this statement it follows that if God has faith, then he must also have hope. Are the Word-Faith teachers willing to say that there are some things that God *hopes* will happen? In any case, the idea certainly cannot be found in the Bible. God is "the God of hope" (Rom. 15:13) not because he *has* hope but because he is the *source* of hope, the God who fulfills the hope of his people.

Third, according to most Word-Faith teachers, faith is something short of knowledge. To have faith or to believe that something is or will be so implies that you do not yet *know* it is so. For example, Hagin has stated, "If you already have it, then you wouldn't have to believe it, for then you would know it."[13] Now put this together with the Word-Faith teaching that God created the worlds by exercising faith in his heart:

a. If you believe something, you don't yet know it.
b. God *believed* that the worlds would exist.

It doesn't take a philosopher or theologian to realize that these two premises lead to the following conclusion:

c. God did not *know* that the worlds would exist.

Thus, the Word-Faith teaching definitely contradicts the essential, biblical doctrine that God knows all things. It is likely that the Word-Faith teachers do not intend to deny the omniscience of God. But in order to uphold the omniscience of God, they must abandon at least one of the premises listed above. They must either disavow the doctrine that God has faith or disavow the idea that faith is not knowledge.

Finally, the Bible teaches quite plainly, and all of the Word-Faith teachers agree, that faith is absent where there is sight (2 Cor. 5:7). Yet, as at least some of the Word-Faith teachers admit, "God lives in ONE ETERNAL NOW."[14] If the past, present, and future are all perfectly known and open to God, then if he "sees" anything, he sees it all. How, then, could he have faith about anything? Again, we may set forth the problem in the following form:

a. If you believe something, you don't yet see it.
b. God *believed* that the worlds would exist.
c. Therefore, God *did not see* the worlds as existing.

The sum of the matter is that the Word-Faith teachers have misunderstood both Mark 11:22 and Hebrews 11:3. But we have seen that this is not merely a case of a friendly disagreement about the interpretation of a couple of verses. The claim that God exercises faith is disastrous theologically. It implies that God is bound by the constraints of time and does not see or know the future until it has happened to him. It implies that God has hopes of his own that he is seeking to realize. Most if not all of the Word-Faith teachers seem unwilling to draw these conclusions explicitly, but here, and elsewhere in their teachings as well, they seem to imply that indeed God is operating under such limitations.

In any case, the whole idea that God has faith is foreign to the Bible. Faith is human beings trusting in a God that they cannot see to do things that he has not yet done. God sees all and knows all from eternity. So God does not have faith. And since God does not have faith, the idea that we must imitate God's "faith" is also unbiblical.

Must God Speak Words to Get Things Done?

The Bible frequently speaks of God creating the universe and accomplishing his purposes through his word. Hebrews 11:3 speaks of creation occurring by or through "the word of God." Genesis 1 repeatedly prefaces God's creative works with the words, "Then God said." These and many other texts are cited by Word-Faith teachers to prove that God himself gets what he wants by speaking words—specifically, "words of faith" or "faith-filled words." And, as has already been explained, they argue that because we are made in God's image, we, too, can get what we want by speaking words of faith.

What seems to have escaped the Word-Faith teachers is that the biblical language about God's "word" is not meant literally. That is, God did not need to vocalize words expressing his will or desire (let alone his "faith") in order to create, nor could he have done so. Think about it this way: For God literally to *speak* words, he would need to make audible sounds. This would require God to vocalize his will in an environment of air (no air = no vibrations = no sounds). Of course, this would be difficult even for God to do before he created air!

The assertion that the biblical statements about God's creative word are not to be taken literally is not based on rationalizing or speculation. It can be proved from the biblical statements themselves. Take, for instance, this verse:

When He utters His voice, there is a tumult of waters in the heavens,
And He causes the clouds to ascend from the end of the earth;

He makes lightning for the rain,
And brings out the wind from His storehouses.

Jeremiah 10:13

Jeremiah, of course, does not mean that God literally has storehouses in heaven where he keeps a supply of wind. Nor does he mean that God literally speaks out with an audible voice to stir up the moisture in the atmosphere. Consider also the following passage:

> Praise Him, sun and moon;
> Praise Him, all stars of light!
> Praise Him, highest heavens,
> And the waters that are above the heavens!
> Let them praise the name of the LORD,
> For He commanded and they were created.
> He has also established them forever and ever;
> He has made a decree which will not pass away.
> Praise the LORD from the earth,
> Sea monsters and all deeps;
> Fire and hail, snow and clouds;
> Stormy wind, fulfilling His word.

Psalm 148:3–8

As I hope is obvious, the sun, moon, and stars, along with the rest of the inanimate creation, do not literally "praise" the Lord. They "speak" of God's glory and creative power without any speech or words (Ps. 19:1–3). Likewise, God accomplishes his will simply by willing it; he does not need to verbalize it. God did not issue a literal "decree" (v. 6) that the inanimate creation is supposed to read and consciously obey!

One passage commonly cited by Word-Faith teachers is the following:

> By the word of the LORD the heavens were made,
> And by the breath of His mouth all their host.
> He gathers the waters of the sea together as a heap;
> He lays up the deeps in storehouses.
> Let all the earth fear the LORD;
> Let all the inhabitants of the world stand in awe of Him.
> For He spoke, and it was done;
> He commanded, and it stood fast.

Psalm 33:6–9

If this passage proves that God speaks literal words to accomplish his will, then it also proves not only, once again, that God has storehouses (apparently with supplies of ocean water as well as wind) but also that God has a literal mouth and literally breathes. If this were taken literally, it would reduce many biblical passages to silliness (e.g., Isa. 40:24). It would also raise the problem mentioned earlier of how God could breathe before he created air.

By no means am I saying that God cannot cause literal words to be heard aloud by his creatures. The Bible includes many historical accounts of God communicating verbally and audibly to human beings. There is no reason not to take these accounts literally. Nor am I denying that God has the ability to communicate intelligently with angels or departed human spirits. What I am saying is that God does not need to speak audible words to do anything, and that in fact it is nonsense to claim that he vocalized literal words with a literal mouth before he created anything.

The importance of this point may be lost on the reader not entirely familiar with the Word-Faith teaching. In the view of the Word-Faith teachers, it is not enough for people simply to believe something in their minds; what they need to do is to put their faith into words—spoken, audible words. Thus, from their point of view, it is absolutely essential to maintain that God literally speaks words of faith, since our speaking words of faith to get our will done is predicated on the assumption that God, our heavenly Father, literally does the very same thing.

The Bible, however, clearly shows that both halves of this Word-Faith teaching are wrong. God does not have faith, and he does not need to speak literal words to accomplish his will. The idea that God is "a faith God," then, is contrary to the faith of the Bible.

8

The God with a Bod

So you see, that faith didn't come billowing out of some giant monster some-where. It came out of the heart of a being that is very uncanny the way he's very much like you and me. Can you conceive that? Not hardly, in the mind, but your heart can; your heart can. A being—a being that stands somewhere around 6–2, 6–3, that weighs somewhere in the neighborhood of a couple hundred pounds, little better.

Kenneth Copeland[1]

The deity of Faith theology bears little resemblance to the God of the Bible. The minute God is assigned physical qualities such as height and weight, He is by definition not the God of Scripture.

Hank Hanegraaff[2]

"But will God indeed dwell on the earth? Behold, heaven and the highest heaven cannot contain You, how much less this house which I have built!"

1 Kings 8:27

In the previous chapter I critiqued the notion that God must literally speak words of faith to create or do anything else. One of the objections I raised was that such an idea implied that God has a literal mouth, which in turn implies that God has a body. It turns out that many Word-Faith teachers actually believe that God does indeed have a body.

Let us be clear what is and is not at issue here. All orthodox Christians agree that God became incarnate in Jesus Christ and as such took to himself a physical body. All Christians agree further that God, before his incarnation, was able at any time to appear to human beings on the earth with a visible form—what are often called *theophanies*. What is controversial about the Word-Faith teaching is its claim that God, as God, has always had a body as part of his intrinsic nature. According to the Word-Faith teachers, this is not a physical body but something called a "spirit body"— a body composed of spirit.

The Development of a Word-Faith Doctrine

The Word-Faith teachers evidently did not take this doctrine from E. W. Kenyon. From what little evidence is available, it appears fairly clear that Kenyon did not agree with it. For example, in one of his writings he says very plainly, "We realize that when He created man, God had no body. . . ."[3] This is one of several respects in which the Word-Faith teaching differs from, and goes beyond, that of Kenyon.

Although he does not dwell on it, Kenneth Hagin does teach that God has a body:

> Even though we say that God is a Spirit, that doesn't mean that He doesn't have a shape or form in the spiritual realm, because He does. Angels are spirits, yet angels have a form or a spirit body. . . . Even though God is a Spirit, we know that He has a face and hands, a form of some kind. He is no less real because He is a Spirit than He would be if He had a physical body.[4]

Notice that Hagin attributes actual face and hands to God, as well as a "form," and in speaking of angelic forms, he asserts that an angel has "a spirit body." Clearly, then, Hagin is saying that God has a body, albeit a spirit one, a body that has a literal face and literal hands.

Of all the Word-Faith televangelists, Kenneth Copeland has probably gone into the greatest detail in his teaching about God's bodily existence. When Copeland says that God has a body, he evidently means it *very* literally. For example, in a letter responding to an inquiry on the subject, Copeland lists a number of bodily attributes that, he says, Scripture indicates God possesses. God, according to Copeland, has back parts, a heart, hands, a finger (only one finger?), nostrils, a mouth with lips and a tongue, feet, eyes and eyelids, a voice, breath, ears, hair, head, face, arms, and loins.

God wears clothes, eats, rests, sits on his throne, and walks.[5] In a taped sermon that Copeland distributes to the public, he even tells us, based on the
statement in Isaiah 40:12 that God "marked off the heavens by the span,"
that God is about six feet, two inches and weighs about two hundred
pounds.[6] On this and other occasions, Copeland has claimed that God lives
on a planet, of which the earth is an exact copy, if on a smaller scale:

> I used to think, I said, "God, how come when you made Adam, why didn't
> you have him live up there where you are?" He said, "I don't want him to
> live up here as a servant. I want to put him down there in his own universe,
> on his own planet, and let him be god to that world. Let him enjoy what I
> enjoy here as God of this world," and he said, "It'll be God and sons!"[7]

> You don't think Earth was first, do you? Huh? Well, you don't think that God
> made man in his image and then made Earth in some other image. There's
> not anything under this whole sun that's new. Are you hearing what I'm say-
> ing? This is all a copy. It's a copy of home. It's a copy of the mother planet.
> Where God lives, he made a little one just like his and put us on it.[8]

The idea of God living on a heavenly planet—an idea never suggested
in the Bible—poses a serious problem: Has this planet always existed or did
God create it? If he created it, this raises the further question of where God's
"spirit body" resided before he made his planet. Remember, in Copeland's
view God has a literal body with literal feet and must be somewhere, sitting or standing. Thus it would seem that Copeland's doctrine requires a
planet that has always existed somewhere for God's home. But if this planet
has always existed, then it is eternal and uncreated, and thus we have at
least two uncreated realities—God and his heavenly planet. Either way,
the doctrine that God lives on a planet somewhere is highly problematic,
theologically unsound, and unbiblical.

Isaiah 40:12

Besides the problem of the heavenly planet, there are several reasons
why Copeland's teaching about God having a body must be rejected as
unbiblical. The main reason is that the very proof texts he uses to back up
his teaching contradict it. Take, for instance, Isaiah 40:12, from which
Copeland confidently concludes that God is about six feet and two or three
inches tall and weighs a little more than two hundred pounds. All of this
is deduced from the word *span* in this passage. But here is what the verse
really says (NASB):

> Who has measured the waters in the hollow of His hand,
> And marked off the heavens by the span,
> And calculated the dust of the earth by the measure,
> And weighed the mountains in a balance,
> And the hills in a pair of scales?

The picture here is dramatically different from the one Copeland imagines. The first line pictures God measuring the waters of the oceans and seas of the earth in the hollow of his hand. The "hollow" of one's hand is the small, depressed area in the middle of the palm that can hold a little water when dipping with one hand. The implication, if this imagery were to be pressed literally, would be that God is at least the size of the Earth if not larger.

The rest of the verse confirms this point. The word translated *span* is literally "cubit," a standard of measurement that was based on a man's hand span—and therefore was *about* nine inches. (Copeland had calculated that God must be slightly bigger than him because Copeland's own hand span was eight and three-quarter inches!) The picture here is of God taking measurements for the universe ("the heavens") using his own hand span. Of course, this would be ridiculous if his hand span were nine miles, let alone nine inches!

Or again, the image of God having a balance or scales on which he could weigh all of the mountains is absurd if taken literally with reference to a man no more than six-feet-two- or three-inches tall. Could anything be clearer than that this passage does not describe God as having a literal hand and using literal scales to measure the material from which he made the earth?

Indeed, the Word-Faith theology cannot take this passage literally any more than can orthodox theology. According to Copeland and all other Word-Faith teachers, God made the heavens and the earth, not by using tools or measuring materials with his hand but by speaking words of faith. How, then, can Copeland take Isaiah 40:12 to be a literal description of the process God used in creation?

Other Passages, Other Problems

As Copeland points out, numerous other passages speak of God's hands, mouth, and even nostrils or loins. But taking these passages literally poses just as many problems as does taking Isaiah 40:12 that way. Are we to suppose that God literally blows smoke out of his nostrils (Ps. 18:8)? If God has "eyelids" (Ps. 11:4), does that mean that he sometimes closes his eyes?

If God literally rests (Gen. 2:1–4), does that mean that God needs to be "refreshed" (Exod. 31:17)? Not if we take literally (as clearly we should) the statement in Isaiah 40:28 that God "does not become weary or tired." The Bible, then, *in the very same passages* cited by Copeland and others to prove that God has a body, makes it very clear that God is being described metaphorically.

A more striking set of problem passages for the view that God has a body are those that say heaven is God's "throne" and the earth his "footstool" (Isa. 66:1; Matt. 5:34–35; Acts 7:49). Obviously, if the earth is God's literal footstool, God is enormous! Not even the nine-hundred-feet-tall "Jesus" that Oral Roberts claims to have seen could use the earth as a literal footstool.

There are other reasons for rejecting the notion that God has a body. I will merely summarize them here. First, the Bible never says that God actually has a body. This fact of itself does not prove that the idea is unbiblical (since arguments from silence are by themselves generally inconclusive), but it puts a certain burden of proof on those who teach it.

Second, the claim that God has a body is incompatible with the omnipresence of God. The Bible says that God is present everywhere (Ps. 139:1–10; Acts 17:28), that the universe cannot contain him (1 Kings 8:27; Isa. 66:1; Acts 7:48–49), and that his presence fills all things (Jer. 23:23–24). True, the Bible also says these things about Christ (Matt. 18:20; 28:20; Eph. 1:23; 4:10; Col. 3:11), and yet he has a body. Christ, though, is omnipresent by virtue of his eternal *divine* nature, whereas he possesses a body only by his having taken on *human* nature (see Heb. 10:5).

Third, the expression "spirit body" is a contradiction in terms: A spirit does not occupy three-dimensional space, whereas a body does. A careful examination of the biblical occurrences of the word *body* will show that it is applied only to physical beings, never to spirits (though human beings possess both a body and a spirit).

These three reasons, in conjunction with the metaphorical sense of the passages that speak of God as if he had bodily parts, make it clear that God in his divine being does not have a body.

The Trouble with the Trinity

The doctrine that God has a body leads to a dilemma for the Word-Faith teaching. The Bible teaches that God is not merely an isolated person but is Father, Son, and Holy Spirit. How are these three to be related as one God if it is asserted that God has a body? There would seem to be only two possible answers within the Pentecostal theological context of the Word-

Faith teaching: Either God has one body only, or the Father, Son, and Holy Spirit each have separate bodies, so that the Trinity is divisible into three entities possessing three separate bodies.

The first of these options naturally leads toward a Oneness view of God, which says that God is really only one person (with one body), and the Son and Spirit preexisted eternally with the Father only as aspects, potentialities, or forms of manifestation of the one God. The one-body position also leads naturally to the view that in the incarnation God's body became a physical one, and in the resurrection it returned to a spiritual one. Although they are not clear on the matter, Hagin and Copeland appear to favor the view that God has only one spirit body, since they always speak of God's body in the singular. This suggests that they will have leanings toward a Oneness view of the Godhead and a spiritualized view of the resurrection of Jesus.

The other choice is to hold that the Father, Son, and Holy Spirit have three separate bodies. This position leads naturally toward a tritheistic view of God. *Tritheism* is the doctrine that there are three Gods, or at least three separable, divisible entities called God. While no Pentecostal admits to being a tritheist, a number of Pentecostal teachers in and out of the Word-Faith movement have exhibited tritheistic tendencies. The most notable such teachers outside the Word-Faith movement are Finis Jennings Dake, who promoted the view in his study Bible, and Jimmy Swaggart, who took it directly from Dake's Bible. Swaggart asserts this view in a book in which he also sharply criticizes some of the doctrines of the Word-Faith movement.[9]

The most notable teacher to teach the three-bodies view is Benny Hinn. Hinn's controversial views on God's bodily nature were first made public in October 1990 when he announced on national religious television the publication by Thomas Nelson Publishers of his book *Good Morning, Holy Spirit*.[10] In his broadcast on the Trinity Broadcasting Network (TBN) on Saturday, October 13, 1990, Hinn affirmed:

> God the Father is a person, God the Son is a person, God the Holy Ghost is a person; but each one of them is a triune being by himself. If I can shock you, and maybe I should, there's nine of 'em. . . . God the Father, ladies and gentlemen, is a person, with his own personal spirit, with his own personal soul, and in his own personal spirit body. . . . Do you know the Holy Spirit has a soul and a body, separate from that of Jesus and the Father? . . . Now *three persons with three separate spirit bodies,* but Jesus Christ is the only one in glory today that is walking around with a glorified body of flesh, because he rose from the dead!

What, then, are we to make of this teaching that God has a body—or three bodies? First, it is simply unbiblical, for the reasons already stated in this chapter. Second, it raises a number of vexing theological problems for those who accept it, not the least of which is how to reconcile it with the doctrine of the Trinity. But third, the God-in-a-bod teaching has a broader significance within the larger context of the Word-Faith theology. If God has a body, then we are a lot more like God than we thought. As we shall see in the next chapter, that is precisely what the Word-Faith teachers claim.

9

Big God, Little Gods

Adam and Eve were placed in the world as the seed and expression of God. Just as dogs have puppies and cats have kittens, so God has little gods. Seed remains true to its nature, bearing its own kind. When God said, "Let us make man in our image," He created us as little gods, but we have trouble comprehending this truth. We see ourselves as "little people" with very little power and dominion. Until we comprehend that we are little gods and we begin to act like little gods, we cannot manifest the Kingdom of God.

Earl Paulk (1985)[1]

Some people have never learned the difference between the error of being a "little god" instead of living as one created "in His image."

Earl Paulk (1987)[2]

Men, why are you doing these things? We are also men of the same nature as you, and preach the gospel to you in order that you should turn from these vain things to a living God, who made the heaven and the earth and the sea and all that is in them.

Acts 14:15

Inevitably linked with one's view of God is one's view of human nature. Since human beings are made in the image of God, what one thinks about God affects what one thinks about people, and vice versa. It is perhaps here that the Word-Faith theology makes its most dramatic and clear-cut departure from traditional Christian doctrine. As we saw in the previous chapter, the Word-Faith teachers think God is a lot more like us than Christians have realized. The converse is also true—they claim that we are a lot more like God than we had thought. To be made in God's image, according to the Word-Faith theology, means to be made by God as "exact duplicates" of God—to exist in God's "class" as "little gods." It is this radically unorthodox doctrine of *deification* (the classification of human beings as gods or potential gods) that will be examined in this chapter.

Little Gods?

Advocates of the Word-Faith teaching sometimes deny that their favorite Word-Faith teachers really say that human beings are little gods. It is therefore important to document exactly what they do say on this subject.

E. W. Kenyon

As has been pointed out before, Kenyon is the grandfather of the Word-Faith movement, and in some ways his teaching differed from that of Hagin and Copeland. However, the roots of the Word-Faith view of man are found in Kenyon's writings. For example, commenting on Genesis 1:26 and Psalm 8:3–4, Kenyon wrote, "In other words, when man was created he was made as near like Deity as it was possible for Deity to create him. . . . Man belongs to God's class."[3] In an earlier chapter we pointed out that Kenyon taught that God and man, because both are spirits, "belong to the same class of being."[4] The significance of this idea for Kenyon is that man has the capacity to exercise dominion over creation by his spoken word:

> Hebrews 1:3 gives to us a suggestion as to the way Adam ruled God's creation. Jesus now upholds all things by the Word of His power. Adam ruled creation by his word. His voice was like the voice of his Creator in its dominion over creation.[5]

In these passages, Kenyon stops short of calling human beings "gods." However, he asserts that God and man "belong to the same class of being" since both are spirits. Further, he teaches that Adam ruled creation by his word—that is, by speaking words of faith, just as God did in creating the world and just as Jesus now does as stated in Hebrews 1:3. Although Kenyon did not develop this teaching to the extent that Hagin, Copeland,

and others have done, it points in the same direction as the modern Word-Faith doctrine.

Kenneth Hagin

Hagin's teaching about the nature of man picks up where Kenyon's left off and goes beyond it. Like Kenyon, Hagin teaches that human beings are "in the same class with God, because God is a Spirit and because man was made to have fellowship with God."[6] Unlike Kenyon, though, Hagin infers from man's likeness to God that man actually was created to be a god:

> God created everything, then He made man, Adam, and gave him dominion over all of it. God made it all for His man Adam. He gave Adam dominion over the cattle on a thousand hills, over the silver and gold, over the world and the fullness thereof. In other words, Adam was the god of this world.[7]
>
> Originally, God made the earth and the fullness thereof, giving Adam dominion over all the works of His hands. In other words, Adam was the god of this world.[8]

Hagin on at least one occasion has disavowed the idea that we are gods. Yet, as the above quotations illustrate, he has repeatedly asserted that human beings were created in God's class and that Adam was the god of this world.

Kenneth Copeland

The doctrine of human beings as little gods comes to full expression in the teaching of Kenneth Copeland, who is not afraid to say that human beings are meant to be gods. For Copeland, as for Hagin, the fundamental premise of his doctrine is that we are in reality spirit-beings just like God:

> According to the law of genesis, every living thing was created by God to reproduce after its own kind. Man was no exception to this rule. God is a Spirit, and Adam was created in God's own image and likeness, a spirit-being.[9]

It might be supposed that the Word-Faith teachers have simply equated being a spirit with being in God's class. If this were so, then the angels, as well as human beings, would in the Word-Faith view be gods. Although this question is not, to my knowledge, addressed directly by Hagin, it has been by Kenneth Copeland:

Man was created in the god class. He was not created in the animal class. He is in the god class. He has a uniqueness about him that even angels do not have—and that is the God-given right to choose his own words, and speak them, thereby setting his own divine destiny, his own destination. . . . All right—are we gods? We are a class of gods![10]

humanism

Copeland says repeatedly and emphatically that Adam was a god and in fact was "God manifest in the flesh." The statements are so surprising that I must quote from them at length.

> Now here's literally what happened. God made this body—I saw it one afternoon in a vision while I was praying. God showed it to me. . . . I saw God standing there holding it by the shoulders. . . . And it looked like God was looking in the mirror. It looked like He had made that thing for himself. . . . Now, when God held that body up there in front of Him . . . it was in His image. . . . I mean, man, they looked just exactly alike. You couldn't tell one of them from the other.[11]

> God's reason for creating Adam was His desire to reproduce Himself. I mean a reproduction of Himself. And in the Garden of Eden, he did that. He [Adam] was not a little like God. He was not almost like God. He was not subordinate to God, even. Now this is hard on the human mind, but I'm telling you what the Bible said. The Bible said, "Let us make man in our image and give him dominion." . . . And Adam is as much like God as you could get—just the same as Jesus when He came into the earth. He [Jesus] said, "If you've seen Me, you've seen the Father." He wasn't a lot like God; He's God manifested in the flesh! And I want you to know something—Adam in the Garden of Eden was God manifested in the flesh! He was God's very image, the very likeness. Everything he did, everything he said, every move he made was the very image of Almighty God. . . . You see, Adam was walking as a god. Adam walked in the gods class. Adam did things in the class of gods. Hallelujah.[12]

> Man was created to function on God's level. . . . Your spirit is just as big as God's because you are born of Him. My son has the same capacity for strength that I have. He has just as many muscles in his body as I have in mine; but at his present age he is not as strong as I am. Why? Because his muscles are not fully developed. He is still growing.[13]

Earl Paulk

Another teacher espousing a form of the "little gods" doctrine is Earl Paulk. It is not clear that Paulk holds to all of the basic doctrines of the Word-Faith movement—for instance, to my knowledge he has never taught that God exercises faith. However, Paulk has taught many of the Word-

Faith teachings, including its view of human beings as little gods by virtue of their creation in the image of God. In *Satan Unmasked,* Paulk expressed this doctrine as follows:

> Adam and Eve were placed in the world as the seed and expression of God. Just as dogs have puppies and cats have kittens, so God has little gods. Seed remains true to its nature, bearing its own kind. When God said, "Let us make man in our image," He created us as little gods, but we have trouble comprehending this truth. We see ourselves as "little people" with very little power and dominion. Until we comprehend that we are little gods and we begin to act like little gods, we cannot manifest the Kingdom of God.[14]

In *Held in the Heavens Until,* Paulk put it this way:

> When I say, "Act like a god," I can hear people saying, "There he goes with the theory of 'the manifest sons of God.'" Forget about theories! Forget about doctrine! Just go back to the simple Word of God! We are "little gods," whether we admit it or not. What are "little gods"? A god is someone who has sovereignty. Everyone is sovereign within certain parameters. . . . We are sovereign in many areas of life because we are "little gods."[15]

The "manifest sons of God" doctrine is the view, taught by some of the Latter-Rain leaders in the 1950s, that Jesus was simply the prototype of many divine sons of God. As Paulk makes clear here and elsewhere, when he says, "Forget about theories! Forget about doctrine!" he is not denying the doctrine but rather the opposite—he is asserting that his teaching is biblical truth and not merely someone's theory.

As important and integral as the teaching that men are little gods is in Paulk's writings, in 1987 Paulk began denying that he had ever taught it! In *That the World May Know,* written to defend himself against the charge of heresy, Paulk claimed that the charge that he taught a heretical view of man was based on a single quotation taken out of context:

> In one of my books, *Satan Unmasked,* I emphasized that man was created in God's image. . . . In keeping with the Genesis account of creation in which each "kind produce their own kind," I wrote, "Just as dogs have puppies and cats have kittens, God has little gods." That one statement quoted by Dave Hunt in *Seduction of Christianity* thrust me into a category with others accused of teaching humanism, rebellion against God, and "seduction" of believers into a cultic mentality! Out of context, perhaps I would have questioned the theological validity of the quote. At least, I would have asked for further development of the analogy.[16]

This statement is misleading because it implies that Paulk wrote of "little gods" only once. As we have seen, he made such statements in two separate books, and throughout both books he says things about the nature of humanity and of the church that support his "little gods" doctrine. Moreover, Paulk is apparently blind to the problem: Even here he explains his view as relating to the concept of beings producing after their own kind, which again implies that Paulk views man as the same kind of being as God. Throughout this same book, Paulk distinguishes between being "in the image of God," which, he says, is the biblical view he has taught all along, and seeking to be "like God" or "little gods," which he says he has always rejected as the lie of Satan.[17] "Some people have never learned the difference between the error of being a 'little god' instead of living as one created 'in His image.'"[18]

As bold as this attempt was to hide the fact that he himself had taught that we are "little gods," his statement in the November 1987 issue of his newsletter *Thy Kingdom Come* was bolder still: "I have never stated that believers are gods."[19] This statement is true only in the sense that Paulk never said that believers *alone* are gods; as we have seen, he has taught in two different books that *all* human beings are gods. It is interesting to compare this statement with his assertion in *Held in the Heavens Until,* quoted above: "We are 'little gods,' whether we admit it or not." One wonders, then, how his statement that he "never stated that believers are gods" can be regarded as anything other than a lie. Earl Paulk said we are little gods, whether *he* admits it or not.

Sorting Out the Issues

So much has been said by so many, both pro and con, on the question of human beings as "gods" that I have found most participants in the controversy are not at all clear about what the real issues are. Before considering the biblical arguments that have been marshalled by the Word-Faith teachers (and others) for regarding human beings as gods, we need to be clear on what such a claim might or might not mean in the context of the Word-Faith theology.

First of all, it needs to be said as clearly as possible that indeed all human beings are made in God's image. The question here is not whether the Bible *says* this but what it *means*.

Next, I wish to make clear that there are certain *unbiblical* notions that are *not* taught by the Word-Faith teachers. Calling human beings "gods" or "God manifest in the flesh" is, I will argue, wrong, but such language can mean different things to different people. Here are some things that, to the best of my knowledge, such language does *not* mean when used by Hagin, Copeland, and other Word-Faith teachers. There are five points to be considered.

First, they do not mean that *human beings preexisted with the Father.* To my knowledge no one has ever accused the Word-Faith teachers of espousing this heresy. This is one elementary way in which the Word-Faith teaching differs, for example, from the Mormon or Latter-Day Saint doctrine of human beings as gods.

Second, they do not mean that *human beings are omnipotent, omniscient, or omnipresent.* Again, to my knowledge no one has characterized the Word-Faith teaching as holding such views. If anything, the Word-Faith teachers have been accused of denying these attributes to God! We have already seen that the Word-Faith doctrine of God having a body is at odds with the omnipresence of God (although the Word-Faith teachers, apparently undisturbed by the inconsistency, try to claim that both are true). In any case, there is no danger of the Word-Faith teachers being accused of attributing these divine attributes to human beings.

On the other hand, at least one Word-Faith teacher, Kenneth Copeland, has intimated that human beings are capable of exercising just as much power as God (however much that may be). Recall, for instance, the statement quoted earlier by Copeland that the spirits of human beings are just as big as God's and simply have not yet developed the same strength as has God.

Third, they do not mean that *human beings are deserving of worship.* Not even the harshest critics of the Word-Faith teachers have suggested they believe this.

Fourth, they do not mean that *human beings are or will become coequal with God.* Some critics have suggested that at least some Word-Faith teachers hold this view. Recall that on at least one occasion Copeland has given them reason to think so—when he asserted that Adam in the Garden of Eden "was not subordinate to God, even." Whatever Copeland meant by this statement, it is evident from the whole body of his teaching that he does not think human beings or Christians are coequal with God. He thinks that they are subject to his laws and answerable to his judgments. He distinguishes, however inadequately, between God as the Creator and human beings as God's creatures. I will argue that Copeland's teaching compromises the distinction between Creator and creature, but it does not do so by making human beings coequal with God.

Fifth, they do not mean that *human beings are divine in their outer man, their material bodies.* To the best of my knowledge this idea has never been attributed to the Word-Faith teachers by anybody.

The Word-Faith doctrine of "little gods" deserves scrutiny. Those who would defend the "little gods" doctrine cannot do so merely by pointing out that they do not hold any of the obviously unbiblical ideas mentioned above.

Having affirmed the biblical truth that we are made in God's image, and having cleared away several possible (though unlikely) misunderstandings of the Word-Faith doctrine, we are ready to focus on the real issue. That issue, simply put, is *whether human beings were created in God's "class" or are composed of the same substance.* Clearly, the Word-Faith teachers answer this question in the affirmative. What we need to know, then, is whether this teaching is biblical. In the remainder of this chapter we will consider this question in detail.

What Does the Bible Say?

The Word-Faith teachers use a variety of strategies to justify the "little gods" doctrine biblically. First of all, they appeal to passages where people appear to be called "gods" (notably Ps. 82:6 and John 10:34). Second, they argue that since both God and people are spirits, human beings exist in the same class as God. Third, they appeal to the biblical theme of human beings as created in the image of God. Any comprehensive treatment of the question of human beings as gods in Word-Faith theology must deal with all three of these arguments.

Are Human Beings Called "Gods" in Scripture?

Both Old and New Testaments are emphatic and explicit in their repeated affirmation that there is only one God, and that there is no other God besides him. The Old Testament statements on this matter use all three of the different Hebrew words for God. The LORD (Jehovah) is the only *el* (2 Sam. 22:32; Isa. 43:10), the only *eloah* (Isa. 44:8), and the only *elohim* (Deut. 4:35, 39; 32:39; Isa. 44:6). In Isaiah 43–46, all three words are used interchangeably in a series of such affirmations, often in the same verse, making it quite clear that there is absolutely only one God (Isa. 43:10; 44:6, 8; 45:5, 14, 21–22; 46:9). The New Testament, which regularly uses the Greek word *theos* for God, is just as emphatic and explicit (Rom. 16:27; 1 Cor. 8:4–6; Eph. 4:6; 1 Tim. 1:17; 2:5; James 2:19; Jude 25). (It should be noted that biblically no distinction can be made between *god* and *God*, since lowercase letters were not used in the original manuscripts.) Therefore, the Bible most definitely rejects any sort of polytheism, including the doctrine of *henotheism*, according to which there are many gods but only one that human beings should worship. Both Mormonism and Jehovah's Witnesses teach henotheism, and it is arguable that the Word-Faith teachers do so as well.

The Scriptures are also very clear in teaching that God is an absolutely unique being who is distinct from the world as its Creator and Maker. As the Creator of the universe (Gen. 1:1; Ps. 33:6; 102:25; John 1:3; Rom. 11:36; Heb. 1:2; 11:3), who made all things by himself (Isa. 44:24), he is to be distinguished from the world that he made (Isa. 40:22; Acts 17:24; Rom. 1:25). Since he is eternal, omnipresent, omnipotent, and omniscient, God is totally unique, so that there is none even like God (Ps. 102:25–27; 139; Isa. 40–46; Jer. 10:6–7; 23:23–24; Acts 17:24–28). The Bible, then, clearly and unmistakably teaches a monotheistic worldview.

While most Word-Faith teachers would probably agree with this monotheistic worldview in principle, their teachings often contradict it. For example, Copeland contradicts the doctrine of God's omnipresence by teaching that God has a body and lives on a planet somewhere.

In the face of so many explicit statements about there being only one God, and in light of his uniqueness, it may seem surprising that anyone would claim that the Bible teaches that people are or can be gods. However, a few passages in Scripture seem to call human beings "god" or "gods." Most or all of these, however, are irrelevant to any doctrine of deification.

In several texts, certain human beings are either called "gods" by unbelievers, denoting improper worship (Acts 12:22; 28:6; 2 Thess. 2:4), or are specifically said not to be gods (Isa. 31:3; Ezek. 28:2, 9). These texts actually serve to further undermine any notion of human deification.

Moses was said to be "as God" to Aaron (Exod. 4:16) and to Pharaoh (Exod. 7:1), but the first is clearly metaphorical and the second just as clearly gives Pharaoh's pagan point of view.

In two texts the messianic son of David is evidently called "God" (Ps. 45:6; compare Heb. 1:8; Isa. 9:6), which in the light of the New Testament should be explained by the fact that the Messiah was in fact to be none other than God himself.

Finally, there are a few texts in which it is thought that *elohim* might have reference to Israelite judges (Exod. 21:6; 22:8–9, 28; 1 Sam. 2:25; Ps. 82:1b, 6; cf. John 10:34–35). It is possible to interpret the Exodus and 1 Samuel passages to mean that in approaching the judges of Israel one was entering the presence of God (compare Deut. 19:17). However, even if one takes the view that the judges are here called "gods," this is a special figurative usage that applies only to them and does not teach that people generally or Christians specifically are gods.

In Psalm 82:6, however, there is no doubt that *elohim* is to be translated "gods," just as it is quoted in John 10:34–35 with the plural *theoi*. Therefore, the question of whether the Bible ever calls human beings "gods" in a positive sense focuses exclusively on Psalm 82 and its citation by Jesus in John 10:34–35. Charles Capps speaks for many when he writes that in quoting Psalm 82 Jesus was teaching "that man was created to be a god over the earth."[20]

Most of the interpretations of Psalm 82 that understand "gods" to be human beings are incompatible with any doctrine of deification. The classical view is that the term refers to Israelite judges by virtue of their position as representing God. This has been the usual view among both Catholic and Protestant expositors. If this view is correct, then, as in the case of the Exodus and 1 Samuel texts, it is a figurative usage that applies only to those judges under the old covenant rule of God and does not apply to people or even to believers in general. This classical interpretation, therefore, contradicts the interpretation adopted in the Word-Faith theology.

An alternative interpretation agrees that the "gods" are Israelite judges but sees the use of the term *elohim* as an ironic figure of speech. Irony is a rhetorical device in which something is said in such a way as to make the assertion seem ridiculous (compare Paul's ironic "you have become kings" in 1 Cor. 4:8, where Paul's point is that they had *not* become kings). That the psalmist's use of "gods" for the Israelite judges is meant to be taken ironically seems evident from the parallel description of them as "sons of the Most High" (when in no biblical sense of the term were they truly "sons" of God), the condemnation of the judges for their wicked judgment, and especially the statement, "Nevertheless you will die like men."

Whichever of these interpretations of Psalm 82 one prefers, it is certainly the case that neither Psalm 82 nor John 10:34–35 teaches that human beings were created as gods, or that they may become exalted to the point of being gods. The Israelite judges were wicked men who were condemned to death by the true God and therefore were not by any definition of deification candidates for godhood. The use of these texts to justify a doctrine of deification, then, is certainly mistaken.

It is interesting to note how one Word-Faith teacher handles the question of deification as it relates to this text. James A. Laine, writing in *Seduction?? A Biblical Response*, a critique of Dave Hunt's *The Seduction of Christianity*, offered the following comments:

> Beside the second verse [Ps. 82:6] I have written in the margin, "DPI." Those who have attended our seminary know what these initials mean—DON'T PREACH IT! Certain things in the Word of God are too hot and too clumsy to be handled. . . . I have seen, historically, that every time people have preached, "you are gods," or "you are the manifest sons of God," such massive error has been produced that many people in the body of Christ have been injured by it. . . . The truth of the matter is that, according to this scrip-

ture, believers are gods. The problem with this is that as soon as you begin thinking that, you are in trouble.[21]

There is something very wrong with an interpretation of Scripture that cannot be preached. Such a conclusion directly contradicts 2 Timothy 3:16, "All Scripture is inspired by God and profitable for teaching," and Romans 15:4, "Whatever was written in earlier times was written for our instruction." The truth is that Psalm 82:6 does not teach that believers are gods, and the correct interpretation can be preached without any embarrassment to orthodox Christians.

If, then, any notion of deification is to be found in Scripture, it will have to appeal to other biblical texts or themes. In general the Bible denies that human beings are or can become gods, and there is no passage in Scripture that gives them the title of "gods" in anything but at best a figurative sense.

Our Spirits, Our Divine Selves?

A basic argument in the Word-Faith theology for viewing human beings begins with the premise that in essence we are spirits. The argument might be set out formally as follows:

a. God is a spirit; that is, God is in the spirit class of being.
b. Man is also a spirit; that is, man is in the spirit class of being.
c. Therefore, man is in the same class of being as God.
d. Any being in the same class as God is a god.
e. Therefore, man is a god.

I have set out the argument more formally than it is found in the Word-Faith teachers' writings and televised sermons, but for most of them this fairly represents their reasoning. Hagin put it this way: "We know this, then: Man is a spirit. We know he is in the same class with God, because God is a Spirit and because man was made to have fellowship with God."[22]

The one Word-Faith teacher who apparently does not employ this argument is Copeland. Since Copeland argues directly from the image of God to the little gods concept, it might be supposed that he would agree that just our being spirits makes us gods. But for some reason Copeland appears to exclude the angels from this status:

Man was created in the god class. He was not created in the animal class. He is in the god class. He has a uniqueness about him that even angels do not have—and that is the God-given right to choose his own words, and speak them, thereby setting his own divine destiny, his own destination.[23]

In any case, since Hagin and other Word-Faith teachers use the argument, it needs to be addressed. The first problem with the argument is that it is highly misleading, if not simply erroneous, to assume that *spirit* designates a "class of being." If it is, then there are actually only two classes of beings, *spirit* and *nonspirit*—or to use Copeland's categories, *god* and *animal,* as in the above quotation. (Again, it is confusing that Copeland seems to exclude the angels from either category.) One might, of course, for some purposes legitimately employ a broad classification of all beings into the two categories of spirit and nonspirit. But to say without qualification or explanation that human beings are "in God's class" is highly misleading.

Second, the premise that human beings are essentially spirits rather than fleshly beings is unbiblical. It is true, as we have seen, that human beings do have a spirit or soul distinct from the physical body. But this does not mean that we are fundamentally spirits encased in physical bodies that are only an outer "shell" (as some Word-Faith teachers have put it).[24] Fundamentally we are material beings, created to inhabit the physical universe and this earth in particular. This is clear, not only from Genesis 1–2 but also from biblical statements such as the following: "For you [Adam] are dust" (Gen. 3:19b). "Thus He remembered that they were but flesh" (Ps. 78:39a). "For He Himself knows our frame; He is mindful that we are but dust" (Ps. 103:14). "Now the Egyptians are men and not God, and their horses are flesh and not spirit" (Isa. 31:3).

The third problem is that the premise "Any being in the same class as God is a god" simply is not true if "class" is defined so broadly as to include all spirits, created and uncreated. The proof for this is easy:

a. Demonic beings are spirits (e.g., the many biblical passages referring to "unclean spirits").
b. Demons are not gods (Gal. 4:8; cf. 1 Cor. 10:20).
c. Therefore, at least some spirits are not gods.

The sum of the matter is this: The argument that we are little gods because we are spirits just as God is a spirit has several holes. Spirits do not constitute a distinctive class of being, we are not simply or fundamentally spirits, and at least some spirits are definitely *not* gods. Spirits come in different varieties, but the most important difference is between *created* spirits and the unique *uncreated* Spirit, the Lord God. Since the Bible says repeatedly that this Lord is the *only* God, we should reject the Word-Faith doctrine that other spirits are in God's class and are themselves gods.

Our examination of this argument has also prepared us to see the error in another, related argument. At least some of the Word-Faith teachers claim that God formed our spirit beings from the substance of his own divine spirit being. To quote again from Kenneth Hagin:

> God took something of Himself and put [it] in man. He made the body of man out of the dust of the earth, but He breathed into man's nostrils the breath of life. The word translated "breath" in the passage concerning man's creation, is the Hebrew word "ruoch." "Ruoch" means "breath" or "spirit," and is translated "Holy Spirit" many times in the Old Testament. God is Spirit, so He took something of Himself, which is spirit, and put it into man.[25]

The Bible simply does not teach this doctrine. God gives all human beings life, including their immaterial spirits, but our spirits are created, not taken out of God's being. God's Spirit is the Creator and Giver of our life, not the stuff of our life. The text to which Hagin refers is Genesis 2:7, which says, "Then the LORD God formed man of dust from the ground, and breathed into his nostrils the breath of life; and man became a living being." As Greg Durand has pointed out, the word translated "breath" here is not *ruach* but *neshamah*.[26] Both words can be translated "breath," but *neshamah*, unlike *ruach*, never refers to the Holy Spirit. However, even had the text used *ruach*, it still would not have been saying that God transferred some of his own *ruach* into Adam as his *ruach*. All the passage says is that God breathed the breath or spirit of life into Adam; it does not say where God got that spirit. Once again, it is important to keep in mind that God does not have a body and does not literally breathe air or anything else.

The Image of God: An Exact Duplicate?

One biblical teaching emphasized by those who teach some form of deification is the doctrine of human beings created and redeemed in the image of God. In Genesis 1:26–27 and 5:1, the Bible states that we were created in the image and likeness of God. The Word-Faith teachers equate this creation in God's image with the notion of things reproducing "after their kind," also found in Genesis 1. But it is not at all clear why these two concepts should be equated. Genesis says that God *created* man, not that God *birthed* man or reproduced himself in man. Genesis says that man was created in God's *image and likeness,* not after God's *kind.*

Nothing else in the Bible supports equating being in God's image with being the same kind of being as God. Genesis 9:6 says that murder is punishable by death because God made man in his image. In the New Testament, James 3:9 speaks of the evil of cursing men, "who have been made in the likeness of God," while 1 Corinthians 11:7 says that man "is the image and glory of God." In some unique sense, Christ is the image of God (2 Cor. 4:4; Col. 1:15), and Christians will by virtue of their union with Christ be conformed to the image of God and of Christ, resulting eventually in glorification (Rom. 8:29–30; 2 Cor. 3:18), moral perfection (Eph. 4:24; Col. 3:10), and an immortal physical body like Christ's (1 Cor. 15:49; cf. Phil. 3:21).

These truths about the image of God are wonderful and profound. Yet the Bible rarely uses the expression "image of God" and says little about its meaning. It is therefore not surprising that orthodox biblical theologians and scholars have some differences of opinion as to how best to define and explain what these passages mean.[27] However, these differences are relatively minor and do not obscure the basic truth of the image, which is that human beings were created as physical *representations* (not physical *reproductions* or exact duplicates) of God in the world. As such, we were meant to live forever, to know God personally, to reflect his moral character—his love—through human relationships, and to exercise dominion over the rest of the living creatures on the earth (Gen. 1:28–30; compare Ps. 8:5–8). But the word *image* does not mean that a human being as God's image has God's nature or essence, any more than a Roman coin with Caesar's "image" has Caesar's nature (compare Luke 20:24). Thus the Word-Faith teachers are simply mistaken when they say that the meaning of the word *image* forces us to the conclusion that a human being is an "exact representation" of God. Their undocumented claim that this is the meaning of the Hebrew is simply false.

From the biblical teaching on the image of God, then, there is nothing that would warrant the conclusion that people are or will ever be "gods," even "little gods," as the Word-Faith teachers have maintained. Of course, if by "deification" one means only that we will be "like God" in those respects indicated in Scripture, such a doctrine is biblical, even if the language used to describe it is not. If, on the other hand, it is taught that human beings as the image of God are essentially the *same kind of being* as God or will be some day, or that a human being is, like God, a being with a "sovereign will" by which he can control his circumstances, then such a teaching is unbiblical in its meaning and language and is clearly heretical. This is apparently how the Word-Faith teachers explain the doctrine of "little gods," though typically such explanations are far from clear. One must also acknowledge that the Word-Faith teachers do not describe human beings as, for instance, potentially omnipotent or omniscient.

It is only the vague and contradictory character of most Word-Faith teachers' explanations that prevents us from concluding definitively that their "little gods" doctrine is itself necessarily heretical. In general, their teachings on this subject appear to range from the rather aberrant (Kenyon) to the outright heretical (almost certainly Copeland). While we must be careful not to overgeneralize the error, there is no getting around the fact that the doctrine of human beings as little gods is indeed seriously erroneous.

10

Dominion and the Devil

Now, Adam committed high treason, used that authority and delivered it into the hands of an alien spirit—a spirit that was already fallen as far as God was concerned. He [Satan] had no right to receive it, but Adam gave it to him. That gave him the right to receive it. . . . And when he [Adam] said, and when he acted on the fact that, and bowed his knee to Satan, and put Satan up above him, then there wasn't anything God could do about it, 'cause a god had placed him there. But in doing so, he bowed his knee to his enemy, to God's enemy and his, Satan, and the nature of Satan then was lodged in his spirit forever unless God could do something about it, because man could not.

Kenneth Copeland[1]

Saying that humans have Satan's nature makes them little more than demonic entities imprisoned in human bodies. This sounds more like Scientology than Christianity.

Michael G. Moriarty[2]

You are of your father the devil, and you want to do the desires of your father. He was a murderer from the beginning, and does not stand in the truth because there is no truth in him. Whenever he speaks a lie, he speaks from his own nature, for he is a liar and the father of lies.

John 8:44

In the previous chapter I argued that the Word-Faith view of human beings as "little gods" is unbiblical. I gave reasons to reject the claim that we were *created* to be gods. This claim is closely related to the Word-Faith teaching that we were *redeemed* to be gods. These claims are so closely related that we might have chosen to discuss them together. But to understand fully the Word-Faith view of redemption, we need to consider first its teaching on the fall of Adam into sin and God's answer to the fall in Jesus Christ. This chapter focuses on the fall, while the following chapter examines the Word-Faith view of Jesus.

The Word-Faith View of the Fall

The Word-Faith teachers claim that God created Adam to be the god (or God) of the earth. As Kenneth Copeland put it, "Man had total authority to rule as a god over every living creature on earth, and he was to rule by speaking words."[3] The reason human beings do not live like gods now is because of the fall.

E. W. Kenyon

I begin with Kenyon's own explanation of this doctrine. According to Kenyon, God gave man a "lease" in which he had a "Time-Limit Dominion" to rule the universe. He finds this idea implicit in several texts (Matt. 8:29; Luke 21:24; Rom. 11:25; Rev. 12:12). When Adam sinned, he legally transferred his lease to Satan, giving the devil universal authority. "We know that Satan is ruling today through fallen man, but, thank God, that Lease is nearly ended and will expire at the Coming of the Lord Jesus."[4] The effects of this treason were threefold. "First, it was the thwarting of God's plan. Second, it was the separation of God and Man. Third, it gave Satan universal Dominion over God's creation."[5] Because God had given dominion to man on a lease and man had transferred that lease to Satan, Satan's dominion is a legal one, and "God is unable to break it until such time as the Adamic lease, so-called, expires."[6]

In addition, Adam's fall into sin resulted in human beings' losing the nature of God and receiving, in a kind of perverted "new birth," the nature of Satan:

It is very noticeable that the moment Man sinned His Nature underwent a complete change. This change has no parallel in Nature except in that which is known as the New Birth, for when one is born of God he undergoes as instantaneous a change. This proves to us that Man was actually Born Again when he sinned. That is, he was born of the devil. He became a partaker of the Satanic Nature just as a man today becomes a partaker of Divine nature when he is born of God by accepting Jesus Christ.[7]

Kenneth Hagin

Hagin's doctrine of the fall is apparently identical to Kenyon's, even using much of the same language to express it. One difference is that Hagin adds the concept of a transferred godhood to the idea of a transferred dominion:

God created everything, then He made man, Adam, and gave him dominion over all of it. God made it all for His man Adam. He gave Adam dominion over the cattle on a thousand hills, over the silver and gold, over the world and the fullness thereof. In other words, Adam was the god of this world.
But Adam committed high treason and sold out to Satan. Thus Satan became the god of this world.[8]

Hagin realizes that it sounds odd to say that Adam had a right to transfer his godhood to the devil. He offers this qualification: "Adam didn't have the moral right to commit treason, but he had the legal right to do so." In any case, "Now Satan has a right to be here and be the god of this world until 'Adam's lease' runs out."[9] Thus, God cannot evict Satan until the lease expires. Were he to do so, Satan could accuse him of wrongdoing: "God doesn't just move in on top of Satan. If He did this, Satan could accuse Him of doing the same thing he did."[10]

Kenneth Copeland

As might be expected from our study of Copeland in previous chapters, his exposition of the doctrine of the fall is bolder in its disdain for traditional Christian beliefs and in some respects goes beyond his predecessors. Nevertheless, his basic doctrine of the fall is the same as that of Kenyon and Hagin.[11] According to Copeland, when Adam sinned and transferred his godhood to the devil, "there wasn't anything God could do about it, 'cause a *god* had placed him there." Once he had committed his godhood to Satan, man "fell below the god class."[12]

In an interesting twist, Copeland teaches that Satan had devised a strategy to gain ascendancy over God that actually might have worked. The devil's plan was to maneuver God into violating Satan's legal lease, thus making God a kind of galactic criminal.

> If He had injected Himself illegally into the earth—what Satan intended to do was to fall for it—pull off an illegal act—and turn the light off in God, and subordinate God to himself. Now, he intended to get God into such a trap that He couldn't get out. That's what he tried to do, and he did it with man.[13]

It is within this context that Copeland made one of his most outlandish statements:

> I was shocked when I found out who the biggest failure in the Bible actually is. . . . The biggest one in the whole Bible is God. . . . He lost His top-ranking, most anointed angel, the first man He ever created, the first woman He ever created, the whole earth and all the fullness therein, a third of the angels at least. That's a big loss, man. I mean, you figure that out—that's a lot of real estate, brother, gone down the drain. . . . Now the reason you don't think of God as a failure is He never said He's a failure. And you're not a failure till you say you're one.[14]

Charles Capps

One of the more interesting expositions of the Word-Faith doctrine of the fall comes from Charles Capps. At times apparently plagiarizing Copeland, Capps also contributes the concept of a "Supreme Court of the Universe" to which even God is subject:

> God couldn't come to earth and say, "Adam, I'm going to wipe out you and Satan. I'm going to get that authority back. I'm going to do this whole thing over and make another man out of the dust of the earth." He couldn't do that because the dust of the earth didn't belong to Him. His man, Adam, had given it to Satan. . . . God couldn't come here in His divine power and wipe them out. He had to move in an area where it would be ruled legal by the Supreme Court of the Universe.[15]

Summarizing the Word-Faith Teaching

From the preceding passages from the Word-Faith teachers, I will now summarize their view of the fall, adding the biblical proof texts used to substantiate their doctrine.

Adam was legally the god of this world until he sinned, when he transferred or forfeited his godship to Satan. This transfer was an act of high treason that made Satan the legal god of this world (John 14:30; 2 Cor. 4:3–4; 1 John 5:19) and denied God legal access to the earth.

According to Kenyon and Hagin, mankind's dominion over the earth as god was on a "lease" basis, for a definite period of time. Now that Satan has become the god of this world, his dominion cannot be terminated completely by God until the lease expires (Matt. 8:29; Luke 21:24; Rom. 11:25; Rev. 12:12). How many Word-Faith teachers espouse this "lease" concept is unknown. Copeland's view seems to be that Adam's dominion was of unlimited duration, so that Satan's dominion is of unlimited duration unless God can do something to reverse the situation legally.

In either case, most or all Word-Faith teachers hold that Satan had upset God's plan for humanity and the earth. God's plan was "thwarted," says Kenyon; God himself was a "failure," asserts Copeland, though he explains that God himself refuses to admit failure but confesses only victory over Satan. God was now legally barred from taking any direct action against Satan. In order to reclaim dominion over the earth, God would have to find some indirect strategy that would satisfy cosmic law—or, as Capps puts it, "the Supreme Court of the Universe."

This strategy would have to be through human beings, since the earth was made for humanity and it was a man that had given Satan godhood in the first place. But in sinning against God and submitting to Satan, Adam had forfeited his own godhood (Copeland says he fell below the level of gods) and taken on the nature of Satan, so that human beings are now Satan's children instead of God's (John 8:44). Thus human beings would seem to be totally incapable of reclaiming dominion over the earth. That, as the Word-Faith teachers see it, was the predicament in which God found himself when Adam sinned.

Evaluating the Word-Faith View of the Fall

Not everything about the Word-Faith doctrine of the fall is unbiblical. Adam did sin against God. Adam's sin was contrary to God's created design for humanity. Adam's sin did result in Satan wielding power over fallen humanity. If the Word-Faith teachers stopped there, no Christian could object to their doctrine. Unfortunately, the Word-Faith teachers go further.

Is Satan the Legal God of the Earth?

The fundamental premise of the Word-Faith doctrine is that Adam was the god of this world. As I hope has been made clear, this premise is unbiblical. But if Adam was not the god of this world, then he could not have transferred legal godhood over this world to Satan.

But does not 2 Corinthians 4:4 call Satan "the god of this world"? Indeed it does. However, two factors call the Word-Faith teachers' conclusion from this passage into question. First, in this passage Paul is not teaching that Satan is *legally* the god of this world. Satan may in some sense be the god of this world, but he has no legal right or title to that position. Second, the expression "god of this world" does not mean "god over this earth," as the Word-Faith teachers appear to assume. The word translated "world" in the King James Version (and most modern versions as well) is not the Greek word *gē* (which does mean "earth") or even *kosmos* (which can mean "world" in the sense of the earth or the universe). Instead, the word Paul uses is *aiōn,* which literally means "age" (compare the NIV), and in this context means something like "world system," referring to the world of fallen humanity with its sin-corrupted history. Thus, Paul's point is not that Satan is legally the god of this planet but that he is the being whom this fallen world of humanity unwittingly follows as if he were its god (see also John 14:30; 1 John 5:19).

The reason we can be confident that Satan is not *really* the god of this world is simple. The Bible plainly says that the Lord is the only true God (Isa. 43:10; 45:5–7; John 17:3; 1 Cor. 8:4–6; 1 Tim. 2:5; James 2:19; 1 John 5:20) and is *still* sovereign over the earth. "The earth is the LORD's, and the fulness thereof; the world, and they that dwell therein" (Ps. 24:1 KJV). Compare this text with Copeland's bold assertion that God "lost . . . the whole earth and all the fullness therein."[16] And Psalm 24:1 cannot be explained as a kind of divine "positive confession" in which God was claiming by faith that the earth was his even when it did not seem that way. If Satan had legal claim to the earth, God had no legal grounds to claim, even by faith, that the earth belonged to him. We must conclude that the idea that God "lost" his world is unbiblical.

Satan may aspire to godhood, and fallen humans may allow him to rule over them *as if* he were their god. But Satan, like all demonic spirits, is by nature no god (1 Cor. 10:20; Gal. 4:8).

Does Satan Have a "Lease"?

At least some of the Word-Faith teachers claim that God is unable to evict Satan from planet Earth until his "lease" runs out—a lease that Satan took over from Adam when Adam sinned. This idea implies that humanity's authorization to exercise dominion on the earth was strictly temporary—an idea nowhere found in Scripture.

The texts adduced by Word-Faith teachers to support the idea of Satan's lease do not make the case. What these texts do indicate (Matt. 8:29; Luke 21:24; Rom. 11:25; Rev. 12:12) is that Satan's rebellion against God's authority will come to an end. But none of them even hints at the idea that God is legally unable to end Satan's rule until some fixed future date. For example, when Jesus spoke of "the times of the Gentiles" (Luke 21:24), he was simply speaking of a period of time when God would allow the Gentiles to dominate Jerusalem. Revelation 12:12 speaks of a time when the devil will know that his time is short, but it does not say that he will know this because he has checked his calendar and seen that his lease is about to expire!

Did God Lose Control of the World?

By itself the idea that Satan has a "lease" of rule over the earth might not sound so bad, even if it happens to be without biblical basis. But in the context of the Word-Faith theology, it is part of the picture of a universe out of God's control, a universe subject to laws that even God cannot change. It may even be viewed as a universe perhaps subject along with God to a mysterious "Supreme Court of the Universe" (Capps), a universe whose Creator is "the biggest failure in the Bible" (Copeland). It is, in short, an idea so antithetical to the biblical view of God as the sovereign Lord of the universe as to make any biblically informed Christian cringe.

Since God's control of the world is so often doubted today, even by many outside the Word-Faith movement, I will draw attention here to just some of the biblical evidence supporting the doctrine of the sovereignty of God.

God's control of nature. According to the Bible, God is in control of such seemingly random or chance events as the casting of lots (Prov. 16:33). He is, therefore, in complete control of the natural realm everywhere, including on the earth. Jesus taught that God even cares about how many hairs are on our heads and about the death of common birds (Matt. 10:29–31). This is not merely a complete knowledge of the *present* (though that is included) but an assurance of God's control and care for Jesus' disciples *in the future* (note especially Matt. 6:34).

God's control of events. Your brothers turn against you, try to kill you, sell you to a drug cartel. You end up in jail, wrongfully accused of attempted rape. Could this be God's will? The Bible says yes, as the story of Joseph clearly illustrates (Gen. 45:4–9; 50:20).

God is in control of the rise and fall of nations and governments (Ps. 33:10–11; Isa. 10:5–15; 14:24–27; Jer. 49:20). Paul made travel plans but recognized that God could override them (Acts 18:21; Rom. 1:10; 15:32). God is in control of the circumstances under which His people suffer (1 Peter 3:17; Gen. 50:20) or are tempted (Matt. 6:13; 1 Cor. 10:13).

God's control of individuals. Not only is God in control of nature and of historical events and circumstances, God is also in control of individuals. He can turn the heart of a king one way or another as he wills (Prov. 21:1). God sovereignly chooses to whom he will show mercy and to whom he will not (Prov. 16:4; John 1:13; 6:44; Rom. 9:6–24; Eph. 1:3–12). God determines what spiritual gifts we have (1 Cor. 12:11; compare 1 Cor. 14:1). God is ultimately in control both of what we say and what we do (Prov. 16:1, 9).

None of this is to deny that we do what we choose to do; it does not mean that God "forces" us to do things we would not otherwise do. It does mean that God's creative, determinative will is somehow back of all that happens, including the free actions of moral agents.

The ultimate example of God's sovereignty: the crucifixion of Jesus Christ. The central event of history is the crucifixion of Jesus Christ. Here, better than in any other event, we can see how God's sovereignty relates to human actions. We may begin with the dastardly betrayal of Jesus by Judas. Who was responsible for this act? Well, Judas, of course; but it was inspired by Satan (Matt. 26:14–16, 24; Luke 22:3; John 13:2, 27). More surprising, however, is that, according to Jesus himself, the betrayal was foreordained *by God* (Luke 22:22).

Again, we may ask, who was responsible for the crucifixion of Jesus? On the one hand, we may quite properly answer that the Jews and Romans conspired together to do it (Matt. 26:1–5; John 11:47–53; Acts 3:13–15). But the Bible also states repeatedly that God planned and ordained for it to happen (Isa. 53:10; Matt. 26:42; Luke 22:42; John 10:17–18; Acts 4:28; 1 Peter 1:18–20). Both are true and can be affirmed together without contradiction, as Peter does in the first Christian sermon (Acts 2:23).

God's knowledge of all future events. If God is in control of all events, obviously he has foreknowledge of all future events. Through the prophet Isaiah the Lord ridicules the false gods of the nations by pointing out that they cannot do what he can, namely, predict the future (Isa. 41:22–23; 42:9; 44:7). As a case in point, God predicts the restoration of the nation of Israel to their land and gives *the name* of the king who will do it—Cyrus (45:1). God not only knew that Israel would be restored to the land and the name of the king, but he also knew *when* they would be restored (Jer. 29:10). He knew it, because he planned it (Jer. 29:11).

Once again, the grand proof of God's foreknowledge is the fact that God planned from the beginning of time to send his Son to earth as a man and that Jesus would be betrayed and crucified (Isa. 53:10; Matt. 26:42; Luke 22:42; Acts 2:23; 4:28; 1 Peter 1:20; Rev. 13:8).

I do not want to be misunderstood as saying that there is only one acceptably Christian way of relating God's sovereignty to our human freedom. I do insist that all Christians ought to acknowledge that God *is* sovereign, that this is our Father's world, that God never "lost control" of it, that God has always known what he was doing, and that God is certainly no failure.

Has Man Traded in God's Nature for Satan's?

The Word-Faith teachers universally agree that when Adam fell, he forfeited God's nature with which he had been endowed in his "spirit being" and took within himself instead the nature of his new god, Satan. Although other texts are sometimes cited as supplementary support, the chief proof text for this doctrine is John 8:44, in which Jesus told his Pharisaic opponents that their father was not God but the devil.

Once again, it is appropriate to note that this doctrine rests on a premise already shown to be false. Adam did not possess God's essential nature prior to his fall into sin and therefore could not have forfeited God's nature for Satan's. Furthermore, in John 8:44 Jesus did not say that the Pharisees actually possess "Satan's nature" in their spirit beings. He did call the devil their father, but in this context Satan is so called because their moral character reflects Satan's—that of murder and lying. If this were all the Word-Faith teachers meant—that since the fall the moral disposition of natural human beings has been satanic rather than divine—once again traditional Christians would have no objection. And it may be that for some advocates of the Word-Faith theology this is how the language about fallen man having Satan's nature is understood.

However, Hagin and especially Copeland are very clear about insisting that Adam possessed God's essential nature—that his very being was created from the same spirit as in the being of God. If this was what it meant for Adam to have "God's nature," then likewise we should conclude that to have "Satan's nature" would mean to possess Satan's essential nature, not just his moral dispositions.

What is really troubling about the Word-Faith teaching at this point—however the language about Satan's nature is interpreted—is that it implies a complete defacing or obliteration of the image of God in the unredeemed. This is unavoidable once it is recognized that in Word-Faith theology man has the image of God only as long as he has God's nature (since these are the same thing in the Word-Faith teaching). It implies that non-Christians are little more than demonized animals. Thankfully, so far as I can tell, the Word-Faith teachers themselves have not followed through at this point and pressed the matter consistently. They seem to recognize, as hopefully their followers do also, that all human beings retain much of the dignity and worth of creatures made in the image of God (as Gen. 9:6 plainly implies; see also James 3:9). But at this point their better instincts run contrary to their basic doctrine.

11

Confessing Jesus—A New Twist

In what may well be the ultimate demotion, Copeland here strips the pre-incarnate Christ of His omnipresence and eternal existence—indeed, of His very Godhood. How can Christ guarantee our salvation if He is not God?

Hank Hanegraaff[1]

This theology of Mr. Hanegraaff is more than unorthodox, it is scary. It profoundly demeans the reality of Jesus being the scriptural unblemished lamb.

Michael Bruno[2]

Be on guard for yourselves and for all the flock, among which the Holy Spirit has made you overseers, to shepherd the church of God which He purchased with His own blood.

Acts 20:28

We have seen that the Word-Faith teachings about both God and humanity are in significant ways highly unbiblical. This leads us naturally to the question of the Word-Faith view of Jesus Christ, the God-man. Since Jesus Christ is God incarnate, faulty views of God and human nature would naturally be expected to be held together with faulty views of Christ. Unfortunately, this is what we find in the Word-Faith movement, as we shall see in this and the next chapter.

The Word-Faith View of Jesus Christ

The Word-Faith teachers generally affirm a more-or-less trinitarian view of Jesus. So far, to my knowledge none has actually denied the Trinity. In the books and tapes of the Word-Faith teachers, statements can be found affirming the preexistence of Jesus Christ, his eternal deity, the legitimacy of worshiping Jesus Christ, and the like. In general, the Word-Faith movement appears to have inherited a basically traditional, orthodox view of Jesus Christ. Michael Bruno, a Word-Faith writer, is adamant on this point. After quoting the Athanasian Creed, he comments, "There is not a teacher of faith or a Christian I know who holds the doctrine of faith who would not agree with the above."[3]

More Trouble with the Trinity

Regrettably, however, this is not the whole story. As we saw in an earlier chapter, Benny Hinn's view of the Trinity is implicitly tritheistic. Bruno's defense of Hinn at this point is fascinating. Replying to Hank Hanegraaff's criticism of Hinn as tritheistic, Bruno agrees that tritheism "is indeed cultic" but insists that Hinn's view is not tritheistic. Hanegraaff's mistake, Bruno explains, is in equating belief "in three separate distinct beings" with belief "in three Gods." Bruno cites some biblical texts that (he says) show that the Father and the Son sit on two separate thrones (e.g., Matt. 22:41–46; Heb. 1:8). Noting that the Holy Spirit is also a person, he concludes that the Bible supports Hinn's teaching that the three Persons are separate and distinct—and implicitly endorses Hinn's doctrine that the three Persons have separate "spirit bodies."[4]

Bruno then goes on the offensive. He suggests that it is Hanegraaff's theology that "is on thin ice."[5] Specifically, Bruno suggests that Hanegraaff's understanding of the Trinity is dangerously akin to that of the Oneness Pentecostals. In particular, Bruno criticizes Hanegraaff's definition of the Trinity as an affirmation of *"one God revealed in three persons."*[6] As Bruno sees it, this formulation implies that Jesus was merely a revelation of God and not that Jesus was God himself.[7]

Bruno's discussion illustrates the point that if one holds to the idea of God as embodied, one must choose between the belief that God is one person and the belief that God is three separate personal beings. Bruno does not seem to consider the possibility that both of these positions are extremes.

On the other hand, he is right about Hanegraaff's language being susceptible to misunderstanding as endorsing a kind of Oneness view. I would
prefer to say that according to the doctrine of the Trinity, God reveals to us
that he exists eternally in (or "as") the three Persons of the Father, Son,
and Holy Spirit.

No Praying to Jesus?

Moreover, many leading Word-Faith teachers have a less than thoroughly orthodox view of the person of Christ. For example, both E. W.
Kenyon and Kenneth Hagin maintain that Christians should not address
prayers to Jesus. Kenyon commented, "I know that the habit of praying to
Jesus is very widespread, but if we want the truth and we desire to pray in
such a manner that we can be sure of our answer, then we must obey the
Scriptures and pray as they teach us."[8] Hagin claims that this is a major key
to getting answers to prayer:

> Paul is telling us [Eph. 5:20] that it is to the Father and not to Jesus that we
> give thanks. . . . A minister friend of mine never gets answers when he prays.
> It is a struggle for him. He prays to Jesus. I pray to the Father in the name of
> Jesus. I've prayed this way for twenty-nine years, and I've gotten everything
> I've asked for.[9]

There is no biblical basis for saying that prayer should not be addressed
to Jesus. In fact, the New Testament clearly teaches that prayers may be
addressed to Jesus Christ (John 14:14; Acts 7:59). Neither Kenyon nor
Hagin mean to deny the deity of Christ, but their teaching at this point at
the very least shows an openness to unorthodox ideas about Jesus Christ.

Denial of Christ's Deity?

One of the teachings of Kenneth Hagin that has been accepted by most
if not all other Word-Faith teachers is that, in becoming incarnate and living as a man on earth, Jesus Christ made no use of his divine nature but
acted as a mere man empowered by the Spirit. This doctrine has sometimes
been expressed in ways that have prompted critics to conclude that the
Word-Faith teachers are actually denying the deity of Christ. If this charge
were true, the movement would indeed be heretical and theologically cultic, as most of its critics allege.

According to Hagin, although Jesus as a person was God, he laid aside
his divine powers and did not "minister" as God:

But what they fail to realize is that He as the Son of God was one thing and He as a person ministering was another thing. He did not minister as the Son of God—He ministered as a mere man anointed by the Holy Spirit. . . . Jesus also had to be anointed before He could heal, because He had laid aside His mighty power and glory as the Son of God when He became a man. Although in person He was the Son of God, in power He was not the Son of God. Even though this may sound like a paradox, can you understand it? . . . Now, as a person, because He is the Son of God, He is in a class by Himself. But in ministry, He is not in a class by Himself. . . . Why has this not been properly understood? We have not thoroughly studied the Word on this subject because we have been religiously brainwashed.[10]

Kenneth Copeland takes the same view: "Jesus did not minister on earth as the Son of God. He could have. He was God manifest in the flesh. The important thing to us is that He didn't. Jesus ministered on earth as a prophet under the Abrahamic Covenant."[11]

The same idea is expressed in more radical and controversial fashion in Copeland's 1987 "prophecy" in which Jesus supposedly said the following:

Don't be disturbed when people accuse you of thinking you are God. . . . They crucified Me for claiming that I was God. But I didn't claim I was God; I just claimed I walked with Him and that He was in Me. Hallelujah. That's what you're doing.[12]

This "prophecy" evoked considerable outrage among the evangelical discernment ministry community. Walter Martin spoke for many when he delivered a lecture condemning Copeland's prophecy. Martin's assessment has often been quoted to show that he agreed with the judgment that the Word-Faith movement is cultic: "For ten years I have warned—and I'm on tape and in print on this—that we were heading into the kingdom of the cults with the Faith teachers. You are no longer heading there, baby, you are there!"[13]

In his last writing before his death, Martin reaffirmed his condemnation of Copeland's prophecy and his conclusion that the Word-Faith movement was cultic:

Prophecies such as Copeland's do not originate with Christ or the Holy Spirit, and Scripture flatly rejects them as false. We are, therefore, warned not to fear false prophets (Deut. 18:22). . . . Those who propagate these erroneous views (the "little gods," the "born again Jesus," and so on) have sadly crossed over into the kingdom of the cults and stand in need of genuine repentance, lest they come under the inevitability of divine judgment.[14]

In a 1988 column in his monthly magazine, Copeland attempted to clarify his statement:

> I didn't say Jesus *wasn't* God, I said He didn't *claim* to be God when He lived on the earth. Search the Gospels for yourself. If you do, you will find what I say is true. He referred to God as His Father (which enraged the Pharisees), but He never made the assertion that He was the most High God. In fact, He told His disciples that the Father God was greater and mightier than He (John 14:28).
> Why didn't Jesus openly proclaim Himself as God during His 33 years on earth?
> For one simple reason. He hadn't come to earth as God, He'd come as man. He'd set aside His divine power and had taken on the form of a human being—with all its limitations. . . . They don't realize, that when Jesus came to earth, He voluntarily gave up that advantage, living His life here not as God, but as a man. He had no innate supernatural powers. He had no ability to perform miracles until after He was anointed by the Holy Spirit as recorded in Luke 3:22. . . . He ministered as a man anointed by the Holy Spirit.[15]

Neither Walter Martin nor Hank Hanegraaff was satisfied with this explanation. Martin's response was to say that Copeland was wrong in asserting that Jesus never claimed to be God, in view of Christ's "I AM" statement for which the Jews sought to stone him for blasphemy (John 8:58–59).[16] Hanegraaff makes the same point, citing other statements in the Gospel of John as well (John 5:18; 10:30, 33).[17]

Ironically, though, the aspect of Copeland's prophecy that both Martin and Hanegraaff criticized was actually a defensible claim. While Jesus did make many statements that implied his deity (as I myself have argued in several books),[18] it remains true that Jesus never said, "I am God," in those or any other words of similar explicitness. Rather, Jesus made his deity evident through his actions (such as forgiving sins or stilling a storm), through his divine modes of speech (such as "Amen, I say to you"), and through references to himself as God's "Son" (note especially John 5:17–18). The "I AM" statements are among the best examples of Jesus' use of divine speech forms that strongly connoted his own deity, but even they stop short of making that claim *explicit*.

Another more important aspect of Copeland's statement is that Jesus did not "come as God" but rather "came as a man" and was limited in all of the ways that other human beings are limited. Walter Martin was oddly silent about this aspect of Copeland's prophecy, but for good reason: *Martin held essentially the same view.* Note the following statements from one of Martin's popular books:

The New Testament irrefutably teaches that Christ did not exercise at least three prime attributes of deity while on the earth prior to His resurrection. These were omniscience, omnipotence, and omnipresence. Had He done so while a man He could not have been perfect humanity. . . .

The miracles of our Lord offer further proof of His limitations as a man, for He did not hesitate to teach that He personally worked none of them, and that it was the Father who performed the works (John 5:19, 30; John 8:28; 10:37, 38; 10:32; 14:10). . . .

It can be said on good biblical ground that all of Christ's miracles, powers, and supernatural information were the result of the Father's action through Him, thus safeguarding our Lord's identity as a true man (John 14:10; John 5:30).[19]

The similarities between Martin's view and Copeland's are striking. They both agree that Jesus did not exercise his infinite powers of deity while he was a man on earth. They both agree that he was, nevertheless, God in the flesh. They both agree that his miracles were not performed by his own power. They both agree that Jesus *could not* have been a true man if he had utilized his divine powers on earth. They both agree that Jesus' non-use of his divine powers was voluntary.

Hanegraaff, criticizing the Word-Faith teachers, strongly denounces the idea that Jesus lacked these divine attributes while he was on earth, arguing that such a position implies that Jesus was not God at all:

To say that Jesus surrendered even one attribute of deity is to assert that Jesus is less than God and is therefore not God at all.

While Christ voluntarily veiled His divine *glory* (Phil. 2:5–11), Scripture insists that He did not surrender His divine *attributes*.[20]

What Hanegraaff may not have realized is that the view he is criticizing here was held by his predecessor, Walter Martin.

Some may object that Martin was only saying that Jesus merely ceased to *use* his divine attributes, while Copeland says that Jesus did not *have* them. But this objection does not appear to be correct. Copeland agrees that Jesus was God and that his becoming a man did not alter that fact. Martin agrees that Jesus could not use his own divine attributes and be a perfect man. The two views, though worded differently, are basically the same. There is, after all, a very thin line (if any at all) between the idea of Christ "surrendering" the divine attributes in order to become a man on earth (a view Hanegraaff says denies the deity of Christ) and the idea of Christ foregoing all use of them for the entire duration of his life as a man on earth (the view held by Martin).

I read the passage from Martin's book to a fellow researcher[21] at the Christian Research Institute (in 1990 or 1991, after Martin had passed away) without telling him what I was reading, and I asked him what he thought. His response was, "That's heresy," to which I said, "That's Walter Martin." The researcher quickly backed away from his initial assessment—and rightly so, since Martin's view is not really heretical (though it might be labeled heterodox, i.e., differing from the usual position held within orthodox circles). After all, Martin stoutly maintained the deity of Christ and affirmed of Jesus that "in His divine nature He was always the Father's equal."[22] But the researcher's *faux pas* is instructive. Perhaps Martin and other critics of the Word-Faith movement were too quick to accuse Copeland of denying the deity of Christ. At the very least, the reasons given for this assessment have been rather superficial.

Christ's Incarnation Not Unique?

The real problem, as I see it, with Copeland's "prophecy" is the claim that Christians can make the same claim Jesus made. "But I didn't claim I was God; I just claimed I walked with Him and that He was in Me. Hallelujah. *That's what you're doing.*"[23] The implication of this statement is that Jesus Christ was not unique in his relationship to God. This idea is not an isolated idea in the Word-Faith movement but appears to be at the very heart of its theology. The idea is that Christians are just as much sons of God and incarnations of God as was Jesus. Kenneth Hagin puts it quite plainly: "Every man who has been born again is an incarnation and Christianity is a miracle. The believer is as much an incarnation as was Jesus of Nazareth."[24] This statement was actually plagiarized from E. W. Kenyon,[25] and it has thus been a part of the Word-Faith doctrine from its inception.

Copeland, as he usually does, makes essentially the same point in much bolder and more obviously unbiblical fashion:

> He said, "A born-again man defeated Satan, the firstborn of many brethren defeated him." He said, "You are the very image and the very copy of that one." . . . And I said, "Well now you don't mean, you couldn't dare mean that I could have done the same thing?" He said, "Oh, yeah, if you'd known that, had the knowledge of the Word of God that He did you could have done the same thing. 'Cause you're a reborn man too."[26]

Even more brazenly, at least twice Copeland has asserted that Christians may say "I AM" just as God and Christ do:

> . . . any time I see in the New Testament where He said "I am," I just jump
> up and say, "Well, I am, too, bless God." Whatever You are I am. Because You
> are means that I can. Because You are means that I am.[27]

> And I say this with all respect, so that it don't upset you too bad, but I say it
> anyway: When I read in the Bible where He says, "I AM," I just smile and say,
> "Yes, I AM too."[28]

Copeland's admission that his statement is likely to "upset" Christians
should alert us that what he is saying here is indeed contrary to what Christians have generally believed. Yet Copeland throws out these statements
without really explaining them. Clearly, he does not mean that Christians
are self-existent or self-sufficient beings—it is because God *is* whatever he
is that we *are* whatever we are *in him*. But it is hard to avoid the conclusion that for Copeland, at least, Christians literally are (at least in potential) whatever Christ is ("Whatever You are I am"). That this is indeed
Copeland's position will shortly become clear.

One other point should be made here. Copeland's view of the incarnation of God in Jesus Christ should be correlated with his teaching that Adam
himself was "God manifest in the flesh." Once it is understood that for
Copeland, Adam, as well as Jesus, was God incarnate, the question of
whether Copeland affirms the deity of Christ in a biblical sense quickly takes
on new potency. William DeArteaga appears to have missed this dimension
of the problem in his eagerness to defend Copeland against Hank Hanegraaff's charge that he denied the deity of Christ in the following passage:

> What [why] does God have to pay the price for this thing? He has to have a
> man that is like that first one. It's got to be all man. He's got to be all man. *He
> cannot be a God* and come storming in here with attributes and dignities that
> are not common to man. He *can't* do that. It's not legal.[29]

Hanegraaff certainly exaggerates when he makes such comments about
the above passage as, "Apparently, almost everyone gets to be God . . .
except Jesus," and when he asserts that Copeland "clearly divests Christ of
every shred of deity."[30] And DeArteaga is correct in pointing out that
Copeland went on to speak of Christ as "a God-man":

> There had to be a man, but it also had to be a man as pure as that first one
> [Adam], and there wasn't anybody left like that but God. Now somehow or
> other there's got to be an incarnation, there's got to be a man filled with
> God—there's got to be a God-man come into the earth.[31]

What DeArteaga has plainly missed here is that in Copeland's teaching, as expressed in this very passage, Adam was also "a God-man" on earth. If Hanegraaff exaggerated Copeland's doctrinal error, DeArteaga exaggerated his doctrinal soundness when he concluded, "In the context of his sermon, Copeland was completely orthodox on this issue."[32]

Confessing the Word into Being

Several Word-Faith teachers have taught a doctrine that seems very close to monarchianism, a heresy rejected by the early church. *Monarchianism* is the view that God was a single, solitary person, and that he became incarnate in Jesus. On this view, Jesus did not preexist as a person distinct from the Father. In effect, the Father did not *send* the Son; he *became* the Son. Oneness Pentecostals (e.g., the United Pentecostal Church, Pentecostal Assemblies of the World, and various "Apostolic Faith" churches) are the largest representatives of this view today.

E. W. Kenyon, whose theology forms the backbone of Word-Faith doctrine, apparently did not teach this doctrine. However, his theology of the "name of Jesus" was so similar to that of Oneness Pentecostalism that some of his works became very popular in Oneness circles. Sometimes Kenyon clearly affirms the preexistence of the Son[33] and the distinct Persons of the Father, Son, and Holy Spirit.[34] At other times Kenyon speaks of God before creation as the Father alone, as a "lonely Father God" who "longed for sons and daughters" and so created the human race.[35] The doctrine of the Trinity, of course, implies that God was never lonely. Thus Kenyon's teaching, while not monarchian, seems to have had some monarchian leanings.

Kenneth Hagin also apparently does not teach the monarchian doctrine. However, at least two popular and influential Word-Faith teachers, Kenneth Copeland and Charles Capps, do teach a doctrine that appears to be monarchian. According to Copeland and Capps, "the Word" of John 1:1 became incarnate through the process of God's people, beginning with Abraham and culminating in Mary, "positively confessing the Word" that the Messiah would come. This implies that "the Word" was not a person before becoming incarnate.

Charles Capps says that Mary *"actually conceived God's Word sent by an angel."* Jesus was therefore

> *the personification of God's Word on this earth . . . Jesus in Word form was the creator of all things.* God used the Word to create. He used the Word to frame the worlds. Then to prove to us that the Word is as powerful on earth as it is in heaven, God clothed His Word with flesh and sent Him to the earth.[36]

Kenneth Copeland teaches a similar doctrine:

> "The Word became flesh and dwelt among us" [John 1:14]. What Word? The Word of the Covenant that God cut with Abraham way back there years before. . . . That covenant was the door that opened up to heaven that caused God to be able to come to Mary and speak words of life to her and that those words that that angel brought to her became seed inside her womb that produced the blood that flowed in the veins of Jesus. Literally produced it. That's the reason He had to be born of a virgin. It was a creative miracle of God. He created with His words the blood that flowed in His veins.[37]

Thus, Copeland says that in the Old Testament, "God was making promises to Jesus, and Jesus wasn't even there. But you see, God deals with things that are not yet as though they already were."[38]

Again, although Kenyon apparently did not teach this doctrine, he hinted at it at least once: "The Word became flesh once. It is becoming spirit in your spirit."[39] Thus the seed of this doctrine appears to have been planted by Kenyon himself.

Evaluating the Word-Faith View

Evaluating the Word-Faith movement's teachings on the person of Jesus Christ is not a simple matter. The movement is far less clear, and much less unified, in its view of the person of Christ than it is in its view on other matters. Specifically, most Word-Faith teachers do not seem to have espoused the monarchian view promoted by Copeland and Capps. In fact, neither Copeland nor Capps seems to have *explicitly* taught monarchianism, nor has either man actually and explicitly denied the doctrine of the Trinity. In fact, it is possible that both men believe in the personal pre-existence of Jesus Christ. Still, unless either or both of these teachers agrees to clarify his position, the evidence seems to indicate that Copeland and Capps have seriously compromised the trinitarian view of Christ, if not implicitly denied it.

The Incarnation of "the Word"

The New Testament clearly teaches the personhood of the Word prior to the Incarnation. John 1:1 says that "the Word was *with God*" *(pros ton theon)*, that is, the Word was a person who existed in the beginning with God. The whole Gospel of John is replete with references to Jesus having come down from heaven, from God, and going back to God (John 13:3; 16:28), implying he was a person before "coming down."

The preexistent personhood of the Word, or Son, is at odds with the notion that human beings brought Jesus into being through their "positive confession" of the Word. The Copeland-Capps view, that Mary positively confessed God's "covenant Word" into physical manifestation, is pure imagination. It was not the word of the angel believed by Mary but the activity of the Spirit that produced the body of Jesus in Mary's womb (Luke 1:35). Mary *submitted to God's will* as his "servant" by saying, "May it be done to me according to your word" (Luke 1:38); she did not *make it happen*. Nor is there any record of Mary "confessing" the angel's words in the manner prescribed by Word-Faith teachers.

Since not all Word-Faith teachers adhere to this false doctrine, the movement as a whole cannot be condemned because of it. On the other hand, Word-Faith teachers who do not agree with the doctrine ought to say so clearly and ought to call on Copeland and Capps to repent of teaching such false doctrine.

Jesus Acting as a Mere Man

The claim that Jesus was God incarnate but did nothing by the use of his own divine powers is held by many Christians today outside the Word-Faith movement. As I noted earlier, even Walter Martin held this same idea. So it would be unwise to appeal to this teaching as proof that the Word-Faith teachers are heretics, unless one is willing to say the same thing about Martin and many other evangelical Christian teachers.

Still, it needs to be pointed out that such a view has some severe problems. One of the claims made on behalf of this doctrine is that Jesus had to give up the use of his divine attributes to be a man. However, Jesus is *still* a man (Acts 17:31; 1 Cor. 15:47; 1 Tim. 2:5). Does that mean that he still does not use his divine powers?

Moreover, the notion that Jesus did everything without drawing on his own divine powers seems to make the incarnation beside the point: If Jesus acted like a mere man his whole life, why couldn't a mere man do what Jesus did? Indeed, the Word-Faith answer to the above question is, at least according to such teachers as Copeland, that in principle such a thing *was* possible.

The doctrine that Jesus never used his own divine powers is usually based on a misunderstanding of Philippians 2:6–7, which speaks of Christ "emptying himself" and taking the form of a servant and being made in the likeness of men. Philippians 2:6–7 is perhaps the most debated passage in the New Testament, certainly in Paul's epistles, and it would therefore not be wise to base a controversial doctrinal conclusion on one debatable interpretation of the precise wording of Paul's statement there.

Given the complexity of the interpretive issues surrounding this passage, I will simply state what I believe is its meaning. When Paul says that Christ "emptied himself," he does not mean that Christ emptied himself of his divine attributes or even that he ceased to make use of them. Rather, he means that Christ exchanged the glorious form of God—the blinding, unapproachable light of his divine glory—for the humble form of a servant, the appearance of an ordinary man. That glorious form was still properly his, and Christ gave the disciples a glimpse of it in the Transfiguration (Matt. 17:1–9; 2 Peter 1:16–18), but for the most part that glory was hidden or veiled from the world while Christ was on the earth.

Finally, the theory that Jesus never utilized his divine powers on earth and did not come "as God" but acted only as a man contradicts the biblical presentation at several points. For example, the Gospels report Jesus knowing all things (John 16:30), doing what only God can do, such as forgiving sins (Mark 2:1–12), and so forth.

Jesus: First of Many Incarnations?

A complete discussion of the Word-Faith teaching that Christians are exactly like Christ must await a later chapter (chapter 13). Still, it may be helpful here to comment on the idea that Christians, like Christ, are "incarnations" of God. The word *incarnation* (from Latin *in carne*, "in the flesh") refers in Christian theology to the unique assumption of human flesh by the preexistent divine person, the Son, called "the Word" in John (1:1, 14). Jesus was therefore God in the flesh—and, as at least most of the Word-Faith teachers sometimes admit, we are not.

So there are only two ways to justify calling Christians "incarnations" of God. One is to agree that Jesus was uniquely God but then redefine the word *incarnation* to apply to all people indwelled with the Spirit. This will work but at the cost of great and needless confusion. The second way would be to deny that Jesus was uniquely God—to hold that Jesus was not a preexistent divine person singularly incarnated but rather the first man in whom God fully dwelled. This second tack would indeed imply a denial of the true deity of Christ in the biblical and historically Christian sense of this doctrine. As we have seen, there are good reasons to believe that at least two Word-Faith teachers—Kenneth Copeland and Charles Capps—have erred in this fashion. If that is true, we can hardly escape the unhappy conclusion that they are indeed heretics.

12

The Fall and Rise of the Born-Again Jesus

Now listen: From the book of Acts, all the way through all of the Epistles, all the way through the Revelation of John, Jesus is no longer called "the only begotten Son of God"; He's called "the firstborn from the dead"; He's called in the eighth chapter of Romans "the firstborn of many brethren." Jesus was the first man to ever be born from sin to righteousness. He was the pattern of a new race of men to come. Glory to God. And you know what He did? The very first thing that this reborn man did—see, you have to realize that He died. You have to realize that He went into the pit of hell as a mortal man made sin. But He didn't stay there, thank God. He was reborn in the pit of hell.

Kenneth Copeland[1]

So where did this teaching of a "born-again Jesus" originate? Clearly it came from below rather than from above. There is zero biblical basis for this despicable doctrine.

Hank Hanegraaff[2]

But God demonstrates His own love toward us, in that while we were yet sinners, Christ died for us. Much more then, having now been justified by His blood, we shall be saved from the wrath of God through Him.

Romans 5:8–9

A t its core, Christianity is all about Christ. What we think about Jesus Christ determines whether our Christianity is genuine or not. If we radically misunderstand who he was or why he came or what he accomplished for us, we have fallen for "a different Jesus" and a counterfeit gospel (2 Cor. 11:4; Gal. 1:6–9). In particular, it is the death of Jesus on the cross and his resurrection from the dead that constitute the central story of the Christian faith.

We have already seen that the Word-Faith movement adheres to unbiblical views of both God and man and that at least some Word-Faith teachers have presented unbiblical ideas about the person of Jesus Christ. It is therefore to be expected that the movement will also entertain unbiblical views about Christ's death and resurrection. Yet the Word-Faith movement, because it originated in a Christian context and draws its followers primarily from the ranks of Pentecostal and charismatic Christian churches, also acknowledges much biblical truth about Jesus Christ. I will attempt to reflect this mix of truth and error as accurately as possible in this chapter.

The Word-Faith Teachers Speak

The general outline of what the Word-Faith teachers say about the death and resurrection of Christ is fairly constant. We will look briefly at some key statements by Kenyon, Hagin, and Copeland and then present an overview of the areas in question.

Jesus Died Spiritually

Kenyon and the modern Word-Faith teachers all teach that Jesus died spiritually as well as physically. For Kenyon this was something of which he was convinced on theological grounds even before he could prove it biblically: "Jesus died twice on the cross. I knew this for many years, but I had no scriptural evidence of it." He eventually found such proof, he says, in Isaiah 53:9, where "the word 'death' is plural in the Hebrew."[3]

Kenyon's theological reason for this belief is that a spiritual death was absolutely essential if mankind was to be saved from its spiritual disease of sin. Kenyon explains: "Sin basically is a spiritual thing, so it must be dealt with in the spirit realm." The implication is that Jesus did not pay for our sins by his physical death on the cross. "If Jesus paid the penalty of Sin on the cross, then Sin is but a physical act. If His death paid it, then every man could die for himself."[4]

Hagin and Copeland teach the same ideas. Hagin has written, "If sin were only physical, then each one of us dying physically could atone for ourselves. But, no, *sin is spiritual*."[5]

These teachers are not quite clear or consistent with one another about what this spiritual death means. In some sense, Jesus is said to have "become sin" and to have been separated from God the Father. It is sometimes said that Jesus received Satan's nature—with the implication being that Jesus no longer possessed the divine nature (an implication rarely if ever stated explicitly). Again, as we saw in the previous chapter, the Word-Faith teachers are not altogether clear about the meaning of a person having Satan's nature. Jesus' spiritual death is also said to have entailed going to "hell" and suffering further under the dominion of Satan.

Lest we misunderstand him, Kenyon flatly denies that our sin was reckoned to Jesus. Commenting on the key text in this discussion, 2 Corinthians 5:21, Kenyon wrote, "Sin was not reckoned to Him. Sin was not set to His account. He became sin."[6] Following Kenyon, Hagin understands 2 Corinthians 5:21 to mean that Jesus experienced spiritual death and "became sin":

> Jesus tasted death—spiritual death—for every man. Sin is more than a physical act; it is a spiritual act. He became what we were, that we might become what He is. . . . Jesus became sin. His spirit was separated from God.[7]

Asked if he believed that "Christ went to hell, submitted to the lordship of Satan and took on Satan's nature, and was born again," Hagin replied, "No, I don't believe that Jesus took on Satan's nature or submitted to his lordship. However, Jesus was forsaken by God or His statement on the cross was a lie."[8]

All the Word-Faith teachers believe that Jesus' experience of spiritual death required him to be susceptible to the real possibility of failure to do God's will. None, though, makes the point more dramatically than Copeland:

> The spirit of Jesus accepting that sin, and making it to be sin, he separated from his God, and in that moment, he's a mortal man—capable of failure, capable of death. Not only that, he's fixing to be ushered into the jaws of hell. And if Satan is capable of overpowering him there, he'll win the universe,

and mankind is doomed. Don't get the idea that Jesus was incapable of failure, because if he had been, it would have been illegal.[9]

Jesus Was Born Again

Another startling aspect of the Word-Faith doctrine of Christ's work is the claim that Jesus was "born again." This is not a figurative reference to Jesus' physical resurrection from the dead. Kenyon asserts "that Jesus was born again before He was raised from the dead."[10] Ironically, at one point Hagin seems to say that Jesus' resurrection was his *first* "birth":

> When was Jesus begotten? Most people think He was begotten when He came into the world as the Babe of Bethlehem. No! Oh, no! Begotten means born. The Son of God was not born as He took on flesh. He preexisted with the Father. He just took upon Himself a body. . . . He was not begotten when He came into the world; He always preexisted with the Father.[11]

Note that here Hagin presupposes the orthodox view that Christ existed before his incarnation as the divine Son of God. As we saw in the last chapter, this is a point on which Copeland and Capps are unclear, to put it charitably. A few pages later, Hagin speaks explicitly of Jesus being "born again." Commenting on Acts 13:33, Hagin writes:

> When was it that He was begotten? When He was raised up! On that Resurrection morn! Why did He need to be begotten, or born? Because He became like we are, separated from God. Because He tasted spiritual death for every man. His spirit, His inner man, went to hell in our place. . . . Physical death would not remove our sins. He tasted death for every man—spiritual death. Jesus is the first person ever to be born again. Why did His spirit need to be born again? Because it was estranged from God.[12]

Copeland adheres to the same doctrine of Jesus' spiritual death and suffering in hell being followed by a new birth:

> Now listen: From the book of Acts, all the way through all of the Epistles, all the way through the Revelation of John, Jesus is no longer called "the only begotten Son of God"; He's called "the firstborn from the dead"; He's called in the eighth chapter of Romans "the firstborn of many brethren." Jesus was the first man to ever be born from sin to righteousness. He was the pattern of a new race of men to come. Glory to God. And you know what He did? The very first thing that this reborn man did—see, you have to realize that He died. You have to realize that He went into the pit of hell as a mortal man made sin. But He didn't stay there, thank God. He was reborn in the pit of hell.[13]

The Word-Faith Teaching about Christ: Pros and Cons

Quotations like these could easily be multiplied, not only from the writings and sermons of Hagin and Copeland but from the other Word-Faith teachers as well. Although the Word-Faith teachers do differ among themselves on some issues, there is an identifiable core of doctrinal ideas about Jesus' death and resurrection that can be discussed and compared with Scripture.

The fundamental and distinctive doctrine to be considered here is that Jesus died spiritually and suffered in hell and was then born again. All of the Word-Faith teachers accept this idea, although some take it further than Kenneth Hagin, for example, may be willing to go. The doctrine that Christ died spiritually and was born again, then, will be the focus of this chapter. This doctrine has been severely criticized by others in the past. While some of these criticisms have been helpful, it has usually been overlooked that at least some aspects of the Word-Faith doctrine are biblical. It will be helpful, as well as much fairer, to begin with these points of agreement, of which there are six.

1. Jesus did die a complete human death. The whole man Jesus died, body and soul. The material and immaterial aspects of the human nature of Christ suffered death.
2. When Jesus died physically, he went down into the underworld, the abode of the dead. This was part of his experience of death, and his work of redeeming us would not have been complete without it.
3. By his death Jesus overcame Satan.
4. In his death Jesus took on himself the curse of our sin, suffering for our sin so that we might be blessed with his righteousness.
5. Jesus suffered the experience of God-forsakenness on our behalf.
6. Jesus' resurrection was in some sense a passing from death to life, and as such it was the basis or foundation of the new birth.

With these six propositions we have no objection. It is where the Word-Faith teachers go from here that is troubling. The problematic aspects of their doctrine may be summarized in six more propositions, each corresponding to the one above:

1. Jesus died spiritually in addition to dying physically.
2. Jesus suffered in hell to complete his suffering for our sins.
3. Jesus took on Satan's nature.
4. Jesus literally became sin.
5. Jesus was literally separated from God.
6. Jesus was born again in hell and then rose from the dead.

I shall examine each of these six propositions in turn.

Biblical Truth	Controversial Faith Doctrine
Jesus died a complete human death. The whole man Jesus died, body and soul.	Jesus died spiritually as well as physically.
When Jesus died physically, he went down into the underworld, the abode of the dead.	Jesus suffered in hell to complete his suffering for our sins.
By his death Jesus overcame Satan.	Jesus took on Satan's nature.
In his death Jesus took on himself the curse of our sin, suffering for our sin so that we might be blessed with his righteousness.	Jesus literally became sin.
Jesus suffered the experience of God-forsakenness on our behalf.	Jesus was literally separated from God.
Jesus rose from death to life and as risen became the source of life in the new birth.	Jesus was born again in hell and then rose from the dead.

Did Jesus Die Spiritually?

The Word-Faith teachers' reasoning to support the idea that Jesus died spiritually is simple and seemingly sound:

a. The punishment for our sin is not merely physical death but spiritual death as well.
b. Jesus died to take our place.
c. Therefore, Jesus must have died spiritually.

In addition to this argument, the Word-Faith teachers assert that Isaiah 53:9 speaks of the future Suffering Servant as undergoing "deaths" and conclude from this plural form that Jesus must have died twice—first physically and then spiritually.

Isaiah 53:9. The Hebrew word translated *death* here in all English translations is indeed a plural form. However, we know that this does not mean that the Suffering Servant was to undergo two deaths, for at least three reasons.

First, in Hebrew usage the plural form of a noun was often used without signifying an actual plurality of the thing named. For example, the Old Testament several times uses the plural form for *life* where it is contrasted with its opposite, *death*—yet the word *death* in these texts is singular, not plural (Deut. 30:15, 19; Prov. 18:21; Jer. 8:3; 21:8). The Old Testament does this with many other words, such as *salvation* (Ps. 68:20 KJV). Most famously it uses the plural form *elohim* with a singular meaning, to refer to one "God"

(Gen. 2:4; Deut. 4:35). I have found one other passage in which it does the same thing with two related Hebrew words for *death,* one of which is the same as found in Isaiah 53:9 (Ezek. 28:8, 10).

Second, in the context of Isaiah 53 the "death" cannot be plural. Isaiah 53:9 itself says, "His grave was assigned with wicked men, yet He was with a rich man in his *death*. . . ." From the New Testament we know that Jesus "was with a rich man in his death" in the sense that his dead body was buried in the tomb of the rich man Joseph of Arimathea (Matt. 27:57–60). This "rich man" had nothing to do with Jesus' alleged "spiritual death" but only with Jesus' physical death. Therefore, "death" in Isaiah 53:9 must be singular in meaning even though it is technically plural in form.

Third, a few lines later Isaiah says that the Suffering Servant "poured out Himself to *death*" (v. 12a), using the singular form of the noun in verse 9. Here again the death must be physical, yet it is connected with the fact that "He Himself bore the sins of many" (v. 12b).

For these three reasons, we can be certain that Isaiah 53:9 does not mean that Christ died two deaths, one physical and the other spiritual. In fact, Isaiah 53 confirms the traditional view that Christ's physical death was the act by which he redeemed us.

The Word-Faith theology argument. But what of the argument used by the Word-Faith teachers that for Jesus to save us from spiritual death he had to undergo spiritual death himself? This argument backfires in that it proves too much. If Jesus had to undergo precisely what we would have without him, then for Jesus to save us he would have needed to suffer eternal punishment in the lake of fire! The Bible simply does not teach the idea that Jesus' suffering had to correspond *exactly* to what we deserve for our sins. Rather, it teaches that God accepted Jesus' death as a satisfactory substitutionary sacrifice for our sins.

The Bible is really quite emphatic that it was Jesus' physical death that constituted his suffering for us. I will mention just two texts in which this is especially clear. In 1 Corinthians 15:3–6 Paul reminds the Corinthians that the gospel says:

> that Christ *died* for our sins according to the Scriptures,
> and that He *was buried,*
> and that He *was raised* on the third day according to the Scriptures,
> and that He *appeared.* . . .

As biblical scholars have noted, the text here lists four events in chronological order: death, burial, resurrection, and appearances. This means the death that Jesus suffered for our sins took place before the burial. On the other hand, for the Word-Faith teachers the critical spiritual death of Christ was suffered both before and after the burial. Moreover, in 1 Corinthians 15:3 the burial is the historical proof of the death, just as the appearances are the historical proof of the resurrection. Clearly, the burial is proof of the physical, bodily death of Christ.

Even more striking and definite is 1 Peter 3:18–19:

> For Christ also died for sins once for all, the righteous for the unrighteous, that he might bring us to God, being put to death in the flesh but made alive in the spirit; in which he went and preached to the spirits in prison (RSV).

According to Peter, the death that Jesus suffered was "in the flesh." Peter repeats this statement a few lines later: "Since therefore Christ suffered in the flesh . . ." (4:1 RSV).[14] Again, it was this fleshly, physical death that was suffered "for sins" and to "bring us to God"; no other death is needed or contemplated.

Indeed, in the best interpretation of this passage Peter actually states the opposite of the Word-Faith doctrine. Whereas the Word-Faith teachers assert that Christ died spiritually, Peter says that Christ was "made alive in the spirit," or in other words, Christ was made alive spiritually. This does not mean that Christ was spiritually dead before! Rather, it means that when Christ died physically, in the physical realm ("in the flesh"), at that moment of physical death he began living spiritually, that is, in the spiritual realm ("in the spirit"). Peter makes this clear in the very next line by saying that in this spiritual state or realm Christ "went and preached to the spirits in prison."[15] In other words, when Christ died he went immediately as a spirit into the spirit realm and proclaimed his victory over sin and Satan to the spirits in the spirit "prison." On this interpretation, then, not only did Christ not die spiritually, but between his death and resurrection he was spiritually alive and triumphantly announcing his accomplished victory on the cross.

I realize that 1 Peter 3:18 has been interpreted in other ways and that its meaning is a matter of considerable controversy. However, one thing is very clear from both 1 Peter 3:18 and 4:1—Christ's suffering and death for our sins was "in the flesh."

Did Jesus Suffer in Hell?

According to the Word-Faith teachers, Jesus did not stop suffering when he died physically. He kept on suffering during the period between his death and resurrection, when he was in "hell." This doctrine is based on some truth. According to Acts 2:27, 31, Jesus did go down into the underworld, what the Old Testament calls *sheol* and the New Testament calls *hadēs*. Since this word is translated "hell" in the King James Version, there is some biblical basis for the idea that Jesus went down into hell between his death and resurrection. However, the confusion comes in the popular assumption that *hell* is necessarily a place of suffering or punishment. There is such a spiritual place, also known as the lake of fire (Rev. 20:10–15), but the word *hell* can also refer to the intermediate abode of the dead, including the righteous dead who are waiting without suffering for the resurrection (Pss. 16:10; 139:8; Rev. 20:13–14, all in KJV). Jesus did go down into hell in the sense of going down into the intermediate abode of the dead, but he did not go to a place of eternal punishment, nor did he suffer between his death and resurrection.

A key text on this point is Luke 23:43, in which Jesus said to the repentant thief on the cross next to him, "Truly I say to you, today you will be with Me in Paradise." The clear implication is that immediately after dying physically, Jesus went to a spiritual place or realm in which he was freed from suffering and enjoyed the presence and love of his Father. This is obviously contradictory to the doctrine that between his death and resurrection Jesus suffered spiritual death and continued separation from the Father.

Indeed, Luke 23:43 is so clearly contrary to the idea of Jesus' spiritual death and suffering in hell that Kenyon was forced to adopt a variation on the Adventist reinterpretation of the text: "You understand there is no punctuation in the Greek. Punctuation is determined by the emphasis. . . . It should read like this: 'I say unto you Today, thou shalt be with me in Paradise.'"[16] Later Kenyon explains that Jesus met the repentant thief in a spiritual Paradise during the forty days between his resurrection and ascension.[17]

Kenyon is correct in saying that there is no punctuation in the Greek manuscripts. However, the traditional punctuation is easily shown to be correct. The expression "Truly I say to you" is a stylized expression used throughout the Gospels by Jesus alone, and it always stands apart from the rest of the sentence following. It functions, that is, as an opening expression similar to "Thus says the Lord" or the medieval "Hear ye, hear ye." For this and other reasons, the word *today* should be understood as part of the statement that follows and indicates when the thief would be in Paradise with Jesus.[18]

Did Jesus Take on Satan's Nature?

We saw earlier in this chapter that Kenneth Hagin has disavowed explicitly teaching that Jesus took on Satan's nature when he died spiritually. We ought, of course, to take Hagin at his word that he finds such a way of expressing his teaching somehow unacceptable. On the other hand, we should not assume too quickly that Hagin disagrees with the *idea* expressed by saying that Jesus took on Satan's nature.

According to Hagin, Jesus was "separated from God," suffered "spiritual death," and then was "born again."[19] Furthermore, he states, "When one is born again, he takes upon himself the nature of God—which is Life and peace. The nature of the devil is hatred and lies. . . . He became what we were, that we might become what He is."[20] If in Hagin's view "what we were" was humanity burdened with "the nature of the devil," then it would seem that for Jesus to become "what we were," he would have to take on Satan's nature.

Moreover, according to Hagin to be born again means to "take upon himself the nature of God," and Jesus was born again. From these two premises it would seem to follow that Jesus went from a situation in which he did not have the nature of God—and therefore, on Hagin's presuppositions, by default had the nature of Satan—to a situation in which he regained the nature of God.

Or again, according to Hagin "spiritual death" means receiving the nature of Satan: "Spiritual death means something more than separation from God. **Spiritual death also means having Satan's nature**."[21] This is about as explicit as he could get. Can we not infer that if Jesus suffered spiritual death, he also had Satan's nature? Nor is this an isolated statement: "When Adam and Eve listened to the devil, he became their spiritual father, and they had the devil's nature in their spirits. This is spiritual death. . . . Man is spiritually a child of the devil, and he partakes of his father's nature."[22] In this same context Hagin goes on to write the following:

> The new Man, Jesus Christ, had no death in Him. He was not born as we are born. He didn't have the spiritual nature of death—the devil—in Him. Yet Hebrews 2:9 says He tasted death for every man. He took upon Himself our sin nature. . . . He took upon Himself our sin nature, the nature of spiritual death, that we might have eternal life.[23]

Here Hagin says clearly that Jesus came to the cross without the nature of the devil, also called spiritual death or sin nature, but then took upon himself that sin nature or spiritual death. Since Hagin has already equated our sin nature and our spiritual death with the nature of the devil, we can only conclude that in Hagin's view Jesus did take on himself the nature of Satan.

It is difficult to know, then, why Hagin denies teaching that Jesus took on Satan's nature, except for the reason that this idea is just too patently unbiblical and offensive to Christians. In any case, the substance of Hagin's doctrine is the same as that of other Word-Faith teachers.

One searches the writings of the Word-Faith teachers in vain for any biblical references supporting the claim that Jesus took on Satan's nature.

The reason for this is simple: There are no such references. The Word-Faith teachers' argument for this idea is strictly indirect: Human beings have Satan's nature (John 8:44); Jesus had to become what we are in order to redeem us; therefore, Jesus had to take on Satan's nature. And since we have already seen that John 8:44 does not mean that human beings have Satan's nature, this line of reasoning fails.

The devastating consequences of teaching that Jesus took on Satan's nature, even for a second (let alone a couple of days), can hardly be exaggerated. If Jesus took on Satan's nature, he must for that period of time ceased to have God's nature. The implication is obvious: Jesus ceased being God while he was "spiritually dead." But if Jesus ever stopped being God, even for a second, then he never really was God (since God cannot stop being God, after all). Instead, Jesus was simply a man in whom God dwelled, a man through whom God spoke and acted, a man in whom God was "manifest"—but not really God himself. While most of the Word-Faith teachers (and all of the prominent ones) shy away from drawing this conclusion explicitly, there is some reason for thinking that this is where their doctrine of Christ is really headed.

Did Jesus Literally Become Sin?

As I just mentioned, Word-Faith teachers cannot produce one text of Scripture even hinting that Jesus took on Satan's nature. They might with some satisfaction claim to be on more solid ground in their view that Jesus became sin. After all, they might argue, Paul said so in 2 Corinthians 5:21, "He made Him who knew no sin to be sin on our behalf, so that we might become the righteousness of God in Him." Doesn't this say exactly what the Word-Faith teachers say?

No, not exactly. Paul uses the same words, "became sin," but he means something different by them than the Word-Faith teachers mean. They mean that Jesus took on a sinful nature, the nature of Satan, so that somehow Jesus himself, without committing any sin (as we may gratefully acknowledge the Word-Faith teachers to recognize), comes to have the character of sin. Their reasoning is that if our becoming "the righteousness of God" means that we are truly made righteous, then Christ's becoming "sin" must mean that he is truly made sinful—again, without ever committing a sin himself.

As sound as this reasoning may seem at first, it does not correctly understand Paul's meaning. There are various ways of looking at the error, but one way is to diagram the sentence. This is how the Word-Faith teachers' interpretation implies the sentence is to be diagrammed:

2 Corinthians 5:21, Word-Faith Theology Reading

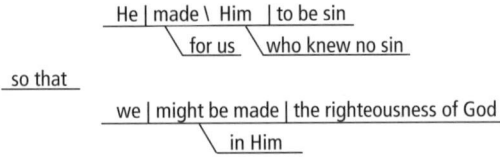

```
        He | made \ Him  | to be sin
                    \ for us  \ who knew no sin
  so that
            we | might be made | the righteousness of God
                           \ in Him
```

I say that this is how their interpretation *implies* that the sentence should be diagrammed, because, as is commonly recognized and even the Word-Faith teachers themselves would probably agree, it should really be diagrammed as follows:

2 Corinthians 5:21, Correct Reading

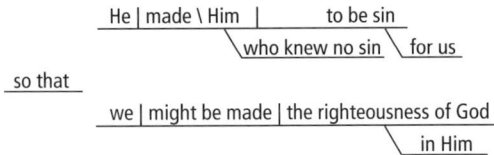

```
        He | made \ Him  |          to be sin
                      \ who knew no sin \ for us
  so that
            we | might be made | the righteousness of God
                           \ in Him
```

What's the difference between these two ways of reading the sentence? In the Word-Faith interpretation, the contrasting nouns *sin* and *righteousness of God* are unqualified, so that Jesus was simply and actually made "sin" and we were simply and actually made "God's righteousness." However, in the correct reading the noun *sin* is qualified by the prepositional phrase *for us,* and the noun phrase *righteousness of God* is qualified by the prepositional phrase *in Him.* And this makes all the difference in the world. On this reading, Paul is saying not that Christ became *sin* but that he became *sin-for-us.* Likewise, he is not saying that we become *God's-righteousness* but rather *God's-righteousness-in-Him.*

For us to become "God's righteousness in Christ" means that, by virtue of our faith relationship with Jesus Christ, God considers us to be right with him. It does not mean that we become righteous in our character or nature, at least not immediately. God's establishing us as right with him through Christ does create the context in which we can develop righteous character, but that does not happen automatically—it takes time.

Christ's having been made "sin for us" means that, in his death on the cross, he suffered for our sin in our place. It means that God inflicted suffering and death on Jesus, his own Son, as if Jesus were our sin. But Jesus, of course, was not sin, nor did he become sinful in character or nature.

Recall Kenyon's explicit denial that God reckoned our sin to Jesus. But this is exactly what 2 Corinthians 5:21 means in context. Paul is not talking about an "exchanged life" (as many evangelicals, even outside the

Word-Faith movement, suppose) but about an *exchanged status*. Paul affirms that God has "reconciled us to Himself through Christ" and that Paul's ministry is one of proclaiming "that God was in Christ reconciling the world to Himself, not counting their trespasses against them" (vv. 18–19). Reconciliation according to Paul refers to God's graciously bringing us out of the position of his enemies deserving of his wrath and into a new relationship in which we are at peace with him (Rom. 5:1–11). The centerpiece of this reconciliation is God's graciously "not counting their trespasses against them" (2 Cor. 5:19). How is it that God does not count our trespasses against us? Paul explains this in verse 21: Christ took our place. In effect, God counted our trespasses against Christ so that he could count Christ's righteousness in our favor. Paul's entreaty to all who would listen was to "be reconciled to God" through faith in Christ's reconciliatory death on the cross.

A correct reading of the text, then, does not conclude that Jesus had to become truly "sin" in order for us to become truly "righteousness." That is not what Paul said, nor does it fit with what the Bible says elsewhere about Christ.

For instance, Hebrews 7:26 states that Jesus, as our high priest in heaven, is "holy, innocent, undefiled, separated from sinners and exalted above the heavens." While this is a description of Christ now, by describing him as "unstained," it implies that he has *never* been anything but pure holiness, pure righteousness. That is why he "does not need daily, like those high priests, to offer up sacrifices, first for His own sins, and then for the sins of the people, because this He did [offered sacrifice for the sins of the people] once for all when He offered up Himself" (Heb. 7:27).

Was Jesus Separated from God?

It is commonly asserted, and not just by advocates of the Word-Faith teaching, that Jesus was literally separated from God when he took on himself the burden of our sins. In the Word-Faith teaching this idea is pressed so literally as to imply that Jesus ceased to be divine himself, at least in some sense, while he was "spiritually dead," possessing "the nature of Satan," and "literally made sin." The claim that Jesus was separated from God is based solely on Jesus' cry on the cross, "My God, My God, why have You forsaken Me?" (Matt. 27:46; Mark 15:34).

Although Jesus' words here may seem to imply that he really was forsaken or abandoned by God, that is in fact not the case. Jesus is actually quoting the first line of Psalm 22. As is commonly recognized, Psalm 22 is one of the several psalms of David that were prophetic of the future Messiah, and it contains the most graphic picture of his suffering on the cross:

> My God, my God, why have you forsaken me? . . .
> All who see me mock me;
>   they hurl insults, shaking their heads:
> "He trusts in the LORD;
>   let the LORD rescue him.
> Let him deliver him,
>   since he delights in him." . . .
> I am poured out like water,
>   and all my bones are out of joint.
> My heart has turned to wax;
>   it has melted away within me.
> My strength is dried up like a potsherd,
>   and my tongue sticks to the roof of my mouth. . . .
> Dogs have surrounded me;
>   a band of evil men has encircled me,
>   they have pierced my hands and my feet.
> I can count all my bones;
>   people stare and gloat over me.
> They divide my garments among them
>   and cast lots for my clothing.
>
> Psalm 22:1, 7–8, 14–18 NIV

Jesus quoted the first line of the psalm, not in order to apply that line alone to himself out of context but because he was applying the entire psalm in its prophetic significance to himself. Just as we might quote the first line of a song and be thinking really of the whole song, Jesus was quoting the first line of Psalm 22 because the whole psalm related to his situation.

Of course, if Jesus is applying the entire psalm in some prophetic sense to himself, this includes the first line as well. But in the context of Psalm 22 as a whole, the psalmist is *not* saying that God had *really* abandoned or forsaken him. Rather, David (and Jesus after him) is giving vent to the feeling that God *seemed* to have forsaken him, although David (and, clearly enough, Jesus also) was confident that God had not really abandoned him at all:

> My God, my God, why have you forsaken me?
>   Why are you so far from saving me,
>   so far from the words of my groaning?
> O my God, I cry out by day, but you do not answer,
>   by night, and am not silent. . . .
> But you, O LORD, be not far off;
>   O my Strength, come quickly to help me. . . .
> For he has not despised or disdained

> the suffering of the afflicted one;
> he has not hidden his face from him
> but has listened to his cry for help.
>
> Psalm 22:1–2, 19, 24 NIV

So Jesus was not implying that God had actually forsaken him. He was, rather, expressing the profound feeling of God-forsakenness, about which the psalmist had written. We have all felt abandoned by God at some time in our life, but if we belong to him, we trust that he has not really abandoned us. Jesus felt especially abandoned because it was the first and only time he had ever experienced anything like abandonment. But Jesus knew that his Father had not and never would abandon him. He knew that the Father loved him just as much at that moment as he ever had. We can be sure that he knew that because he had chosen to lay down his life—no one had forced him to die (John 10:17–18).

On the cross Jesus suffered not only physically but also emotionally and personally as he took on himself the burden of our sins. He felt the wrath of God against our sin falling on him. But he was not literally separated from God in the process. God cannot be separated from God. Jesus was not merely God manifest in the flesh; he was God himself, the eternal person of the Son come in the flesh for the express purpose of dying for our sins. As God the Son, he could not be literally separated from God the Father, though by virtue of his human nature he could *feel* separated from God.

One last point should be made here. Some Word-Faith teachers focus on Jesus' descent into hell as the time when he was separated from God. As we have seen, the Bible does teach that Jesus descended into Sheol or Hades, the intermediate abode of the dead. But in fact no one can be literally separated from God just by being in Sheol (Ps. 139:7–8). Moreover, Jesus had supreme confidence that God would not abandon him in Sheol either. This confidence was based on Christ's own prophetic word through David. Peter explained this on Pentecost:

> But God raised him from the dead, freeing him from the agony of death, because it was impossible for death to keep its hold on him. David said about him:
>> "I saw the Lord *always* before me.
>> Because he is at my right hand,
>> I will not be shaken.
>> Therefore my heart is glad and my tongue rejoices;
>>> my body also will live in hope,
>> because you *will not abandon me* to the grave [literally, 'to Hades'],
>>> nor will you let your Holy One see decay. . . ."
>
> Acts 2:24–27, quoting Psalm 16:8–10 NIV; emphasis added

Here David, speaking prophetically for Christ, expresses the confidence that God would not abandon Christ. It is therefore simply false to say that God abandoned Jesus, either on the cross or in "hell," because, as the psalm puts it, the Lord was *always* with Jesus.

Was Jesus Born Again?

The last aspect of the Word-Faith teaching on Jesus' death and resurrection we will consider is its claim that Jesus was born again in hell and then was raised from the dead. The idea that Jesus was born again is connected in the Word-Faith teaching to the idea that he had become sin— and so *needed* to be born again. Having seen that Jesus did not die spiritually, we must conclude that he did not need to be born again. Still, the Word-Faith teachers do cite certain proof texts that they think establish this idea biblically, and we shall consider them.

The first line of reasoning by which the Word-Faith teachers try to justify the born-again Jesus doctrine biblically begins with the statement in Psalm 2:7, "You are My Son, today I have begotten You." This statement, spoken by God in the context of the psalm to his anointed king of Israel, is applied to Jesus in the New Testament in the context of his resurrection from the dead (Acts 13:33; Heb. 1:5). From this fact the Word-Faith teachers deduce that Jesus was literally "begotten" as God's Son at his resurrection; and, since he had been God's Son before, they conclude that Jesus was begotten *again* as God's Son at his resurrection.

This line of reasoning, if pursued with other biblical texts consistently, proves to be self-defeating. At least some of the Word-Faith teachers (including Hagin) agree that Jesus was the Son of God even before his birth in Bethlehem. But in Luke 1:35 an angel tells Mary, "The Holy Spirit will come upon you, and the power of the Most High will overshadow you, and for that reason the holy child shall be called the Son of God." Does this mean that Jesus only became the Son of God through his virgin birth? The Word-Faith teachers who believe (as I do) that Jesus was already the Son of God before his birth would have to say no; but if they read Luke 1:35 the way they read Hebrews 1:5 and Acts 13:33, they would have to say yes.

A better way of understanding these texts is to see that they speak not of Jesus literally becoming the Son of God but of the critical moments in which his being the Son of God was revealed to the world. On this reading Luke 1:35 is saying that Jesus became incarnate in the virgin birth as the son of Mary in order to become known as the Son of God. Likewise, in the resurrection Jesus was vindicated to the world as the Son of God. This is exactly the meaning of Romans 1:4, which says that the one who already was God's Son (v. 3) "through the Spirit of holiness was declared with power to be the Son of God by his resurrection from the dead" (NIV). It is also clearly the meaning that fits the context of Psalm 2:7, which has to do with the coronation of the Davidic king as God's anointed "son" sitting on his throne in Jerusalem.

The same phenomenon is at work in a text such as Acts 2:36, in which Peter says concerning the resurrection of Jesus, "Therefore let all the house of Israel know for certain that God has *made* Him both Lord and Christ—this Jesus whom you crucified." On the Word-Faith reading of Acts 13:33 and Hebrews 1:5, we would have to conclude that Jesus became the Lord and Christ at his resurrection. Or did he become Lord and Christ again? In Luke 2:11 the angel announced the birth of Jesus to the shepherds by saying, "Today in the city of David there has been born for you a Savior, who *is* Christ the Lord" (emphasis added). Did Jesus stop being Lord and Christ and then begin again when he was raised from the dead? No; he was always Christ the Lord but was officially recognized or announced as such by God when he raised Jesus from the dead.

Once again, we see that the Word-Faith teaching implies, even if some of its advocates shy away from saying so, that Jesus ceased being the Lord while he was dead and then regained his divinity when he rose from the dead.

The other line of reasoning used to support the born-again Jesus teaching appeals to those texts that call Jesus the "firstborn from [among] the dead" (Col. 1:18; Rev. 1:5). The Word-Faith teachers think these texts imply that Jesus, as Copeland puts it, "is no longer called 'the only-begotten Son of God,'" and that Jesus was "the first man to ever be born from sin to righteousness," or from spiritual death to spiritual, eternal life.

Copeland is wrong in his assertion that after the resurrection Jesus "is no longer called 'the only-begotten Son of God'" (see 1 John 4:9). More importantly, he is mistaken in thinking that the word *firstborn* implies that Jesus was literally born. This is no more true than it would be to say that because Jesus is called the *firstfruits* of the resurrection (1 Cor. 15:20, 23) that he literally was or became fruit! What all of these texts are saying is that Jesus is the first person raised from the dead to unending physical life (cf. Rom. 6:9). Other persons were raised from the dead (most notably by Jesus himself; see Matt. 9:18–25; Luke 7:11–15; John 11; see also 1 Kings 17:17–24; 2 Kings 4:18–37), but Jesus is the first person raised from the dead who will never die again. As such he has become, as Paul puts it in Colossians 1:18, the "beginning" (Greek, *archē*), the fountain or source of resurrection life to all who believe in him.

To say that Jesus was the first person raised to immortal life is a far cry from saying that he was the first person to be born again. One searches the Bible in vain for any statement to the effect that Jesus was born again. We do find that *we* are born again through Christ's resurrection: "According to His great mercy [He] has caused us to be born again to a living hope through the resurrection of Jesus Christ from the dead" (1 Peter 1:3). But this does not mean that Jesus himself was born again. We need to be born again because we are spiritually dead in our own trespasses and sins (Eph. 2:1); Jesus has never had any need to be born again. In fact, it is precisely because Jesus was without sin and died for the sins of others that his resurrection could be the fountain of resurrection life for others. The teaching that Jesus was born again, therefore, is contrary to the very heart of the gospel of salvation through the death and resurrection of Christ.

Orthodox Precedent?

In order to defend the Word-Faith doctrine of Jesus dying spiritually and being born again, both James Spencer and William DeArteaga claim that this doctrine has significant precedent in orthodox Christian theology. Specifically, both argue that the Word-Faith doctrine is a version of the "ransom" theory of the atonement, a venerable position held by a majority of the early church fathers.[24] The ransom theory held that Jesus' death was a ransom paid *to the devil* to free us from his dominion.

Of the major theories of the atonement in church history, the Word-Faith view is closest to the ransom theory. But it is a *non sequitur* to conclude on that basis that the Word-Faith view is orthodox. It all depends on what is done with the ransom theory. The Jehovah's Witnesses, for example, hold to a thoroughly heretical version of the ransom theory. In their view Jesus' death had to be a "corresponding ransom," requiring that he be a mere perfect man, not God incarnate.[25]

In the case of the Word-Faith movement, its doctrine that Jesus died spiritually and was given into the hands of Satan in order to secure redemption is not heretical *merely* because it uses a form of the ransom theory. Again, it is legitimate for Spencer and DeArteaga to criticize Hanegraaff for the overgeneralization that the ransom theory itself is heretical.[26] But the Word-Faith doctrine may still be heretical due to the specific objectionable elements in its formulation, such as its claim that Jesus became sin and was born again in hell. We need to see the Word-Faith position in its larger theological context. Although the Word-Faith teachers acknowledge that Jesus was God incarnate, they typically hold that in his "spiritual death" Jesus somehow ceased to have the divine nature and took on Satan's nature. This is not, as we might say, your father's ransom theory! The whole point of the patristic ransom theory was that Jesus' death overcame Satan because Jesus was actually not a mere man but was God incarnate, *even in death*.

DeArteaga takes the historical precedent argument one intriguing step further when he claims that Kenyon's doctrine that Jesus died spiritually has precedent in the theology of the sixteenth-century Protestant Reformer, John Calvin. He finds Calvin teaching this idea in his classic work, the *Institutes of the Christian Religion:*

> If Christ had died only a bodily death, it would have been ineffectual. No— it was expedient at the same time for him to undergo the severity of God's vengeance, to appease his wrath and satisfy his just judgment. For this reason, he must also grapple hand to hand with the armies of hell and the dread of everlasting death. . . . Therefore, by his wrestling hand to hand with the devil's power, with the dread of death, with the pains of hell, he was victorious and triumphed over them, that in death we may not now fear those things which our Prince has swallowed up.[27]

DeArteaga admits that Calvin's teaching was not identical to Kenyon's. He notes that Calvin held that Jesus' "descent into hell" was experienced on the cross, not between the cross and the resurrection. Yet DeArteaga thinks the similarities are sufficient to justify the conclusion, "To call Kenyon's theory heretical and dangerous is to say the same of Calvin's theory."[28]

In fact, the dissimilarities run even deeper than DeArteaga acknowledges. Calvin does not describe Jesus as undergoing a "second" or "spiritual" death. When he says, "If Christ had died only a bodily death, it would have been ineffectual," his point is that Jesus' death had to be a *complete* human death, one of both body and soul. For "surely, unless his soul shared in the punishment, he would have been the Redeemer of bodies alone."[29] Note that Calvin was a dichotomist, not a trichotomist; Jesus died a complete death by dying body and soul. This is a point of no small importance, because in Calvin's view Jesus did not die "spiritually" at all. What Jesus did was to experience the mental and emotional pain of bearing the sins of the world on the cross. He "paid a greater and more excellent price in suffering in his soul the terrible torments of a condemned and forsaken man."[30]

Nor does Calvin allow for the idea that Jesus took on Satan's nature. Rather, Calvin affirms that Jesus "bore *our* nature" and did so in order to suffer and die in our place.[31] Because Jesus was the "uncorrupted" Son of God, his suffering did not "in the least detract from his power." His self-imposed weakness was "pure and free of all vice and stain."[32]

As we noted above, Calvin held that Jesus experienced "in his soul the terrible torments of a condemned and forsaken man." Yet Calvin, in contrast to the Word-Faith teachers (and many others today), makes it clear that Jesus was never truly abandoned by God. On the cross Jesus "knew that he stood accused before God's judgment seat for our sake" and as a result experienced pain and fear in our place. Yet this "feeling of pain and fear was not contrary to faith. . . . For feeling himself, as it were, forsaken by God, he did not waver in the least from trust in his goodness."[33] In other words, Calvin affirms that Jesus knew that although he felt abandoned by God, the Father continued without interruption to love him.

> Yet we do not suggest that God was ever inimical or angry toward him. How could he be angry toward his beloved Son, "in whom his heart reposed" [cf. Matt. 3:17]? How could Christ by his intercession appease the Father toward others, if he were himself hateful to God?[34]

Clearly, the overall context and meaning of Calvin's teaching about Christ's sufferings of "hell" are substantially different from the Word-Faith doctrine. Calvin does not teach a spiritual death and rebirth; he does not teach a change in Christ's nature; he does not teach a ransom theory of the atonement, orthodox or otherwise. There is no basis for DeArteaga's claim that to denounce the Word-Faith doctrine as heresy implicates Calvin in heresy as well.

There is an interesting irony here, with which I close this chapter. DeArteaga rightly criticizes McConnell, Hunt, and Hanegraaff for basing their judgments of the Word-Faith movement on slender, selective parallels between the Word-Faith teachings and those of the metaphysical cults. Yet he commits a similar error in reverse: He appeals to slender, selective parallels between Kenyon's teachings and those of the church fathers and of Calvin in order to vindicate Kenyon. Both sides appear to be guilty of the same fallacious methodology.

13

Just Like Jesus?

The Spirit of God spoke to me and He said, "Son, realize this"—now follow me in this; don't let your traditions trip you up. He said, "Think this way: A twice-born man whipped Satan in his own domain." . . . He said, "A born-again man defeated Satan, the firstborn of many brethren defeated him." He said, "You are the very image and the very copy of that one." I said, "Goodness gracious, sakes' alive," and it just began—I began to see what had gone on in there [hell]. And I said, "Well now you don't mean, you couldn't dare mean that I could have done the same thing?" He said, "Oh, yeah, if you'd known that, had the knowledge of the Word of God that He did you could have done the same thing. 'Cause you're a reborn man too."

Kenneth Copeland[1]

That utterance is glaringly blasphemous. It is astonishing to me that anyone with the barest knowledge of biblical truth could accept it as true revelation.

John MacArthur[2]

For it was the Father's good pleasure for all the fullness to dwell in Him [Christ], and through Him to reconcile all things to Himself, having made peace through the blood of His cross.

Colossians 1:19–20

179

We have seen that the Word-Faith teachers hold that human beings were made in God's class, that Adam was the god of this world, and that human beings are or were created to be little gods. But Adam forfeited his (and our) godhood over the earth by submitting to the lordship of Satan, taking on Satan's nature, and crowning Satan the god of this world. For this reason, Jesus Christ came into this world to take on Satan's nature in death in order that we might be freed from Satan's rule.

As might be expected, then, the Word-Faith teaching also holds that the goal of the redemptive work of Jesus Christ is to restore us to the realization of our godhood. According to Word-Faith theology, this restored godhood is "in Christ"—that is, we are gods because we are Christians, members of the body of Christ. In this context the Word-Faith teachers assert that we are incarnations just as was Jesus and that we are meant to be able to do and say the same kind of things Jesus did when he was on earth. It is this doctrine that will be examined in this chapter.

The Word-Faith Teaching

Kenneth Hagin

One of Kenneth Hagin's most controversial statements, which he plagiarized from E. W. Kenyon, is the following: "Every man who has been born again is an incarnation and Christianity is a miracle. The believer is as much an incarnation as was Jesus of Nazareth."[3]

For Hagin, this claim must be understood in the context of his view of the church as the body of Christ. Commenting on 1 Corinthians 12:12, 1 Corinthians 6:14–15, and 1 Corinthians 6:17, he has this to say:

> If the Church ever gets the revelation that we are the Body of Christ, we'll rise up and do the works of Christ! Until now, we've been doing them only limitedly. . . . We are Christ. He's calling the body, which is the Church, Christ. . . . The believer is called "Christ," and the unbeliever, "Belial." . . . We are one with Christ. We are Christ.[4]

Jesus is the Head. We are the Body. The Head and the Body are one. A person's head doesn't go by one name, and his body by another. People wouldn't call a man's head, James, and his body, Henry. Christ is the Head—we are the Body—and the Body of Christ is Christ. He that is joined to the Lord is one Spirit. We are one with Him.[5]

In at least one place Hagin does try to qualify this teaching that we are Christ:

In fact, in the Epistles, the Church is called Christ! The Church has not yet realized that we are Christ. No, we're not divine as He is, but we're joint-heirs with Him—we're His body sent forth to work in the earth on His behalf. . . . The believer is called Christ! We are identified with Him! The Church is called *believers*. The Church is called *righteousness*. The Church is called *light*. The Church is called *Christ!* That's who we are! We are His representatives on earth. Christ is the Head; we are the body. We are one with Christ. We're not gods, but we've been given the right to use Jesus' Name and to act on His behalf.[6]

It is striking in this passage that Hagin explicitly denies that we are gods and that we are "divine" like Christ. Yet, as we have seen, he does teach that human beings were created in God's class, that Adam was the god of this world, that Christians are just as much incarnations of God as was Jesus, and that the church is Christ. There is evidently a tension here in Hagin's teaching.

A recurring theme in Hagin's writings is that because we are the body of Christ on earth, Christ is powerless to do anything on the earth except through us.

In fact, Christ can't do His work on the earth without us! Someone will argue, "Well, He can get along without me, but I need Him." No, He can't get along without you any more than you can get along without Him. . . . What if your body said, "I can get along without the head. I don't need my head." No, your body can't get along without your head. And what if your head said, "Well, I can get along without my body. I don't need the rest of it; I can get along without hands and feet." No, you can't. Likewise, Christ can't get along without us, because the work of Christ and God is carried out through the Body of Christ.[7]

Just in case someone thinks Hagin means merely that Christ *chooses* not to work on earth except through the church, Hagin tells a story about Jesus appearing to him in a vision and refusing to do anything about a demon that was interfering with their meeting. Finally, Hagin commanded the demon to leave.

possibly a dream? ↵

Jesus looked at me and said, "If you hadn't done something about that, I couldn't have." That came as a real shock to me—it astounded me. I replied, "Lord, I know I didn't hear you right! You said You *wouldn't*, didn't you?" He replied, "No, if you hadn't done something about that, I *couldn't* have." I went through this four times with Him. He was emphatic about it, saying, "No, I didn't say I *would* not, I said I *could* not."[8]

Hagin tells us that he refused to accept this teaching from Jesus without New Testament proof texts, which Jesus gladly supplied. One of these was Matthew 28:18, about which Jesus supposedly said the following: "'But I immediately delegated my authority on earth to the Church, and I can work only through the Church, for I am the Head of the Church.' (Your head cannot exercise any authority anywhere except through your body.)"[9]

On the basis of this revelation, Hagin consistently maintains that Jesus can do nothing on earth except through us. ". . . The Head is totally dependent on the Body for carrying out His plans."[10] "Actually, the only way He could have authority on the earth—He's not here—is through His body."[11]

Hagin, then, teaches that we are Christ, in the sense that we are Christ's body on earth, through whom he works exclusively to do the same kinds of works that he did when he walked the earth personally (for Hagin, most notably, this means healing people). Furthermore, each one of us is just as much an incarnation of God as was Jesus, because we are in fact extensions of Christ, being his body. As Hagin sees it, Jesus is unique in his divine person, but not at all unique in what he was able to do on the earth.

> When people say, "Well, yes—but Jesus was the Son of God," that puts Him *in ministry* in a class by Himself. That would mean that *nobody else could minister that way*—or even come close to it—if Jesus in ministry is in a class by Himself.
>
> Now, *as a person,* because He is the Son of God, He *is* in a class by Himself. But *in ministry,* He is *not* in a class by Himself. . . .
>
> Why has this not been properly understood? We have not thoroughly studied the Word on this subject because we have been religiously brainwashed.[12]

Kenneth Copeland

Like Hagin, Copeland teaches that the true meaning of redemption is the restoration of human nature to godhood. Jesus Christ's status as the Son of God is not unique in Copeland's view, since the purpose of God incarnating himself in Jesus was to produce many divine sons. For example, Kenneth Copeland asserts that "Jesus is no longer the only begotten Son of God."[13] He is even clearer in the following recorded statement:

Peter said it just as plain, he said we are "partakers of the divine nature." That nature is life eternal in absolute perfection. And that was imparted, injected into your spirit man, and you have that imparted into you by God, just as same as you imparted into your child the nature of humanity. That child wasn't born a whale—born a human. Isn't that true? Well now, you don't *have* a human, do you? No, you *are* one. You don't *have* a God in you—you *are* one.[14]

Copeland has made even more astonishing statements along these lines, including the following comment that has provoked many to cry blasphemy: "And I say this with all respect, so that it don't upset you too bad, but I say it anyway: When I read in the Bible where He says, 'I AM,' I just smile and say, 'Yes, I AM too.'"[15]

At times, Copeland explains the significance of this teaching in a way that seems practical:

This is the key to the mystery: The Father was in Jesus and Jesus was in the Father—*they were one.* Jesus' will conformed completely to the will of God. They walked together and worked together in total harmony. This is how believers are to live with God. . . . Jesus goes on in John 17:23 and prays, "Father, show them that You love them as much as You love Me." God loves you *as much* as He loves Jesus! He sees you as equal with Jesus—there is no difference in His eyes.[16]

But there is no denying the fact that sometimes his affirmations are scandalously heretical:

The Spirit of God spoke to me and He said, "Son, realize this"—now follow me in this; don't let your traditions trip you up. He said, "Think this way: A twice-born man whipped Satan in his own domain." And I threw my Bible like that [laughs]; I said, "What?" He said, "A born-again man defeated Satan, the firstborn of many brethren defeated him." He said, "You are the very image and the very copy of that one." I said, "Goodness gracious, sakes' alive," and it just began—I began to see what had gone on in there [hell]. And I said, "Well now you don't mean, you couldn't dare mean that I could have done the same thing?" He said, "Oh, yeah, if you'd known that, had the knowledge of the Word of God that He did you could have done the same thing. 'Cause you're a reborn man too."[17]

Paul Crouch

In 1986 Copeland had the following exchange with Paul Crouch, the president of Trinity Broadcasting Network, which airs Copeland's and many other Word-Faith teachers' programs:

Crouch: He [God] doesn't even draw a distinction between Himself and [us]—
Copeland: Never, never. You can never do that in a covenant relationship.
Crouch: Do you know what else there's settled then tonight? This hue and
cry and controversy that has been spawned by the devil to try and bring dis-
sension within the body of Christ, that we are gods. I *am* a little god.
Copeland: Yes, yes.
Crouch: I have His name.
Copeland: The reason we are—
Crouch: I'm one with Him. I'm in covenant relation—I *am* a little god. Crit-
ics, be gone!
Copeland: You are anything that He is!
Couch: Yes.[18]

Four years later Crouch went even further, if that is possible:

That new creation that comes into new birth is created in His image. That's
what died in the Garden when Adam and Eve sinned, isn't it, that God-created
image. And when that's recreated at the new birth, it, too, is out of time,
because it is joined, then, with Jesus Christ. Is that correct? And so in that
sense—I saw this many years ago—whatever that union is that unites Father,
Son, and Holy Spirit, He says, "Father, I want them to be one with Me even
as You and I are one in Us." So apparently what He does, He opens up that
union of the very Godhead and brings us into it![19]

Sorting Out the Issues

As with the "little gods" question, there seems to be much confusion as
to what the real issues are regarding Christians or the church being incarnations of God.

Four Biblical Truths

Certain biblical truths in this discussion must be affirmed. I want to make
it as clear as possible that I fully agree with these truths and that the real
issues are something else again. There are four of these biblical truths that
I wish to affirm here.

1. Christians are indwelled by the Holy Spirit, and thus by God.
2. Christians are in some senses like Christ: They are called "sons of
   God," and like Christ they will eventually be sinless, immortal, and
   glorified.
3. Christians are "born again" and receive a new nature that is becoming Christlike in character.

4. Christians are members of the church, which is called in Scripture "the body of Christ."

All of these biblical teachings are taken for granted here. The question again is not whether the Bible *says* these things but what they *mean*.

Four Real Issues

Having affirmed several biblical truths that the Word-Faith teachers insist they are trying to uphold, we are ready to focus on the real issues. Once again, there are four of these.

1. Are Christians incarnations or sons of God just as Jesus was?
2. Are Christians individually or corporately Jesus Christ on earth?
3. Are Christians brought into the unity of the Godhead?
4. Are Christians capable of doing any and all of the works Jesus did?

Clearly, the Word-Faith teachers answer all four of these questions in the affirmative. What we need to know, then, is whether any of these teachings is biblical.

Biblical Truth	Controversial Faith Doctrine
Christians are indwelled by the Holy Spirit, and thus by God.	Christians are incarnations or sons of God in the same sense that Jesus was.
Christians are in some senses like Christ: they are called "sons of God"; like Christ they will eventually be sinless, immortal, and glorified.	Christians are individually or corporately Jesus Christ on earth.
Christians are "born again" and receive a new nature that is becoming Christlike in character.	Christians are brought into the unity of the Godhead.
Christians are members of the church, which is called in Scripture "the body of Christ."	Christians are capable of doing any or even all of the same works that Jesus did on earth.

What Does the Bible Say?

The Word-Faith teachers offer four biblical lines of justification to support their doctrine of the nature of the believer and of the church:

1. Christians as "sons of God" (on the theory that sons of God may be called gods).

2. The close relationship between Christ and the Christian, or Christ and the church (e.g., Christians as "like Christ," the church as the "body of Christ").
3. The indwelling of God in the believer.
4. The statement in 2 Peter 1:4 that Christians are "partakers of the divine nature."

We will consider each of these issues in turn.

Sons of God: Like Begets Like?

Human beings are never called "gods" in an affirmative sense in Scripture. However, believers in Christ are called "sons" or "children" of God (Hosea 1:10; Matt. 5:9, 45; Luke 6:35; John 1:12; 11:52; Rom. 8:14–23; 9:8, 26; 2 Cor. 6:18; Gal. 3:26; 4:5–7; 1 John 3:1–2, 10; 5:2; Rev. 21:7). On the assumption that children are of the same nature as their parents, some have concluded that since believers are children of God, they must also be gods—or, at least, "sons" of God in the same sense that Jesus is God's "son." This line of reasoning might seem to be confirmed by those passages in John's writings that speak of believers as being "born" or "begotten" of God (John 1:13; 3:5–6; 1 John 2:29; 3:9; 4:7; 5:1, 4, 18). If Christians are begotten by God, doesn't that prove that they have received God's nature and are therefore gods?

As convincing as this argument may seem, it actually goes beyond the Bible's teaching on Christians as the "sons of God." The above Scriptures do not mean that the "sonship" of believers is a reproduction of God's essence in people, for the following reasons.

First, in one sense all human beings are God's "offspring" (Acts 17:28), so that even Adam could be called God's "son" (Luke 3:38). But, as was pointed out when discussing the image of God, human beings were not literally birthed by God and so are not his literal offspring. It is therefore jumping to conclusions to decide that the word *son* signifies that human beings possess the same nature as God.

Second, Paul speaks of our sonship as an "adoption" (Rom. 8:15, 23; Gal. 4:5), which of course suggests that we are not "natural" children of God.

Third, John, who is the only biblical writer to speak of Christians as having been "begotten" by God, also tells us that Jesus Christ is the "only begotten" or "unique"[20] Son of God (John 1:14, 18; 3:16, 18; 1 John 4:9). At the very least, this means that we are not sons of God in the same sense that Christ is the Son of God, nor will we ever be. Christ was careful to distinguish between his Sonship and that of his followers. He spoke frequently of "my Father" and also often of "your Father"—but he never spoke in relation to himself and the disciples together of "our Father" (in Matt. 6:9 he was instructing his disciples how they should pray). Thus, after his resurrection, he stated, "I ascend to My Father and your Father, and My God and your God" (John 20:17).[21]

Fourth, although the word *begotten* can sometimes mean to produce a child from one's own substance, it does not always have this meaning. For example, Jesus Christ, who was already the unique Son of God during his earthly life (Luke 1:35; 3:22; 9:35; John 1:14; 3:16, 18; etc.), is said to have been "begotten" by God when he raised him from the dead (Ps. 2:7, quoted in Acts 13:33; Heb. 1:5). As we have already seen, Jesus was already in the fullest possible sense of the term God's Son and did not need to be "born again" as God's Son, which the Word-Faith teachers typically claim. Therefore, the statement "Today I have begotten You" (Ps. 2:7) means that at that time God publicly and formally declared to the world that Christ was his Son by raising him from the dead (cf. Rom. 1:4). This example suggests that the "begettal" of Christians by God as his sons refers to something other than a reproduction of his essence in them.

Finally, the sonship of believers is a spiritual regeneration (or new birth) that results, not in a conversion of people into gods but in human beings whose lives are characterized now by moral likeness to God produced by the indwelling of the Holy Spirit. Thus, 1 John tells us that those who have been "begotten" as sons of God will practice righteousness, love, and obedience (1 John 2:29; 3:9; 4:7; 5:1–5). Christ's own teaching on the sonship of believers in the Sermon on the Mount focused on purity of heart (Matt. 5:8), love of enemy (5:44), dependence on God to provide for our needs (6:8, 32; 7:11), and obedience to God (6:10; 7:21). Paul explains the adoption of believers as sons of God as an indwelling of the Holy Spirit whose leading we now experience and through whom we know God as our Father (Rom. 8:14–17; Gal. 4:6–7).

The biblical doctrine that believers in Christ are children of God is a glorious teaching, to be sure, and what it means we do not yet fully know (1 John 3:2). But we do know *something* about what it means, as well as what it does not mean. A new life, eternal, Christlike in holiness and love, in which the full potential of human beings as the image of God will be realized—our sonship means all this at least. But it does not mean that human beings shall be gods.

Is Christ's Body Also Christ?

The doctrine that Christians are adopted sons of God is closely related to the doctrine of the spiritual union between Christ and believers. This union is expressed both as a union between Christ and the individual believer and as a union of Christ and the church. Paul in particular teaches that Christians are "in Christ" (a phrase that occurs over 160 times in Paul's letters) and "with Christ" in his death, burial, resurrection, and ascension (Rom. 6:3–8; Eph. 2:5–6). He also teaches that Christians corporately are the "body" of Christ (Rom. 12:4–5; 1 Cor. 12:12–27; Eph. 1:22–23; 4:12; Col. 1:18). Individually Christians have Christ, or the Spirit of Christ, dwelling within (Rom. 8:9–11; 1 Cor. 3:16; 6:17–20; 2 Cor. 13:5; Eph. 3:16–17), so that Christ himself is their "life" (Gal. 2:20; Col. 3:4). On the basis of this teaching, many have concluded that Christians are in fact either a corporate extension of the incarnation (as the church) or replications of the incarnation (as individual Christians) or both. Does the Bible support such conclusions?

As with the doctrine of Christians as the sons of God, such ideas go far beyond the teaching of Scripture. To say that believers are "in Christ" means that they are somehow spiritually united *to* Christ, not that they *are* Christ. When Paul says that we have been crucified, buried, raised, and ascended with Christ, he is obviously not speaking literally. He means simply that by virtue of our faith relationship with Christ we benefit by his death and resurrection. The teaching that the church is the body of Christ is also to be taken figuratively and not to be pressed to imply that the church is Christ or even an essential part of Christ. The Spirit indwells the believer, to be sure, but the believer does not become a divine person as a result. Christ is our life, not in the sense that our individuality is replaced by his person but in the sense that we have eternal life through our spiritual union with him.

The doctrine of the church as the body of Christ, in particular, has often been interpreted to teach that the church is an extension of the incarnation. This understanding of the church is, in fact, a common teaching in the Roman Catholic church (though it has a quite different application in Catholicism than in the Word-Faith movement). Nevertheless, the idea that the church is an extension of the incarnation is unbiblical.

Earlier in this chapter Kenneth Hagin was cited as interpreting 2 Corinthians 6:14–15 to teach that the church is Christ. The church is not, however, called "Christ" in this text, which simply asks the rhetorical question (to which the answer "none" is expected), "Or what harmony has Christ with Belial [Satan], or what has a believer in common with an unbeliever?" Believers are no more Christ than unbelievers are Belial.

A text more commonly cited to identify the church as being Christ is 1 Corinthians 12:12, "For even as the body is one and yet has many members, and all the members of the body, though they are many, are one body, *so also is Christ*" (emphasis added). This statement is thought to mean that "Christ" is no longer one person but rather a corporate body of many individuals, with one member (Jesus) as the Head. Paul is understood to mean that *Christ* "is one and yet has many members." On this basis it is then concluded that the body is just as much Christ as the Head is (though it is admitted that the body remains subordinate to the Head). This is a prominent theme in the Manifest Sons of God doctrine and is taught by many if not all of the Word-Faith teachers.

Once again, the conclusion goes beyond the biblical teaching. More than once we are told that Christ is the Head (Eph. 1:22–23; 4:15; Col. 1:18) and the church the body (Rom. 12:5; 1 Cor. 12:27; Eph. 1:23; 4:12), but *never* is "the body" said to be Christ. Instead, the body is always said to *belong to* Christ—it is "the body *of Christ*" or "*Christ's* body." First Corinthians 12:12 does say that Christ has a "body" composed of many members but not that this body or its members are literally identical to Christ himself.

It is crucial in understanding the doctrine of the church as the body of Christ to recognize that the term *body* is used metaphorically (as it is when the communion bread is called "the body of Christ"). That this is so is confirmed by the fact that Paul himself uses other metaphors to picture the relationship between the church and Christ: a bride and her groom; a building and its foundation (or its cornerstone); a priesthood and its high priest; a flock of sheep and its shepherd; and the branches of a vine. Rather than build a superstructure of doctrinal speculation about the church being deified or made Christ on the basis of some of these metaphors, it is better to consider all of them together and in doing so realize that Christ and the church, though very closely related, are not identical.

One other point should be made about the church's characterization as the body of Christ. As we have seen, Hagin makes this description the basis for his claim that Christ *cannot* act in the world or do anything on the earth except through the church. A simple reading of the passages in which Paul calls the church the body of Christ will reveal that this idea is far from what Paul is saying. Not once does he, or any other biblical writer, hint that Christ is limited on earth to what he can do through the agency of the church. The church is called the body of Christ to emphasize the interdependence of its members and its absolute dependence on Christ—but never is it suggested that Christ is powerless to do anything on the earth except through his church. This inference, which sounds plausible based on the metaphor of the body, simply goes beyond the point of the metaphor as Paul himself used it and is therefore unwarranted.

The only other text cited by Hagin to prove that Christ is limited on earth to working through the church is Matthew 28:18–19. But this text does not say that Christ transferred or delegated all of his authority on earth to the church, as Hagin claims. Rather, Christ simply commissions the church to go as duly authorized representatives of himself without ever suggesting or implying that in doing so he has barred himself from personally working on the earth in any other way.

Reference has also been made to the claim that Jesus was the "firstfruits" of the incarnation, thus implying that the incarnation is incomplete without the church. However, while Jesus is called the "firstfruits" in Scripture, it is always with reference to the resurrection from the dead, not the incarnation (1 Cor. 15:20, 23). Earl Paulk also paraphrases 1 John 4:17 to the effect, "As He was in the world, so are we." Paulk uses this statement to mean that we are an incarnation of God in the world just as Jesus was. However, in context John is stating the assurance that God has the same love for us even while we are here in the world as he has for the Son of God. While this is a tremendous promise and assurance of our eternal security in the love of God, it does not make us gods.

Does God's Indwelling Make Us Incarnations?

The notion that each believer is somehow a duplicate of the incarnation is a key teaching of the Word-Faith theology. The rationale for this view is usually that an "incarnation" is defined as the indwelling of God in a human being. And since, we are told, this is as true of the Christian as it was of Christ, it follows that the Christian, as Kenneth Hagin puts it, "is as much an incarnation as was Jesus of Nazareth."[22]

The error in this reasoning lies in the definition of *incarnation*. In orthodox Christian theology, the incarnation is defined as the coming of the person of Jesus Christ, the Second Person of the Trinity, into the world as a man, "in the flesh" (Latin, *in carne*, hence "incarnation"). This event was totally unique, and only one person is God incarnate—Jesus Christ. Nor was Christ merely God dwelling in a human being, a heresy the early church condemned because it meant that the Word did not actually become flesh (John 1:14) but only joined himself to a human being. The incarnate Christ was one person in whom were perfectly united two natures; the Christian is a person with one nature, human, in whom God the Holy Spirit (and through him, the Father and the Son) dwells.

A related argument used by some Word-Faith teachers appeals to 1 Corinthians 6:17, which says, "But the one who joins himself to the Lord is one spirit [with him]." From this statement and the biblical teaching that the Holy Spirit, who is also the Spirit of Christ, indwells us (Rom. 8:9–11), it is inferred that we are literally an extension of Christ on the earth.

This inference, which once again seems plausible on the surface, misunderstands the idiomatic way in which Paul was speaking. In Philippians 2:2, for example, Paul exhorts the Philippian Christians to be "of the same mind, maintaining the same love, united in spirit, intent on one purpose."

Here the exhortation to be "united in spirit" (or it could possibly be translated "in the Spirit") should not be read to mean that they were not already, in some sense, one in God's Spirit. Nor should it be read to mean that they should aspire to lose their individual identities (as all the Word-Faith teachers would agree we should not) and literally become one spirit. Instead, it should be read as an exhortation to grow so close that our unity is not merely external (belonging to the same church, saying the same words) but internal, of the heart or spirit (believing the same things, sharing the same values, committed to the same God). Likewise, in 1 Corinthians 6:17 Paul was simply saying that the person who is joined to the Lord enters into a personal relationship with him characterized by a spiritual union. Of course this spiritual relationship is made possible by the Holy Spirit's indwelling our hearts; nevertheless, it remains a relationship between two very different kinds of being, one of whom is God and the other of whom is most definitely not divine at all.

Does Partaking of the Divine Nature Make Us Gods?

In 2 Peter 1:4 we are told that through God's promises Christians may "become partakers of divine nature, having escaped the corruption that is in the world in lust."[23] This text, even more than Psalm 82, has suggested to many a doctrine of deification. Indeed, if by deification one means simply "partaking of the divine nature," then such "deification" is unquestionably biblical. The question, then, is what does Peter mean by "partakers of divine nature"?

The most radical interpretation of 2 Peter 1:4 is that Christians will eventually possess the essential nature of God himself. "Partakers" would be interpreted to mean "possessors," and "divine nature" would mean "God's essence." This interpretation, however, is not in keeping with the exact wording of the text, as can be seen by examining both the word "partakers" *(koinōnoi)* and the expression "divine nature" *(theias physeōs).*

The word *koinōnoi,* "partakers," is related to the Greek words *koinos* ("common"), *koinōneō* ("to share, participate"), and *koinōnia* ("sharing, participation," usually translated "fellowship" or "communion"). It is instructive to note the way these words are used in Scripture. Christians "share" in Christ's sufferings, without being crucified or even literally suffering, if by faith they receive the blessings of forgiveness and cleansing available through Christ's sufferings (2 Cor. 1:7; Phil. 3:10; 1 Peter 4:13). We can "share" in another's sins or wicked works (1 Tim. 5:22; 2 John 11) without actually doing them; all we need do is encourage or support the evildoer in his or her sinful activity. Christians experience "the fellowship of the Holy Spirit" (2 Cor. 13:14) without becoming spirits. Examples could be multiplied.

The point is that the phrase "partakers of the divine nature" need not, on the assumption that "divine nature" refers to God's essence, mean that Christians are to possess God's essence in themselves. When the Book of Hebrews says that Christ "partook" of human nature, for example, it uses a different Greek word (*meteschen*, Heb. 2:14). Rather, God's essence will dwell in them (through the Holy Spirit) and in so doing will transform their lives.

The other question is what "divine nature" means. The phrase is usually translated "partakers of the divine nature," which of course suggests to the English reader that *divine* here means "of God." Some interpreters have suggested that "divine nature" reflects the usage of the word *divine* in the literature of Greek-speaking Jews of the first century, whose language was heavily influenced by Greek thought. In their terminology, "divine nature" was the nature of divine or heavenly beings, which could refer either to angelic spirits or to people who had gained immortality. It might possibly be that Peter is adopting this language (without approving of the pagan Greek belief that all heavenly or immortal beings were gods) and saying that Christians have the hope of being made immortal and perfect. This interpretation does fit the context, since Peter links this "deification" (if it may be called that) to escaping the corruption of the world due to sin.

However, the word *divine* is used earlier in the same sentence ("his divine power," v. 3), and there it must mean "of God." Moreover, the word *divine* in any of its forms is always used elsewhere in the New Testament to refer to God's being or nature (*to theion*, Acts 17:29; *theiotēs*, Rom. 1:20; *theotēs*, Col. 2:9). Therefore, it is best to take "divine nature" in verse 4 to mean God's own nature.

Lastly, some comment on the meaning of "nature" *(physeōs)* is needed. The word is used quite rarely in the New Testament (eighteen times, counting adjectival and adverbial forms) and always with the simple meaning of what is intrinsic or essential or "natural" (Rom. 1:26–27; 2:14; 11:21, 24; 1 Cor. 11:14; Gal. 2:15; 4:8; Eph. 2:3; James 3:7; 2 Peter 1:4; 2:12; Jude 10). Peter, then, is speaking of God's essence and is saying that Christians are to experience the benefits of having the essence of God dwelling in them. This is a reality that has already begun, but its full realization will come when we have fully "escaped the corruption in the world by lust," that is, when we are made incorruptible and immortal. It is a marvelous truth that the actual essence of God dwells in the believer.

However, this falls short of the notion that the believer possesses the essence of God as the believer's own essence. The believer's own essence remains human, but he is united to God in his essence through the Holy Spirit dwelling in him. The Word-Faith teachers obscure or deny this distinction, and it is in that respect that their teaching goes astray.

14

The Faith Debate

God is not going to do anything about it, because He already has done something about it. He has done something about salvation, the Holy Spirit, healing, and deliverance from demons. It is now up to you to plug in. Faith is the plug, praise God. Just plug in. How do you plug in? *Say it. Do it. Receive it.*

Kenneth Hagin[1]

Unlike the cold steel vending machine, God demands more than a few simple steps; He demands relationship.

Demos Shakarian[2]

All these died in faith, without receiving the promises, but having seen them and having welcomed them from a distance, and having confessed that they were strangers and exiles on the earth.

Hebrews 11:13

The Word-Faith movement is best known for its views on faith, healing, and prosperity. We will be discussing these matters in this and the following chapter. But notice that in looking at what the movement's teachers say about God, human nature, humankind's fall into sin, Jesus Christ, and the church, we have already learned a great deal about what they think about faith. Unfortunately, much of what we have seen is unbiblical.

In this chapter, we will focus on the matter of faith itself. Here again, it must be observed that the critics of the Word-Faith doctrine have not always been careful to represent the doctrine accurately or charitably.

The Word-Faith Doctrine of Faith

We begin by summarizing what the leading Word-Faith teachers say about faith. It will be most convenient to summarize the doctrine under three headings: faith, confession, and prayer. As we proceed in this summary, I will make note of the major biblical texts used by Word-Faith teachers to support each point.

Faith

One distinctive aspect about the Word-Faith view of faith is *who* is said to have it. First of all, as we have already seen, God himself is said to have faith. The kind of faith to which the Word-Faith movement calls Christians is the kind of faith God has (Mark 11:22). Specifically, we are to have the kind of faith that God had in creating the world (Heb. 11:3; cf. Rom. 4:17).[3]

Actually, according to the Word-Faith teachers, Christians already have this kind of faith. Such supernatural faith is a gift of God (Rom. 12:3; Eph. 2:8). It is a mountain-moving faith that God gives to every Christian.[4]

On the other hand, the Word-Faith teachers also say that *anyone* who believes can have what he says, even if he is not a Christian, because Jesus said "whosoever" (Mark 11:23 KJV).[5] Faith is a spiritual law that works for (or against) believers and unbelievers.[6] Hagin speaks for the movement when he writes:

> It used to bother me when I'd see unsaved people getting results, but my church members not getting results. Then it dawned on me what the sinners were doing: They were cooperating with this law of God—the law of faith.[7]

The Word-Faith teachers, although they have a reputation as faith healers, are at pains to encourage Christians to have faith for themselves. Rather than looking to a pastor or evangelist to pray for them, Christians ought to learn to pray in faith for themselves. As Hagin puts it, "That's what you've got to learn to do to get things from God: *Have faith in your faith.*"[8]

What, then, is faith? Here we find that at least some of the leading Word-Faith teachers define faith as a "force."[9] What this force of faith does is described in somewhat varying fashion. Faith may be said to make the unreal or nonexistent to become real or existent (Rom. 4:17).[10] Sometimes faith is said to make the spiritual become physical (cf. Eph. 1:3)[11] or to make the invisible become visible or manifest.[12]

All of the Word-Faith teachers insist that true faith ignores the physical facts (Rom. 4:19; 2 Cor. 4:18; 5:7)[13] and reason (Prov. 3:5)[14] if they contradict God's Word.

In Word-Faith understanding, faith is oriented in the present tense ("*Now* faith *is*," Heb. 11:1), in contrast to hope, which is oriented in the future tense. Thus, faith is taking what is *already* ours (Mark 11:23), not waiting for what God has promised for the future.[15] As Hagin puts it, "Quit hoping," and instead start believing that you already have what you want.[16]

Confession

It is a basic maxim of the Word-Faith doctrine that *whatever* we believe and confess, we possess (Rom. 10:10). This is a "formula" or "law" that may be used to get whatever we want.[17] What we get—good or bad—is determined by our faith (Matt. 9:29) as expressed *in words*.[18]

Two lines of argument are used in Word-Faith theology to prove the importance of one's confession. First, God's use of words to create the world (Gen. 1:3, etc.; Ps. 33:6, 9; Heb. 11:3) is said to show that words are the most powerful things in the universe.[19] Second, a variety of biblical passages speak of the importance of what human beings say. The words we say have the power of life and death (Prov. 18:21). Scripture tells us that we need to be very careful what we say, lest our words bring us harm (Prov. 6:2; Matt. 12:37).[20]

Prayer

A fundamental principle of Word-Faith teaching is that we should *not* ask God for things he has already given or ask him to do things he has already done. He has already provided salvation, forgiveness, healing, and prosperity through the redemptive work of Christ, so he has already done everything he is going to do in such matters. The rest is now up to us.[21]

To *ask* God for things implies that we are uncertain as to whether he has already provided them. Likewise, we should not pray, "If it be Thy will," because we already know it is God's will to save, forgive, heal, and prosper us. Rather than asking God for things, we should determine what God's will is from Scripture and then confess those things to be ours by faith. One way of doing this in prayer is to "demand" (which is said to be the real meaning of "ask" in John 14:13–14 and 15:7) or "command" God to honor his Word.[22] Copeland makes the point in this way:

> As a believer, you have a right to make commands in the name of Jesus. Each time you stand on the Word, you are commanding God to a certain extent because it is His Word. Whenever an honest man gives you his word, he is bound by it.[23]

Reformulating Faith

We begin our response to the Word-Faith doctrine of faith by considering who, according to the Bible, has faith.

Who Has Faith?

First, *God does not have faith*. As we saw in chapter 7, the Bible never says that God has faith. Faith is putting one's trust in someone or something; it is dependence, reliance, confidence in someone or something. Of course, in a broadened sense one might use the word *faith* with reference to God in the sense that God is supremely confident of his own power and wisdom. God knows what he is doing! But this is *not* what the Word-Faith teachers mean by faith. As they use the term, faith is a power or force that works according to immutable spiritual laws through the agency of spoken words to bring into reality or manifestation what the person believing and speaking wants. This force of faith is something that God has and that we also can have, according to the Word-Faith teachers. But the Bible says nothing to support this idea.

Next, we must insist that *Christians have saving faith but not necessarily miraculous faith*. Faith is indeed a gift of God, as the Word-Faith teachers rightly point out (Rom. 12:3; Eph. 2:8). But God has not given "mountain-moving faith" to every Christian. Paul lists such faith among the spiritual gifts (1 Cor. 12:9; 13:2; cf. Rom. 12:3, 6), and he goes out of his way to make it clear that Christians do not all have the same gifts (Rom. 12:4–6; 1 Cor. 12:4–6, 14–19, 28–30).

When Jesus spoke about faith that could move mountains (Matt. 21:21; Mark 11:23), he did not mean that anyone could have such faith. His point was that anyone who had such faith could have what he believed. But such faith comes only from God and only as he sovereignly wills (1 Cor. 12:11). I agree that God sometimes gives a Christian a supernatural assurance that God intends to do something that is humanly difficult to believe. But Jesus did not say that God would do this for every Christian or that this would be a routine function of every Christian's life.

Finally, for clarity's sake it would be best to say that *non-Christians do not have faith*. Scripture consistently speaks of non-Christians as those who do *not* believe. This is because faith is not something everyone has but fails to utilize; it is, rather, the God-given confidence in Jesus Christ as Savior and Lord.

What Is Faith?

Faith is never spoken of in Scripture as a "force" or other power. The idea in Word-Faith teaching that human beings can, by using faith, make the unreal become real or the spiritual become physically manifest is contrary to Scripture. Let me illustrate the problem using two of the proof texts cited by Word-Faith teachers in support of their view of faith.

The Word-Faith teachers often cite Romans 4:17 and claim that Christians should seek to imitate God's creative word. But this very text presents God as the only one who can make the unreal or nonexistent become real or existent. Paul explicitly says that Abraham believed *God* precisely because it *was* God (*not* Abraham) who "gives life to the dead and calls into being that which does not exist." It was God who promised it, and it was God alone who was able to perform it (vv. 20–21).

Ephesians 1:3 is sometimes cited to prove that Christians have health and prosperity waiting for them in spiritual form, needing only a confession of faith to make them materialize. If anything, this is an even more bizarre misunderstanding of Scripture than our previous example. The spiritual blessings that Paul says we have in Christ in Ephesians 1:3 are adoption (v. 5), redemption and forgiveness (v. 7), knowledge of his will (v. 9), the status of heirs (v. 11), and the indwelling Spirit (v. 13). These are not physical blessings of bodily health or financial prosperity waiting to be moved by the force of faith from the invisible to the visible realm.

One of the most troubling and potentially destructive aspects of Word-Faith theology is its teaching that true faith may be contrary to the facts or reason. Certainly there is a grain of truth in what these teachers are saying. We ought indeed to believe God no matter what. But faith does not *ignore* physical facts. Rather, faith refuses to allow facts or circumstances to shake our confidence in God's ability to do what he promised.

Consider Paul's teaching about Abraham in Romans 4 again. Abraham did not deny or ignore the fact that his body was too old to produce children if nature simply took its course. Abraham did not "confess" that, in spite of appearances and his feelings, he was really a virile man! Rather, he confessed that God could produce new life even from his body, though it was as good as dead (v. 19).

Word-Faith teachers are fond of quoting Paul's statement that "we look not at the things which are seen, but at the things which are not seen" (2 Cor. 4:18a). But to interpret Paul's words here as a policy of denying the reality of physical facts is a classic case of taking a statement out of context. Paul goes on immediately to say why he did not "look at" the seen but the unseen: "for the things which are seen are temporal, but the things which are not seen are eternal" (v. 18b). When Paul says that he does not "look at" the things he sees, he is clearly speaking figuratively—since one cannot see something if one does not look at it! What Paul means is that he does not live his life based merely on what he can see or allow the immediate, temporal concerns of life to derail him from fulfilling God's calling on his life. Far from denying the reality of the temporal and visible, Paul forthrightly acknowledges it. Note his statement just two verses earlier that "our outer man is decaying" (v. 16). This is what the Word-Faith teachers might call a "negative confession"—it is a frank admission that the body is decaying and falling apart. Evidently, Paul thought there was nothing wrong with making such admissions.

To "walk by faith, not by sight" (2 Cor. 5:7), then, does not mean to deny the reality of what we see. It is, rather, to trust in God's eternal vindication and blessing despite the hard fact that life is not now always what we would like. It means to live in the confidence that God will fulfill his promise to give us immortal, glorious life in the resurrection (vv. 1–8).

It is also a mistake to claim that faith will be contrary to reason. Faith is never irrational, because it is an attitude of confidence in the God who created everything and who rules the world in truth. Rather, faith refuses to depend solely on what our limited reasoning ability can discover. To "lean on your own understanding" (Prov. 3:5) does not mean to think rationally. It means to live as if you are competent to run your own life apart from the wisdom of knowing and fearing God (compare vv. 6–7).

Finally, the Word-Faith teaching that faith is exclusively oriented to the present must be rejected as simply unbiblical. The usual argument for this idea appeals to the words *Now* and *is* in Hebrews 11:1, but this argument is flawed. The word *Now* in Hebrews 11:1 is a transitional "now" (like the one in 1 Cor. 7:1), not a chronological "now." The word *is* does not limit faith to a present-tense aspect. Rather, the word *is* functions here somewhat like an equal sign (=); it indicates that what follows is a definition or description of faith.

Scripture speaks of faith as having past-, present-, and future-tense aspects. Of course, faith does have a present-tense aspect: It is a present confidence in God (and particularly in Christ) as presently loving us, as abiding with us, as guiding us, and so forth (Rom. 15:13).

Faith also has a past-tense aspect, since it involves believing that Christ died and rose from the dead for our redemption (Rom. 10:9; 1 Cor. 15:1–11).

Finally, and most relevant here, faith has a future-tense aspect, since it involves trusting in God to fulfill promises that we may never see fulfilled in our lifetime—trusting in his future reward (Heb. 11:6). That was the chief characteristic of the faith of the Old Testament saints (Heb. 11:8–10, 13–16), and it is an aspect of our faith as well (Rom. 6:8; 2 Tim. 1:12). This future-tense faith is grounded on the past-tense faith (1 Thess. 4:14).

Once we understand that faith includes confidence in God's future fulfillment of his promises, we can see that it is a mistake to insist that faith involves taking what is already ours. Rather, faith is trusting in God to provide for us, whether in the present or in the future. Mark 11:23–24 (which is speaking of an exceptional faith) does not speak of taking but of *receiving* (from God). The tense of "you have received" is not present but past tense and emphasizes the certainty of the matter, not its having a present reality. Note what Jesus says in verse 23: the disciple is to "believe that what he says *is going to* happen" (emphasis added), speaking in the future tense.

Reconsidering Confession

The concept of confession is so central to the Word-Faith doctrine that critics often call it "positive confession." Once again, the Word-Faith position does contain certain elements of truth, but at its heart the teaching is unbiblical.

One of the most popular proof texts for positive confession is Romans 10:10, "For with the heart man believeth unto righteousness; and with the mouth confession is made unto salvation" (KJV). Somehow the Word-Faith teachers generalize this statement into a "formula" or "law" that may be used to get whatever we want. But the immediate context proves this is not so. The Jews believed and confessed that they had righteousness by their works of the law, but that just wasn't true (Rom. 9:30–10:3). Believing and confessing that you have something doesn't make it so. There is undeniable proof of this principle in this very text: The substance of the faith and confession that Paul says is needed is acknowledging that Jesus is Lord and that "God raised him from the dead." But these things are true *whether or not we believe and confess them*. James Kinnebrew, a critic of the Word-Faith movement, points out that the Word-Faith interpretation mistakenly assumes that, as Kenneth Hagin put it, a person "is not saved until he confesses he is saved."[24]

Nor is Jesus' statement to the blind men, "It shall be done to you according to your faith" (Matt. 9:29), a spiritual law covering all beliefs. When the men approached Jesus, he did not ask them if they believed that they had their healing or to confess that healing was theirs. Nor did he ask them if they believed that Jesus *would* heal them if only they had faith. Rather, he asked them, "Do you believe that I am *able* to do this?" (v. 28, emphasis added). This simple distinction is at the root of the problem with the Word-Faith view of faith. The blind men were healed, not by their faith but by Christ. They were asked to believe, not that healing was theirs or that it was guaranteed but that Christ *could* heal them. The rest was up to Christ. Their faith was a necessary condition but not a sufficient condition for them to receive from Christ the healing they sought.

The Word-Faith teachers base their belief in positive confession on statements in the Bible concerning the power of words. There are, first of all, statements about the power of God's words. I am almost embarrassed at having to point this out, but God's "words" are the most powerful things in the universe *because he is God* (see Rom. 4:16–21 again), not because words in and of themselves are powerful. That "He spoke, and it was done; He commanded, and it stood fast" (Ps. 33:9) is something that the psalmist says should cause everyone to "fear" and "stand in awe" of God (v. 8). God nullifies and frustrates the counsels and plans of the nations, while his own counsel and plans stand forever (vv. 10–11). The point is simple and obvious: What God says, goes; what people say, may or may not happen. Nor does the psalmist suggest that this is a deficiency we can overcome by learning to have what we say by faith. Rather, he urges Israel to fear the Lord, to hope for his mercy, and to wait for his help (vv. 16–22).

Another famous passage that speaks about the power of God's word is Isaiah 55:11, in which God states that his word will not return to him empty but will accomplish what he intends. As biblical scholar Anthony Thiselton points out, "If words in general could not return empty, the writer is saying little or nothing which is remarkable or even informative about God."[25] The point of God's statement is to encourage Israel to turn to him for mercy in the confidence that his promise of restoration will be fulfilled (vv. 6–13). It is because God transcends our world and his ways are as high above ours as the heaven is above the earth that we can be assured that what he says will be so (vv. 8–9).

The Book of Proverbs does not teach that words have some sort of spiritual energy or power. Various texts in Proverbs teach that human words by themselves are powerless (see Prov. 14:23; 17:10; 26:23, 26; 29:19).[26]

Proverbs 6:1–2 is simply speaking of a person who is trapped in an awkward financial obligation by his foolish agreement. The tongue has the power of life and death (Prov. 18:21), not because it can convey the force of faith but because when we speak our words have consequences: Foolish talk can lead to fights and ruin a person's life (vv. 6–7).

Another text commonly used to teach positive confession is Matthew 12:36–37, in which Jesus warned the Pharisees about the dangers of speaking careless words. From this warning the Word-Faith teachers extract a principle of negative confession: that you must be very careful what you wish for, because if you say it, you will get it! But this is far from Jesus' point. The careless words of which he warns are exemplified by the Pharisees' sin of blaspheming the Holy Spirit (vv. 31–32). The result of their blasphemous words was not some negative consequence caused by their spoken word itself but that they became subject to the personal judgment and condemnation of God. Words do not have power except as people believe and act on them, but we will be held *accountable* for our words.

There is much evidence in Scripture against the whole idea of positive and negative confessions bringing about reality. If this doctrine were true, it would follow, as Charles Capps puts it, that "if it's the devil you are quoting, you are releasing the ability of the devil. It's just that simple. . . . *Faith in the devil could come by hearing the words of the devil.*"[27] But a rather obvious objection suggests itself: If quoting the words of the devil releases his ability and evokes faith in him, why does *the Bible* quote the devil?

One may also ask why, on Word-Faith premises, Jesus would tell the Laodiceans, "You are wretched and miserable and poor and blind and naked" (Rev. 3:17b). Isn't that a lie of the devil, according to their doctrine? Ironically, as James Kinnebrew points out, the Laodiceans had been making positive confessions.[28] They had been saying, "I am rich, and have become wealthy, and have need of nothing" (v. 17a). But saying so did not make it so.

Rethinking Prayer

It is true that we should not ask God to do things he has already done. He has already sent Jesus Christ and does not need to provide atonement again. However, we do need to ask God to make the blessings of his accomplished work of salvation effective in our lives. There is a simple reason why this is necessary: God does not give the blessings of salvation to everyone. It is therefore necessary to approach God in humility, recognizing that he does not owe any of us anything; much less does he owe us his mercy (Rom. 9:15–18; James 4:6–10).

One argument that the Word-Faith teachers use to prove their doctrine of prayer is based on a faulty word study. The word translated "ask" in John 14:13–14 and 15:7 *(aiteō)* does not mean "demand." In some contexts the asking may be an insistent demanding (Luke 23:23), while in other contexts it may be more like begging (Luke 23:52). Context is determinative here. The KJV and modern translations almost always render the word as *ask* (see especially Matt. 7:7–11). Nor does the Bible ever encourage us to "command" God to honor his Word.

It is also true, as the Word-Faith teachers insist, that we should not pray "if it be Thy will" where God has clearly stated his will. For example, we should not ask God to forgive us "if it is your will," since we already know that it is his will. The question is whether the Bible clearly promises that we will be healed of any disease or relieved of any financial problem if we confess those things to be ours by faith. That we should conduct our daily lives in the mode of "if it be God's will" is clear from James 4:15.

In Mark 11:24 Jesus says, "All things for which you pray and ask, believe that you have received them, and they shall be granted you." Does this mean that faith is a force that makes whatever we believe and say come to pass? No, it does not. According to Jesus' own words here, it is God, not the believer, who actually brings the thing about. Thus, Jesus says, "They shall be *granted* you," not "*you* will do them"; "believe that you have *received* them," not "believe that you have *taken* them." And this will happen when we *pray*, that is, when we ask God. So, our faith is to be in God, not in our faith or in our words.

Elsewhere the Bible clearly stipulates conditions for receiving answers to prayer. For example, we are told that we must abide in Christ and have his Word abiding in us (John 15:7); that we must not ask with wrong motives (James 4:3); that we must have our earthly relationships in order (1 Peter 3:7); and that what we ask must be according to his will (1 John 5:14). While it is wrong to use these verses as excuses never to ask God for things, it is also wrong to ignore these verses and teach that one can get anything one wants through prayer.

Our understanding of prayer must be based on everything the Bible says. God is a personal, sovereign Father who loves us, who knows better than we do what is best for us, and who works mysteriously through even evil circumstances to bring blessing to us and to others. We cannot twist God's arm, nor are we little gods who can command whatever we wish into being. We are God's little children who must depend on him for everything and trust him even when our prayers seem unanswered.

How Bad Is It?

The Word-Faith doctrines concerning faith, confession, and prayer rest on half-truths. It is true that God can do marvelous things when we trust him. It is not true that God is obligated to do marvelous things when we trust him. It is true that thinking and speaking positively is a generally healthy way to live. It is not true that there is some spiritual, immutable law that says that positive confessions bring positive results while negative confessions bring negative results. It is true that we should pray with confidence that God wants to bless us. It is not true that we can demand anything from God.

I do not wish to overstate the errors of the Word-Faith teachings in these matters. Some critics have, I think, overreacted to these erroneous ideas. They have accused the Word-Faith teachers of depersonalizing God, or of making him into our cosmic servant. Perhaps at their worst, some Word-Faith teachers have treated God in these ways. At their best, though, most of the Word-Faith teachers emphasize personal dimensions to our relationship with God—especially his Fatherhood.

Still, the Word-Faith doctrines of faith, confession, and prayer are easily and naturally applied in ways that can only be regarded as presumptuous. If a person believes that confession works as an immutable spiritual law, he is acting quite consistently if he confesses that he is healed even while writhing in pain from an operable disease. The Word-Faith doctrine clearly discourages people from praying in an attitude of humble dependence on God's mercy.

Perhaps the most serious danger of the Word-Faith position is that, since it is unbiblical and unrealistic, those who believe it are in for serious disappointment. The result can be—and often has been—disillusionment. How many people have given up on faith in God because "it doesn't work"? The Word-Faith teachers set people up for a fall when they tell them that God promises them that they can have what they say.

15

On Being Healthy, Wealthy, and Wise

Paul said, "I am not ashamed of the good news, for it is the power of God." Good news is the power of God. It is the gospel. And the gospel, of course, is faith, and it is prosperity, and it is healing. All of these are involved in salvation.

Charles Capps[1]

While there is a germ of truth in their message (God does heal; He does promise to supply needs; and a positive attitude is healthy), the faith teachers have so watered that seed that it has overgrown, obscured, and uprooted all other truths. Purporting to preach the "full gospel," they seldom sound more than one note: "Faith is the avenue to health, wealth, and all success."

James Kinnebrew[2]

I am not ashamed of the gospel, because it is the power of God for the salvation of everyone who believes: first for the Jew, then for the Gentile. For in the gospel a righteousness from God is revealed, a righteousness that is by faith from first to last, just as it is written: "The righteous will live by faith."

Romans 1:16–17 NIV

We have examined the theological system of the Word-Faith movement and found it to be seriously unbiblical on various crucial matters. But the movement is best known for its "health and wealth" message. Our

205

interest here is primarily in how the movement's teachings about healing and prosperity relate to crucial issues in biblical theology.

The Word-Faith Doctrines of Health and Wealth

The Word-Faith doctrines concerning healing and material prosperity are based on five main lines of argument. We will summarize each of these before presenting our critique.

The Power of Positive Confession

The primary basis on which the Word-Faith teachers rest their views on health and wealth is their doctrine of faith and confession. If "faith-filled words" can produce what they say, then it follows that a person who believes that he has healing and speaks a positive confession to that effect will experience health. The same logic applies in matters of financial or material prosperity.

We have already shown that this doctrine is unbiblical. God does not create reality by speaking words of faith, and there is no biblical encouragement for us to do so. Positive thinking may indeed help the body heal or help us succeed in business, but this legitimate truth falls far short of a spiritual law of positive confession.

The Lifting of the Curse

The second argument advanced by Word-Faith teachers focuses on the fact that Jesus lifted the curse of the law from us. Commenting on Galatians 3:13, Kenneth Hagin writes:

> What is the curse of the law? The only way to find out is to go back to the law. The expression "the law" as found in the New Testament usually refers to the Pentateuch, the first five books of the Bible. As we go back to these books—or the law—we find that the curse, or punishment, for breaking God's law is threefold: poverty, sickness, and spiritual death.[3]

If we are freed from the curse of the law, and the curse included poverty and sickness, then it follows that in principle we have been freed from poverty and sickness. The primary Old Testament text thought to support this interpretation is Deuteronomy 28. Note, for example, what Kenneth Copeland says about this passage:

Remember what was listed under the curse in Deuteronomy 28? Poverty of every kind, political failure, drought, war, every calamity known to mankind; and Jesus has redeemed us from it all. ALL sickness and ALL disease, even those not mentioned there, come under the curse. Therefore, we are redeemed from all sickness and all disease. You need to fight the temptation to be sick just as you would fight the temptation to lie or to steal.[4]

Healing in the Atonement

The third argument focuses especially on health, although most of the Word-Faith teachers extend it to include wealth. In common with the evangelical faith-cure teachers of the nineteenth century and many Pentecostals in this century, the Word-Faith movement holds that healing was provided in the atonement. Key biblical passages are thought to show that the believer has been freed from physical sickness no less than he has been freed from condemnation for sin (Isa. 53:4–5; Matt. 8:16–17; 12:15–16; 1 Peter 2:24). Hagin speaks for the entire movement when he writes:

> Through natural human truth a person realizes that he is sick, that he has pain or disease. But God's Word reveals that "Himself took our infirmities, and bare our sicknesses" (Matt. 8:17), and that by His stripes we are healed (1 Peter 2:24). Isn't God's Word just as true one time as it is another? Isn't it just as true when you have sickness and are suffering as when you are well? By believing what your physical senses tell you, you would say, "I don't have healing; I am sick." But by believing the truth of God's Word you can say, "I am healed. By His stripes I have healing."[5]

From the doctrine of healing in the atonement, the Word-Faith teachers draw the inference that healing is already available to us and that it is now entirely up to us whether we experience healing or not. Again, Hagin's statement is typical:

> Although healing is manifested in the physical, it is really a spiritual blessing, because it is spiritual healing. God is not going to heal your body. He is not going to do one thing about healing you. He's already done all He is ever going to do about healing you. He laid on Jesus your sickness and disease. He has already done something about it. Jesus has already borne them and by His stripes "ye *were* healed." Get your believing in line with what God's Word says. Quit hoping.[6]

The King's Kids Rule

The fourth reason Word-Faith teachers give why we should be healthy and prosperous in this life is perhaps its most appealing. We are God's children, and God has abundant life and all the wealth of the universe at his disposal. How, then, could we not be healthy and rich?

According to Word-Faith teaching, our life of poverty and sickness was a result of Satan's dominion over us. Recall that according to these teachers, when humankind fell into sin, Satan became the legal god of this world, giving him power over us. For Word-Faith teachers it is a basic, elementary truth that Jesus' redemption frees us from Satan's dominion and restores rightful rule or dominion to us. As Hagin puts it:

> Jesus, however, came to redeem us from Satan's power and dominion over us. . . . We are to reign as kings in life. That means that we have dominion over our lives. We are to dominate, not to be dominated. Circumstances are not to dominate you. Poverty is not to rule and reign over you. You are to rule and reign over poverty. Disease and sickness are not to rule and reign over you. You are to rule and reign over sickness. We are to reign as kings in life by Christ Jesus, in whom we have our redemption.[7]

Health and Wealth as God's Will

Fifth, Word-Faith teachers cite a variety of texts to show that God wants his people to experience health and wealth in this life. For example, the apostle John prayed "that in all respects you may prosper and be in good health, just as your soul prospers" (3 John 2). The Word-Faith teachers cite a number of other texts to back up this claim (e.g., Pss. 103:2–3; 107:20; Mark 10:29–30). One of the most important passages for the doctrine of healing is James 5:10–20. A statement commonly quoted from this passage in support of a blanket guarantee of healing is "the prayer of faith shall save the sick" (James 5:15 KJV). This statement is commonly understood to mean that God guarantees healing for those who pray with faith.

As I have already noted, the first of these five lines of argument for the Word-Faith doctrine of guaranteed health and wealth has already been refuted biblically in previous chapters. In the rest of this chapter I will examine the other four lines of defense.

No More Curse

It is true that Paul teaches that Christ died to remove the curse of the law from us (Gal. 3:13). However, Paul says nothing about this meaning an immediate guarantee of physical healing for believers. In context the blessing that comes as a result of the end of the curse is the reception of the Spirit (v. 14). Likewise, the blessing of Abraham (v. 15) that Paul speaks of in context is not physical healing or financial prosperity but the righteousness of faith (v. 6).

Of course, if it could be proven that all sickness and poverty was a result of the curse of the law, the Word-Faith argument would still have some merit. But this is not the case. The key chapter here in the Old Testament law is Deuteronomy 28. The blessings that God promised would come on Israel were national blessings that he would bestow on them as a nation if the people as a whole obeyed his law (Deut. 28:1–14). There is no basis for individualizing these blessings and applying them to Gentile or Jewish Christians. Likewise, the curses of which Deuteronomy 28 speaks are those that were to come on Israel if they did not obey the law. These curses were *extraordinary* diseases, calamities, and poverty (Deut. 28:15–68; see especially vv. 20–21, 36–37, 45–48, 58–59).

Moreover, it is striking that Deuteronomy affirms that these curses would be brought on Israel by God himself—contrary to the Word-Faith doctrine that disease and poverty come from Satan and not God. Some sixteen times Moses says "*the LORD* will" do these things (vv. 20–22, 24–25, 27–28, 35–36, 49–61, 64–65, 68; cf. v. 63).

Healing in the Atonement

It is possible to overreact to the doctrine of healing in the atonement. Some Christians, legitimately troubled by the teaching that any Christian who is sick has failed to exercise true faith, have sought to dissociate healing from the atonement entirely. I believe that this extreme, while not nearly as harmful theologically or practically as its opposite, is nevertheless also mistaken.

My position is that believers are promised on the basis of Christ's redemption that *eventually* they will experience unlimited health and prosperity, but these promises will not be completely fulfilled until the resurrection of our bodies. It seems to me that this can be easily shown to be the biblical position. Paul says that our bodies before the resurrection are corruptible, humiliating, and weak—in short, they are "natural." In the resurrection our bodies will be incorruptible, glorious, and powerful—in short, they will be supernatural, Spirit-empowered ("spiritual") bodies (1 Cor. 15:42–45). Until that time we live in a creation subject to suffering and decay and await "our adoption as sons, the redemption of our body" (Rom. 8:18–23).

These and other Scriptures clearly teach that *our bodies have not yet received the benefits of our redemption*. We do have as a present possession spiritual redemption, including forgiveness of sins, justification, and other spiritual blessings (Rom. 3:24; Eph. 1:3–14; Col. 1:12–14). However, the full redemption that has been promised us is still future. The decisive proof of this is that, except for those Christians who are living when Christ returns, *every Christian suffers physical death* (1 Thess. 4:13–17). Until the time of Christ's return, we have the Holy Spirit dwelling in us as a spiritual "down payment" or guarantee of the future, complete redemption of body and soul that has been promised to us (Eph. 1:13–14; 4:30). A down payment guarantees that we will *eventually* receive what was promised, but it also reminds us that we do not yet have all that was promised.

Thus, I think it is actually correct to teach that healing is guaranteed to us by Christ's atonement. I would simply qualify this guarantee as prospective.

Now, in the meantime, of course we often do experience physical healing and material blessings from God. These are foretastes of the full redemption to come. They are reminders of God's love and power, and God also uses them to encourage others to believe in Christ. But the Bible never promises that we will experience health and prosperity *in their fullness in this life.*

With this perspective in mind, let's look at the biblical texts adduced by the Word-Faith teachers. I understand Isaiah 53:5 to be speaking primarily of spiritual "healing," with physical sickness as a type representing or picturing sin as a kind of sickness. This seems clear enough when the whole statement is read in context. Note the parallelism employed in the verse:

> But he was pierced through for our *transgressions,*
> He was crushed for our *iniquities;*
> The chastening for our *well-being* [peace] fell upon Him,
> And by His scourging we are *healed.*
> Isaiah 53:5, emphasis added

The first pair of lines speaks of our sins using two synonymous terms, "transgressions" and "iniquities." The second pair of lines speaks of the positive results of the Servant's death, again using two synonymous terms, "well-being" (*shalom,* "peace") and "healed." It seems best to understand the second pair of lines to be speaking positively of the same blessing as the first pair: deliverance from sin.

This interpretation appears to be confirmed in 1 Peter 2:24, which says nothing about diseases but only of Christ bearing our *sins* on the cross. The word *healed* here clearly refers to healing from sin.

What, then, shall we say about a passage like Matthew 8:16–17, in which Jesus' healing people of physical sicknesses and diseases is said to be a fulfillment of Isaiah 53:4–5? I would suggest that the ambiguity of the words used in Isaiah is utilized by Matthew to make the point that Christ healed people physically as a way of showing that he had the power and the authority to heal people spiritually as well. This understanding of Matthew

8:16–17 is confirmed in the very next chapter, where Jesus forgives the paralytic's sins and then heals his body to prove "that the Son of Man has authority on earth to forgive sins" (9:1–7, citing v. 6). In other words, Jesus healed everyone who came to him for physical healing as a way of encouraging them (and us) to believe that anyone who comes to him for spiritual healing will find it.

Thus, I do not deny that Isaiah 53:5 implies that one of the blessings that can come from Christ is the removal of sickness. I would simply suggest that Christ does this in different ways and to differing extents at different times. Christ gave physical healing to all who came to him while he was on earth in his own physical body. Those whom he healed in this way, however, did not receive permanent health—their bodies were still weak, corruptible, natural, mortal bodies. In the resurrection, Christ will give all who in this life believed in him glorified, immortal, incorruptible, supernatural bodies that will never be sick or infirm again. Between Christ's resurrection in A.D. 33 and our future resurrection, Christ grants physical healing as he chooses to give us a foretaste of the perfect health we will enjoy only in the resurrection.

Christ's death on the cross has to do primarily with releasing us from the punishment due our sins. However, one of the implications of that redemption is that ultimately we will be freed from the consequences of sin, including sickness. Jesus foreshadowed this ultimate redemption and symbolically presented himself as the Suffering Servant by healing everyone who had faith in him. But this does not mean that healing is available *now* to *anyone* who "claims" it on the basis of Christ's redemptive work.

Praying for Reign

Kenneth Hagin and other Word-Faith teachers understand Paul in Romans 5:17 to be saying that Christians are to "reign in life" now. Christ's redeeming death has freed us from the devil's dominion, and consequently we should not allow the devil to continue destroying our lives.

It should be pointed out, first of all, that Paul says that we "*will* reign in life" through Christ—not that we are reigning *now*. Paul goes on in the next chapter to exhort Christians not to let *sin* reign in our mortal bodies. Nothing is said about not letting *sickness* reign in them (6:12–13).

In his epistle to the Corinthians, Paul mocks the Corinthian Christians who were claiming that they had already begun reigning. Paul notes that he and his associates were weak and going hungry, thirsty, poorly clothed, and homeless for Christ's sake (1 Cor. 4:8–13).

A helpful theological concept that would go a long way to correcting the Word-Faith teaching on this score is that of the tension between the "already" and the "not yet." This is a central theme in Paul's theology.[8] While Christ "gave Himself for our sins so that He might rescue us from this present evil age" (Gal. 1:4), we nevertheless find ourselves still living in it. We must therefore make an effort not to "be conformed to this age" (Rom. 12:2, literal translation). The life of God's Spirit is in us now, yet we are still mortal (Rom. 8:9–11). The Word-Faith doctrine, in its insistence that we are to reign now, glosses over this important tension in biblical theology.

Promises, Promises

Finally, we will consider a number of texts that Word-Faith teachers use to prove that health and wealth are guaranteed to God's people if they speak words of faith.

Live Long and Prosper (3 John 2)

One of the more popular such proof texts is the apostle John's prayer for his friend Gaius: "That in all respects you may prosper and be in good health, just as your soul prospers" (3 John 2). There is certainly nothing wrong with praying for people to be prosperous and healthy. But it must be pointed out that John does not say that his prayer will be certainly and immediately answered. John is, after all, praying for someone else, not for himself. Even on Word-Faith grounds—or perhaps especially on Word-Faith grounds—it is difficult to see how John's prayer could guarantee Gaius's health and wealth.

Of course, the fact that John prayed in this matter shows that he believed Gaius's prosperity and health was up to God, not up to Gaius! John did not tell Gaius to claim his health and prosperity.

The Hundredfold Blessing (Mark 10:29–30)

A text that enjoys wide use by teachers emphasizing financial prosperity is Mark 10:29–30. In that text Jesus told his disciples:

"Truly I say to you, there is no one who has left house or brothers or sisters or mother or father or children or farms, for My sake and for the gospel's sake, but that he will receive a hundred times as much now in the present age, houses and brothers and sisters and mothers and children and farms, along with persecutions; and in the age to come, eternal life."

Jesus certainly did not mean that if you left your house to follow him, you would literally receive a hundred houses; or that if a man left his mother to follow Christ, he would receive a hundred mothers! What Jesus is saying is something like this: If it becomes necessary to leave behind one's property or blood relatives to follow Christ (as it literally was for the Twelve, and as it sometimes is for his followers today), the believer doing so will find himself part of a much larger "family." That family is the church, whose people will be for him brothers, sisters, mothers, fathers, and children, and who will open their homes to him and feed him from their fields. This is the experience of faithful itinerant evangelists and foreign missionaries throughout the centuries.

God Is the Healer (Psalm 103:2–3; 107:20)

Next, let's consider two texts from the Psalms. In Psalm 103:2–3 David is reminding himself that God is the one who forgives all his sins and heals all his diseases. It's not at all clear that this is a blanket promise that God will heal all of the diseases of all believers through all history. In the very next verse, David reminds himself that God "redeems your life from the pit" (v. 4), but this certainly is not a guarantee that God will never let David die. Again, eventually God will "heal" all believers of every disease or infirmity by raising them from the dead with perfect bodies. In the meantime, every healing we do experience, whether natural or supernatural, is a blessing from God.

In Psalm 107:20 a very different point is being made. The psalmist is speaking of men who rebelled against God and who "suffered affliction because of their iniquities" (NIV), and as a result came near to dying (v. 18). Then they cried out to God and he saved them from this untimely death (v. 19). There is no blanket promise here of physical healing for everyone regardless of circumstances.

The Patience of Job (James 5:10–11)

We turn finally to James 5:10–18, a major passage for the doctrines of faith and healing. We look first at James's comments about Job, the Old Testament saint who suffered greatly although he was righteous. The Word-Faith claim that persons living by faith may experience "sufferings" but not "sicknesses" does not fit Job's case, since his sickness was a major part of his "sufferings" (vv. 10–11). Not surprisingly, for many Word-Faith teachers Job was actually an example of unbelief. James, however, does not agree with that assessment. Rather, Job is an example of the endurance (v. 11) that is the mark of true faith (compare James 1:3–4).

We might explain briefly why the Book of Job cannot be fairly interpreted to teach that Job brought his miseries on himself. After Job said, "The LORD gave and the LORD has taken away," and "Shall we indeed accept good from God and not accept adversity?" we are told that Job *did not sin in anything he had said* (Job 1:21–22; 2:10). Thus, the claim that Job had brought his suffering on himself because of a "negative confession" cannot be sustained. It is true that in Job 3:25, Job said that what he had feared would happen to him had occurred. However, nothing is said to suggest that his fear was in any way the cause of his suffering.

It is true that *after* his friends had tried to explain his suffering, Job became self-righteous and eventually had to repent of his arrogance (40:3–5; 42:1–6). But then God told Job's friends that they had not spoken of him what was right as Job had (42:7). Since Job's friends had argued that Job had brought his suffering on himself because of his sin, again that idea is proved false.

A Dozen Things James Does **Not** Teach about Healing

We come finally to what may be the most important passage in the New Testament dealing with healing. What is perhaps surprising about this passage is what James does *not* teach about healing. Virtually every aspect of the contemporary Word-Faith movement's approach to healing is undermined if not outright contradicted by James.

1. There are no *itinerant healing ministries* in James. The elders are called to the bedside of the sick (v. 14); the sick are not called to the tents of the healer. Of course, it is true that there were itinerant Christian ministers in the first century who were gifted to heal. However, all the ones that we know of were *apostles*. So far as I can determine, there is no biblical basis for itinerant healing ministries in the New Testament.

2. There are no *gifted healers in the congregation* in James. Again, it is the elders, without distinction, that are to be called (v. 14). Evidently people with gifts of healing were not common. Paul does mention such persons in one epistle (1 Cor. 12:9, 30), but he does not elaborate at all on their ministry.

3. There are no *healing services* in James, since again the elders are called to the bedside of the sick. The practice of scheduling "healing services" or other meetings in which people are promised that healings will occur is utterly without basis in the New Testament. It implies that one can "book" the Holy Spirit to come perform miracles. Of course, holding meetings in

which Christians pray for one another's healing is a perfectly legitimate practice (James 5:16).

4. The elders do not *command the sickness to leave* in James. Instead, the elders are to pray to the Lord (v. 14).

5. It is apparently not necessary to perform *healing by laying on of hands*. The apostles did this in the Book of Acts, but the elders are not instructed to do so. Laying on hands as a gesture of love and concern for the sick is fine; laying on hands as a sign of supposed authority to heal is without biblical basis unless the person is a prophet or apostle.

6. It is false *that all sickness is the result of sin*. Note again the example of Job discussed previously (vv. 10–11). It is true enough that *some* sickness may be the result of sin (as vv. 15–16 may imply), but not *all* sickness. James says "and *if* he has committed sins," implying that he might not have committed sins. We may not always be able to make a connection between sickness and some specific sin. Sickness, then, may be a consequence of sin (cf. John 5:14), but it need not be (John 9:1–3). The Lord has a purpose *(telos)* in everything, even in suffering and sickness (James 5:11b). Sins may be relevant for at least three reasons:

- Sin may directly cause sickness; for example, drug abuse directly damaging the body.
- Sickness may be a divine alarm meant to stop the sinner in his tracks and bring him to repentance.
- The sickness itself may not be related directly or indirectly to any personal sin, but it gives the person the opportunity to lie quietly and reflect on his life and to confess sinful shortcomings.

7. It is false *that sickness is always the result of a demon*. It may in some sense and in some cases be from the devil (Job's afflictions were indirectly the work of the devil), but even then it is going too far to attribute all or even most sickness to the invasion of a demon. Thus James tells us that the elders should pray for healing, not cast out a demon.

8. It is false *that Christians should rely on prayer and faith instead of medical means of treatment*. Nothing in the text implies such a thing.

At this point we should comment on the Word-Faith teachers' view on the matter of seeking medical help. Officially, as it were, the leading Word-Faith teachers do not tell people that they should not seek medical help. However, "unofficially," the Word-Faith doctrine encourages people to try to experience healing without going to a doctor or using medications. Take, for instance, the following statement by Hagin:

The last headache I had was in August 1933, but don't misunderstand me: I'm not opposed to doctors. Thank God for them. Medical science will help people as much as it can. If I'd have needed to go to a doctor in the past half century, I would have gone—but I haven't needed to. I've sent other people to the doctor, however, paid their bills, and bought their medicine. (Doctors often can keep people alive until we can get enough Word in them to get them healed.)[9]

It should be obvious what statements like the last sentence quoted above imply. The Christian who takes Hagin's teachings seriously as the truth will want to try to live without medical help to prove that they have "enough Word in them." Thus, despite comments endorsing the legitimacy of medicine, the thrust of the Word-Faith teaching is such that it discourages Christians from seeking medical attention when they have health problems.

9. It is false *that one's healing is always dependent on one's own faith*. In James it is the elders whose prayer of faith is the instrument of God's healing, not the prayer of the sick person. Of course, he should pray for himself as well (v. 13).

10. It is also false *that perfect character and faith are necessary for the prayer to be answered*. James denies this when he holds up as an example of an effective prayer that of Elijah, "a man with a nature like ours" (v. 17). Elijah's life was filled with spiritual ups and downs, but he was right with God, and he knew it, and that made his prayers effective.

11. It is false *that healing is always God's will*. James does not address this idea explicitly, but his answer is already implicit in 4:15. By "the prayer offered in faith" James does not mean a prayer that assumes without question that healing will take place. Rather, he means a prayer that is characterized by unwavering trust in God, confidence in his love and care for us—a prayer that is unwavering and unselfish in wanting whatever God wants.

How do we know this is what James meant? Because this is how he describes faith elsewhere (James 1:6–8; 4:3). James is saying that prayers for the sick are to be offered by elders of the church with their trust in God. As a rule God responds to such prayers of faith by making the person well. But this does not mean that healing is always God's will, for two reasons.

First of all, we will die from our last sickness, if something else doesn't kill us first. James has already said that we cannot know whether we will even live tomorrow (4:14).

Also, James is discussing only one scenario involving a need for healing, that of a bedridden Christian suffering from a sickness. He does not discuss persons with sickness who can leave their house, or persons who are blind or missing an arm. Thus James's statement cannot be generalized to mean that healing is always God's will.

12. It is false *that God's healing in response to prayer is always overtly miraculous*. It may be, but it need not; the passage says nothing about how they

will be healed, or whether it will be instantaneous or gradual. B.B. Warfield[10] compares this passage to James 1:5, where the Christian is told to pray for wisdom: James does not mean that we must wait for wisdom to be dropped into our heads! All healing, being good, comes from God (compare James 1:17).

Healing the Divide

Everyone talks about finding a "balance" in controversies of this nature, but of course everyone has his or her own idea as to what the right balance is. The table below represents one person's attempt to strike a balance on some of the matters discussed in this chapter.

In setting forth this analysis of the extremes, I must admit that I find some extremes less troubling than other extremes. For example, forced to choose between the extreme of denying that miracles occur today and the extreme of affirming that miracles should be a regular part of every Christian's experience, I would without hesitation choose the former over the latter. The reason for this preference is simple: Scripture contains dire warnings against errors associated with the latter error but says little or nothing against the former error. Jesus and the apostles warned about false prophets and false Messiahs performing apparent miracles so as to mislead people (Matt. 7:15, 22; 24:24; 2 Thess. 2:9). On the other hand, there are no warnings at all in the New Testament about a miracle-free Christianity.

Formalism	In Search of Balance	Fanaticism
No healing in the atonement	Healing in the atonement realized in part now, in full in the resurrection	Healing in full now guaranteed by the atonement
God wants Christians to be poor	God wants Christians to be faithful; in some cases this means rich, in some cases poor	God wants Christians to be rich
God does not do miracles today	God does miracles today, but they cannot be predicted and should not be expected	Miracles should be a regular part of the Christian experience today
Sickness has no relation to sin or unbelief	Some sickness is related to sin or unbelief	All sin is related to sin or unbelief

Fortunately, we do not need to choose between the two extremes. We can—and should—affirm the reality of the overtly supernatural as a factor in God's dealings in the world today, while recognizing that the primary way in which God works today—and has throughout church history—is by the supreme miracle of changing people's hearts.

Conclusion
By Their Fruits

Faithful are the wounds of a friend,
But deceitful are the kisses of an enemy.

Proverbs 27:6

But the fruit of the Spirit is love, joy, peace, patience, kindness, goodness, faithfulness, gentleness, self-control; against such things there is no law. Now those who belong to Christ Jesus have crucified the flesh with its passions and desires.

If we live by the Spirit, let us also walk by the Spirit. Let us not become boastful, challenging one another, envying one another.

Brethren, even if anyone is caught in any trespass, you who are spiritual, restore such a one in a spirit of gentleness; each one looking to yourself, so that you too will not be tempted. Bear one another's burdens, and thereby fulfill the law of Christ. For if anyone thinks he is something when he is nothing, he deceives himself. But each one must examine his own work, and then he will have reason for boasting in regard to himself alone, and not in regard to another.

Galatians 5:22–6:4

In this book I have concentrated on providing an analysis of what I have called the "roots" and the "shoots" of the Word-Faith movement—its origins and doctrinal ideas. In this concluding chapter, I will discuss the question of the "fruits" of the movement—the practical results of the movement's teachings—and offer an assessment of the movement's theological orthodoxy.

Checking the Fruit

A definitive scholarly analysis of the practical effects of the Word-Faith movement would involve a thorough sociological study of the movement's people and institutions. Such a study is rather beyond my competency and the scope of this book. However, I can offer some guiding principles for assessing the fruit of the movement, as well as some preliminary assessments based on the information available to me.

Claims of Good Fruit

Various kinds of good fruit have been suggested as providing positive evidence in support of the validity of the Word-Faith movement. In my opinion, none of these offer convincing or even plausible evidence supporting the movement's claims.

One such type of fruit consists of the testimonies of healing or of prosperity experienced by persons involved in the movement. As I noted earlier in the book, Jesus explicitly warned against viewing miracles—which would obviously include miracles of healing—as good fruit (Matt. 7:20–23). And even though I would not regard Jesus' warnings about material riches (Luke 6:24–25; 12:15–34; 16:13–14, 19–31; 18:22–30) as generalizations condemning all wealth, I certainly think they prove that wealth is no evidence of righteousness!

There are good reasons for skepticism about the value of healing and prosperity testimonies in the Word-Faith movement. If thousands upon thousands of cases of dramatic healings were being reported each year, that would be good cause for at least taking the movement's claims seriously. But the trickle of testimonies reported by the major ministries is no more than we would normally expect without any miraculous element.

Think of it this way. Suppose thirty thousand people pack a convention center to hear Benny Hinn. Many of these people will come in the hope of obtaining healing. Let us suppose for the sake of illustration that 1 percent of the attendees have serious diseases or infirmities from which they want relief. (The number is presumably higher.) Out of those three hundred people, if nothing at all happens out of the ordinary, a good many of them will get better. For example, some people with cancer will have it go into remission. The point is that out of that crowd of thirty thousand, what would really be surprising would be if no one left feeling significantly better!

If healing ministries are to make even a credible case for themselves on the basis of results, those results must be significantly higher than what we would otherwise expect on the basis of the statistical probabilities. From what I can tell, none of the faith-healing ministries of the modern era can pass such a test.

Please understand that I am *not* denying that some people have received remarkable, even miraculous healing when attending a Benny Hinn crusade or when watching Kenneth Copeland or Fred Price on TBN. There certainly is no law that says that God can't heal people in those situations. But it would be a terrible mistake to infer from the scattering of apparent healings in such contexts that God has put his seal of approval on these ministries.

An equally valueless type of "fruit" is the explosive growth of Word-Faith ministries. There is no denying that these organizations have enjoyed numerically measurable successes. Millions of viewers tune in to watch Word-Faith televangelists and then send millions of dollars into their ministry organizations to keep them broadcasting. Word-Faith books occupy a significant place in most Christian bookstores across America. But the financial and numerical successes of these organizations prove nothing about the truth of their teachings or the validity of their ministries. After all, Mormonism is growing much faster; Roman Catholicism is still much bigger; and some anticharismatic evangelical ministries are also very successful. I very much want good ministries to succeed, and I do not count a ministry's success *against* it; but neither do I think it counts as evidence in its favor.

A much better type of fruit would be souls won to Christ through the ministry of Word-Faith teachers or churches. I have no hard information on this matter, but I freely concede that people have been won to faith in Christ through the ministries of the teachers whose theology has been criticized in this book. But in addition to some concerns that I will raise on the "debit" side shortly, I would advise caution about assuming that the winning of souls *in* the movement is a validation *of* the movement. After all, souls are won to Christ by anticharismatics too! We may rejoice that God uses even bad or false teachers to bring people to salvation without excusing their poor or heretical teaching. Only if there was evidence of *extraordinary* numbers of people coming to faith in Christ through Word-Faith ministries would such conversions be legitimately viewed as evidence of God's blessing and validation on the movement.

Undeniable Bad Fruit

In my opinion there is substantial evidence of bad fruit emerging from the Word-Faith movement. The many different kinds of bad fruit that I will identify do not characterize all of the people in the Word-Faith movement or all of its organizations or institutions. However, these problems plague the movement as a whole to such an extent that I cannot see how a positive assessment of the movement's fruit can be justified.

Keep in mind here that in what follows I will be assuming that the distinctive teachings of the Word-Faith movement are false. These criticisms are presented, not to prove that the teachings are false (that has been shown from Scripture) but to show that these false teachings have negative consequences.

1. *Division in the church (Rom. 16:17).* Word-Faith teaching has sparked heated divisions not only among evangelical Christians generally but also within charismatic and Pentecostal circles. Whole churches have been split over the issue. Of course in all divisions there are two sides. However, the New Testament is quite clear as to who receives the blame in cases of doctrinal division: the false teachers (Rom. 16:17). If, as we have argued, the Word-Faith teaching is false—if it inculcates erroneous ideas about God and a distorted view of the Christian life—then the divisiveness of the issue must be charged to the account of those who promote that false teaching.

2. *Self-centered spirituality (Rom. 16:18; 1 Tim. 6:9–10, 17).* At their best, the Word-Faith teachers encourage their supporters to pursue health and prosperity not for selfish reasons but as means to facilitate ministry. But there is no getting around the fact that these teachers also encourage people to pursue faith as a means to their own ends. What else are we to say about books and booklets with titles such as John Avanzini's *The Wealth of the Wicked: Yours for the Taking,* Kenneth Hagin's *How to Write Your Own Ticket with God,* Rex Humbard's *Your Key to God's Bank,* E. W. Kenyon's *Sign Posts on the Road to Success,* and T. L. Osborn's *How to Have the Good Life?*

By no means is the Word-Faith movement alone troubled by self-centeredness. That is an aspect of the sinful disposition of all people, which all of us need to overcome. But the problem here is that Word-Faith theology clearly encourages such self-centeredness. The teaching that you can have what you say if you simply learn to think and speak according to the formula of faith cannot avoid appealing to people who want something for themselves.

Although most of the well-known critics of the Word-Faith teaching have tended to exaggerate the point, there is also no denying that at times the leading teachers in the movement have made cross appeals to people's self-interests. The fund-raising tactics of the major Word-Faith ministries, especially the televangelists, are notorious.

3. *Acceptance of false prophecies (1 Thess. 5:20–22).* Most of the Word-Faith teachers claim to speak prophetically, and several of them have said things under the guise of prophecy or "revelation knowledge" that are just plain false. Yet their followers uncritically accept these prophecies at face value as revelations from God.

4. *General lack of discernment (1 Tim. 1:7).* On the positive side, it must be acknowledged that the Word-Faith teachers constantly tell their followers to check out their teachings in the Bible. But this process, where it goes on at all, evidently occurs on such a superficial level that no real critical discernment is exercised. On the negative side, the Word-Faith teachers' claims to be prophets and apostles, to have regular conversations and private Bible studies with Jesus and the Holy Spirit, and to be God's "anointed" (who must not be "touched") all have the effect of discouraging discernment.

My own experience in talking with people in the movement is that they consistently make excuses for their leaders' more egregious errors and fail to see the real problems in Word-Faith teaching. The parade of guests who are featured on Paul and Jan Crouch's TBN programming runs the gamut from the serious, sound Christian thinkers and ministers to the superficial, silly, and outright heretical. How many viewers can tell the difference? How many care to try? Spiritual gullibility is widespread throughout our culture, of course, but the Word-Faith movement is part of the problem, not part of the solution.

5. *Anti-intellectualism (Mark 12:30).* Closely related to the lack of discernment is a general anti-intellectualism that characterizes the Word-Faith movement. Here my biggest problem is not convincing Word-Faith adherents of the truth of my claim but rather proving to them that it is a problem! When Jesus, in quoting the Greatest Commandment (Deut. 6:4–5), stated that we are to love God with our whole *mind* (Mark 12:30), I take this to mean that we ought to consecrate our intellect to the study and advocacy of the truth. The constant denigration of reason by the Word-Faith teachers, as they argue that the Word of God can actually contradict reason, encourages people to suspend their critical reasoning and accept whatever sounds good or makes them feel good.

6. *Spiritual and doctrinal arrogance and elitism (1 John 2:20, 27).* To observers on the outside, one of the most disturbing things about Word-Faith ministers is the sheer arrogance of the claims they make. The bottom line here is that people like Hagin, Copeland, and Price tell us that they have developed their faith to such an extent that they experience the miraculous all the time. They expect us to believe that the reason they are prosperous and healthy (so they tell us, at any rate) is that they know how to get what they want from God—and the rest of us don't. If there was clear evidence from Scripture that their teachings were true—and significant evidence for the success of their teachings—it would be reasonable to accept their claims. But given that their teachings are in error, and given the lack of hard evidence that their teachings really work "as advertised," their claims to have achieved such heights of spiritual power must be viewed as either insincere or displays of blind arrogance.

7. *Discouragement of Christians' faith (2 Tim. 2:18).* The spiritual elitism of the Word-Faith teachers in presenting themselves as spiritual success stories to be imitated can and has resulted in discouraging many Christians' faith. It is devastating to think that you can overcome financial difficulties or become free of a debilitating disease if you follow these teachers' examples and prescriptions, only to find that they often don't work. Just as I do not have hard figures for the number of people converted to faith in Christ through Word-Faith ministries, I also do not have hard figures for the number of people who have given up on Christianity because the Word-Faith version of it didn't pan out. But we all know that such people exist.

8. *Testimonies of people dying due to the Word-Faith error (Prov. 3:13–16).* When children of members of the Christian Science cult die from lack of treatment, most of us recognize such an occurrence as devastating proof that Christian Science is a false religion. I do not know how we can avoid making similar judgments about Word-Faith churches where members die because they are trying to put the message into practice.

9. *Diversion of Christians from sound teaching and growth (1 Tim. 1:3–7).* Think of all the time and resources that have been diverted from teaching Christians sound theology to promote the Word-Faith doctrines. Millions of Christians in America and around the world are biblically and theologically illiterate. In every Sunday school class I have headed for the past ten years, I have surprised my class by asking them to write out the Ten Commandments from memory. Most can't come up with five. Again, this problem is pandemic throughout the church, but the Word-Faith movement exacerbates the problem.

10. *Unnecessary embarrassment to the church (Rom. 2:24).* There is no need for us to be embarrassed by the true gospel, even though the world will say all sorts of mean and false things about us because of it. But do we need to give the world an excuse to ridicule Christianity and hold it up to contempt? I'm afraid that is what the "health and wealth" preachers do.

I realize that advocates of the Word-Faith teaching will regard this list of ten negative consequences of that teaching as an attack. I would only invite those who may be offended by this list to do what, in my better moments, I try to do when I feel I have been unjustly criticized. Look at the criticisms and consider whether some of them might not have some merit. Ask yourself—and ask God in prayer—whether some of these criticisms might not apply to you, to your church, or to a Word-Faith ministry that you are supporting.

Christian or Cultic?

We come to the point of discernment. Throughout this book I have interacted critically both with the Word-Faith teachers and with their most strident critics. I have tried to point out where the critics have caricatured or misunderstood the Word-Faith position. I have also stated plainly where I think the Word-Faith position is unbiblical. As I explained at the beginning of the book, my opinion is that no simple, unqualified assessment of the movement as soundly Christian or thoroughly cultic can be justified. In concluding this book, I will review the evidence for that opinion and state how I think the movement should be viewed.

Factors Making Assessment Difficult

Some factors, when taken sufficiently into consideration, make sweeping generalizations or a simple "thumbs-up" or "thumbs-down" approach to the Word-Faith movement difficult if not impossible.

First of all, there is some significant diversity of beliefs within the Word-Faith movement. One of the reasons for this diversity is the tendency in a movement claiming to be on the spiritual cutting edge to give rise to individuals making more and more outlandish claims. Thus, Kenneth Hagin takes matters to a more extreme point than E. W. Kenyon did, and in turn Kenneth Copeland has taken Hagin's ideas and pushed them further than Hagin seems willing to go.

Another factor making a simple assessment problematic is the general lack of clarity and consistency in teaching. What do the Word-Faith teachers mean when they talk about Jesus taking on "Satan's nature"? Most of the time, they offer no clear explanation of what they mean.

It is natural for critics to construe the Word-Faith doctrine in the worst possible light and for defenders of the doctrine to construe it in the best possible light. Unfortunately, both approaches tend to add to the confusion. If I must err, I will try to err on the side of viewing the Word-Faith doctrine too sympathetically. But the ideal is to see the doctrine for what it really is. I do not pretend to have done this perfectly. I do, though, entertain the hope that I have done so better than previous critics.

Defense of an "Aberrant" Classification

Back in the 1980s, in concert with other researchers at the Christian Research Institute (when it was still headed by Walter Martin), I developed a formal set of definitions and criteria for differentiating between orthodox and heretical doctrine. In formulating these distinctions, some doctrines clearly did not fit neatly into either category. We used a variety of terms at CRI for such doctrines, the main one being *aberrant* or *aberrational.* Closely related terms include *heterodox, suborthodox,* and *unsound.* The point of having all these terms is that some doctrinal systems are neither fully orthodox nor fully heretical. In early 1992 (ironically, at the very time that I was leaving CRI), I published a book[1] that discussed the use of these terms and outlined a case for making such judgments in the spirit of speaking the truth in love (Eph. 4:15).

Since 1987 I have maintained that the Word-Faith movement as a whole should be classified as aberrant or suborthodox, while at the same time recognizing that at least some of the leading teachers of the movement do teach heresy.[2] I still hold this opinion; let me explain why.

First of all, *none of the Word-Faith teachers explicitly rejects orthodox doctrine.* This fact does not automatically clear them of heresy, but it does place a significant burden of proof on those who would make that charge. To my knowledge, for example, no Word-Faith teacher has denied the Trinity or salvation by grace. In the absence of clear evidence that their doctrines directly overthrow orthodox essentials, I think we must hold back from pronouncing a movement or an individual as heretical, at least without qualification.

Second, *the Word-Faith teachers at times affirm orthodox doctrine.* That is, one can find in their writings, sermons, television broadcasts, and conference speeches affirmations of the basic doctrines of orthodoxy. They all clearly affirm the virgin birth, Christ's sinless life, his physical death, bodily resurrection, and second coming. They all affirm salvation by grace alone through faith in Jesus Christ alone. Certainly there is a substantial body of orthodox truth present in the teaching of the Word-Faith movement.

Third, as I argued at length in the early chapters of this book, *the Word-Faith movement is a radical wing of an orthodox tradition.* If you regard the evangelical faith-cure tradition of the nineteenth century and the (trinitarian) Pentecostal tradition of the twentieth century as orthodox Christian traditions, then I think you have to concede that the Word-Faith movement is at least rooted in orthodoxy. But I hasten to note that this fact alone does not guarantee the movement's orthodoxy. Oneness Pentecostalism is, I would maintain, a sobering case in point. Despite its origins within early Pentecostalism, the Oneness tradition has developed into a religious system that openly and vehemently rejects the doctrine of the Trinity.

Fourth, *the Word-Faith movement teaches patently unbiblical ideas about the nature of God, the nature of human beings, and the person and redemptive work of Jesus Christ.* If the errors of the movement were restricted to its presumptuous and extreme views of health and wealth, I think we would have to regard it as fanatical but not heretical. If it taught erroneous doctrines about secondary theological issues such as the timing of the rapture or the validity of speaking in tongues today, such errors would not disqualify them from being considered soundly orthodox.

On the other hand, to teach significant errors about the nature of God, such as the idea that God has a body or that he must speak words of faith to get anything done, places the movement's orthodoxy in serious question. To teach that human beings are exact duplicates of God and have the capacity to create physical realities by speaking them into existence in the same way that God created the world is to teach a false doctrine that seriously undermines the basic biblical distinction between Creator and creature. To teach that Jesus died spiritually to complete our salvation, and to teach that Christians are just as much incarnations of God as was Jesus, is flagrant error on such central issues as to threaten the very integrity of the faith of those who believe such error.

Fifth, *some of the Word-Faith teachers have espoused blatantly heretical and even blasphemous ideas.* Try as I might, I cannot see how the teaching of Copeland and Capps is compatible with an orthodox doctrine of the person of Christ. Specifically, as we have seen, Copeland and Capps teach that the "Word" that "became flesh" in Jesus of Nazareth (John 1:14) was the word of faith that God confessed about becoming incarnate, a word that Mary herself had to confess in order for Jesus to be conceived. This teaching flatly contradicts the orthodox and biblical teaching that the Word was a divine person preexisting with the Father before creation (John 1:1–2), the eternal Son of God. Moreover, I have not found any evidence to show that Copeland or Capps elsewhere clearly affirms an orthodox, trinitarian view of Jesus as the preexistent, personal Son of God. In short, there seems to be no way of avoiding the conclusion that these two Word-Faith teachers, at least, are guilty of teaching heresy.

Finally, as we argued in the first part of this chapter, *the Word-Faith teaching is demonstrably detrimental to a sound Christian life,* though in varying degrees. While the rank and file of people following the Word-Faith teachers appear to be Christians, there is every reason to conclude that the integrity and maturation of their Christian life is severely undermined by the false teachings and claims of the movement's teachers.

In light of the above six considerations, I believe that we should draw the following conclusions about the Word-Faith movement.

1. The movement as a whole is suborthodox and aberrant. By *suborthodox* I mean that its teachings in certain crucial respects fall below the standards of orthodoxy. By *aberrant* I mean that its teachings in other respects deviate from orthodoxy in ways difficult to classify easily. The doctrine that God has a spirit body is an example of a suborthodox view. The doctrine that full healing is guaranteed in this life in the atonement I would classify as aberrant.

2. Some of the teachers in the movement, as well as on its fringes, are clearly teaching heresy. This would be my assessment of the theologies of Kenneth Copeland, Charles Capps, and Earl Paulk (the last of whom is on the fringes of the movement).

3. Many of the Christians who participate in the movement are ortho-dox, if theologically uninformed. My own experience of talking to people in the Word-Faith movement is that many, if not most, of them do not believe the heretical and near-heretical ideas espoused by the leaders. For example, I have yet to meet a member of a Word-Faith church, or a devo-tee of a particular Word-Faith teacher, who agreed with Copeland's view of Jesus as having been positively confessed into existence. Typically such persons find it difficult to accept that their favorite teacher espouses such ideas.

4. The Word-Faith movement should not be described as cultic. As bad as some of the teaching is in the Word-Faith movement, this movement simply does not belong in the category of cults along with the Jehovah's Witnesses, Mormons, and Christian Science. When heretics are found within a Christian tradition, it is not correct to label the whole tradition or movement cultic. For example, in my estimation the ultraliberal Episcopal bishop John Shelby Spong is an outright heretic, but that does not make the Episcopal church (which regrettably tolerates him) a cult.

To those who have read this book and find themselves disagreeing with its assessment—whether you think it is too harsh or not harsh enough—I hope that this book can be at least a catalyst for dialogue. Out of disagree-ment can come mutual enlightenment if the parties are willing to listen and learn from one another. There are many aspects of "the Word-Faith controversy" that could not be thoroughly explored here. What I have tried to do is move the debate forward in a more constructive manner. If it helps to further such constructive debate, I will be satisfied.

Notes

Introduction:
The War of the Words

1. Hank Hanegraaff, *Christianity in Crisis* (Eugene, Ore: Harvest House, 1993), 10, 14.

2. Benny Hinn, "Miracle Invasion Rally," Anaheim Convention Center, 22 November 1991, cited in Hanegraaff, *Christianity in Crisis*, 336.

3. Kenneth E. Hagin, *Understanding the Anointing* (Tulsa: Kenneth Hagin Ministries—Faith Library Publications, 1983), 4–6.

4. Kenneth Copeland, "What Happened from the Cross to the Throne," tape #02-0017 (Fort Worth: Kenneth Copeland Ministries, 1990), side 1.

5. James R. Spencer, *Heresy Hunters: Character Assassination in the Church* (Lafayette, La.: Huntington House, 1993), xi.

6. Charles Capps, *Authority in Three Worlds* (Tulsa: Harrison House, 1982), 2.

7. Kenneth E. Hagin, *The Believer's Authority* (Tulsa: Kenneth Hagin Ministries, 1984), 30.

8. Frederick K. C. Price, "Prayer: Do You Know What Prayer Is . . . And How to Pray?" in *The Word Study Bible* (Tulsa: Harrison House, 1990), 1178, cited in Hanegraaff, *Christianity in Crisis*, 85.

9. Kenneth Copeland, TBN, 9 August 1987.

10. Kenneth Copeland, "Praise-a-thon," TBN, April 1988, cited in Hanegraaff, *Christianity in Crisis*, 125.

11. Benny Hinn, TBN, 13 October 1990.

12. Randy Frame, "Best-Selling Author Admits Mistakes, Vows Changes," *Christianity Today* (5 October 1991): 44.

13. Benny Hinn, "Praise the Lord," TBN, 23 October 1992.

14. Kenneth E. Hagin, *I Believe in Visions* (Old Tappan, N.J.: Revell, 1972), 115.

15. "Praise-a-thon," TBN, 8 November 1990.

16. Hinn, "Miracle Invasion Rally," cited in Hanegraaff, *Christianity in Crisis*, 336.

17. "Praise the Lord," TBN, 2 April 1991.

18. D. R. McConnell, *A Different Gospel: A Historical and Biblical Analysis of the Modern Faith Movement* (Peabody, Mass.: Hendrickson, 1988), xviii.

19. See, for example, Dave Hunt, *The Seduction of Christianity* (Eugene, Ore.: Harvest House, 1985), 88; this theme is sounded in many of Hunt's writings.

20. Judith Matta, *The Born-Again Jesus of the Word-Faith Teaching*, rev. ed. (Fullerton, Calif.: Spirit of Truth Ministry, 1987), viii.

21. Ibid., 130.

22. Albert James Dager, *Vengeance Is Ours: The Church in Dominion* (Redmond, Wash.: Sword, 1990), 25, 76.

23. Rod Rosenbladt, "Who Do TV Preachers Say That I Am?" in *The Agony of Deceit*, ed. Michael Horton (Chicago: Moody, 1990), 112.

24. John MacArthur, *Charismatic Chaos* (Grand Rapids: Zondervan, 1992), 290.

25. Hanegraaff, *Christianity in Crisis*, 10.

26. Ibid., 14.

27. For example, ibid., 27, 58, 63, 80, 108–10, 116, 175.

28. Ibid., 130.

29. Ibid., 41.

30. MacArthur, *Charismatic Chaos*, 268.

Chapter 1
Understanding the Word-Faith Teaching

1. Hanegraaff, *Christianity in Crisis*, 10, 14.

2. Kenneth E. Hagin, attachment to letter from Kenneth Hagin Jr. to Hank Hanegraaff, 4 January 1991.

3. The terminology "roots and fruits" has been used often; see Charles Farah, "A Critical Analysis: The 'Roots and Fruits' of Faith-Formula Theology," *Pneuma* 3 (spring 1981) 3–21.

4. William DeArteaga, *Quenching the Spirit: Discover the Real Spirit behind the Charismatic Controversy* (Lake Mary, Fla.: Creation House, 1996), 246. The book was originally published as *Quenching the Spirit: Examining Centuries of Opposition to the Moving of the Holy Spirit* (Lake Mary, Fla.: Creation House, 1992); the quotation is found on page 230 of this edition.

5. DeArteaga, *Quenching the Spirit* (1992 ed.), 18–20, 230; (1996 ed.), 18–20, 246.

6. McConnell, *Different Gospel*, 51–52.

7. DeArteaga, *Quenching the Spirit* (1992 ed.), 223–27; (1996 ed.), 236–39.

8. Ibid. (1992 ed.), 228–29; (1996 ed.), 244–45.

9. McConnell, *Different Gospel*, 7.

10. Ibid., 69.

11. Robert M. Bowman Jr., *Orthodoxy and Heresy: A Biblical Guide to Doctrinal Discernment* (Grand Rapids: Baker, 1991), 33–46.

12. See ibid., 37–39.

13. See ibid., 40–43.

14. Hanegraaff, *Christianity in Crisis*, 19–27.

15. Ibid., 17.

16. Ibid., 19–27.

17. A similar approach to describing the Word-Faith teaching was taken by Bruce Barron in his book *The Health and Wealth Gospel* (Downers Grove, Ill.: InterVarsity Press, 1987),

64–76. While Barron's doctrinal summation was incomplete, it was fair and accurate.

Chapter 2
The Man behind the Message

1. DeArteaga, *Quenching the Spirit* (1996 ed.), 218–19, 223; cf. (1992 ed.), 208, 212.

2. McConnell, *Different Gospel*, 50.

3. Ibid., 3–14.

4. Hanegraaff, *Christianity in Crisis*, 331.

5. DeArteaga, *Quenching the Spirit* (1992 ed.), 200; (1996 ed.), 212.

6. On Kenyon's life and thought, see especially Dale H. Simmons, *E. W. Kenyon and the Postbellum Pursuit of Peace, Power, and Plenty*, Studies in Evangelicalism 13 (Lanham, Md., and London: Scarecrow, 1997), especially 2–61. This is a revision of Simmons's 1988 Drew University dissertation. For other reviews of Kenyon's life and thought, see McConnell, *Different Gospel*, 30–56; DeArteaga, *Quenching the Spirit* (1996 ed.), 212–23.

7. See, for example, Kenneth E. Hagin, *Seven Vital Steps to Receiving the Holy Spirit*, 2d ed. (Tulsa: Kenneth Hagin Ministries, 1980); *How You Can Be Led by the Spirit of God*, 2d ed. (Tulsa: Kenneth Hagin Ministries, 1993). See also Norvel Hayes, *The Gift of Tongues and Interpretation of Tongues*, The Gifts of the Spirit 9 (Tulsa: Harrison House, 1980).

8. DeArteaga views the Word-Faith movement as charismatic, even though he argues that Kenyon, whom he regards as the father of the movement, was not Pentecostal; see DeArteaga, *Quenching the Spirit* (1996 ed.), 222–23. Kenyon died before the rise of what would be called the charismatic movement *per se*.

9. Charles Farah Jr., *From the Pinnacle of the Temple: Faith vs. Presumption* (Plainfield, N.J.: Logos International, 1979); Farah, "Critical Analysis" (1981).

10. Barron, *Health and Wealth Gospel*.

11. Bruce Barron, "Sick of Health and Wealth," a review of Hank Hanegraaff, *Christianity in Crisis*, in *Christianity Today* (22 November 1993): 27–28.

12. The two earliest writings I have found arguing that the roots of the Word-Faith doctrine are in the metaphysical cults are H. Ter-

ris Neuman, "An Analysis of the Sources of the Charismatic Teaching of 'Positive Confession'" (unpublished paper, Wheaton Graduate School, 1980); James S. Tinney, "The Prosperity Doctrine: An Accretion to Black Pentecostalism," *Evangelical Review of Theology* 4 (1980). Neuman updated his analysis in "Cultic Origins of Word-Faith Theology within the Charismatic Movement," *Pneuma* 12 (1990): 32–55.

13. Dave Hunt and T. A. MacMahon, *The Seduction of Christianity* (Eugene, Ore.: Harvest House, 1985), 150–54; Dave Hunt, *Beyond Seduction* (Eugene, Ore.: Harvest House, 1987), 51–66.

14. Hanegraaff, *Christianity in Crisis*, 29–30, 47–50, 67, 331.

15. Daniel R. McConnell, "The Kenyon Connection: A Theological and Historical Analysis of the Cultic Origins of the Faith Movement" (master's thesis, Oral Roberts University, 1982).

16. McConnell, *Different Gospel*, especially 15–56.

17. Curtis I. Crenshaw, *Man as God: The Word of Faith Movement* (Memphis: Footstool Publications, 1994), 11.

18. Robert Jackson, "Prosperity Theology and the Faith Movement," *Themelios* 15 (1989): 16.

19. Ibid., 17.

20. MacArthur, *Charismatic Chaos*; Word-Faith teachers figure on pages 10, 14–16, 24–26, 28–31, 49–50, 56–57, 83, 121–22, 152–61, 197–98, 204, in addition to the climactic chapter on health and wealth (264–90).

21. Ibid., 265.

22. Ibid., 289–290.

23. Ibid., 290.

24. Ibid., 291–292.

25. Simmons, *E. W. Kenyon*, xi.

26. Ibid., 304–5.

Chapter 3
A Metaphysical Mind-Set?

1. Hunt, *Beyond Seduction*, 58.

2. DeArteaga, *Quenching the Spirit* (1992 ed.), 239; (1996 ed.), 255.

3. Ibid. (1992 ed.), 203. The passage is reworded in the 1996 edition, but the idea is still acknowledged indirectly (214).

4. MacArthur, *Charismatic Chaos*, 290.

5. McConnell, *Different Gospel*, 25, emphasis in original.

6. John Kennington and Ern Baxter, quoted in ibid., 25–26.

7. E. W. Kenyon, *The Wonderful Name of Jesus* (reprint, Lynnwood, Wash.: Kenyon's Gospel Publishing Society, 1964), 69–70.

8. McConnell, "Kenyon Connection," 90; the first and last sentences are quoted in *Different Gospel*, 30.

9. Kenyon, *Wonderful Name of Jesus*, 70.

10. Kenyon, *The Hidden Man: The New Self. An Unveiling of the Subconscious Mind*, ed. Ruth A. Kenyon (Lynnwood, Wash.: Kenyon's Gospel Publishing Society, 1970), 35, quoted in McConnell, "Kenyon Connection," 103.

11. Kenyon, *Hidden Man*, 35.

12. E. W. Kenyon, *The Two Kinds of Life* (reprint, Lynnwood, Wash.: Kenyon's Gospel Publishing Society, 1971), 143. I owe this quotation to McConnell, *Different Gospel*, 15.

13. J. Stillson Judah, *The History and Philosophy of the Metaphysical Movements in America* (Philadelphia: Westminster Press, 1967), 12–19; Martin A. Larson, *New Thought Religion: A Philosophy for Health, Happiness, and Prosperity* (New York: Philosophical Library, 1987), 129–31; Charles S. Braden, *Spirits in Rebellion*, 9–11, 14–18. Judah's perspective is that of a historian seeking a balanced view; Larson's is that of an insider; and Braden's is that of a critic. These three each present a list of New Thought tenets, and the three lists overlap considerably.

14. McConnell, *Different Gospel*, 20.

15. Ibid., 51.

16. Ibid., chs. 6–10.

17. The metaphysical writer McConnell quotes most often is Ralph Waldo Trine (some thirty-two times). He quotes about thirteen times from Eddy and about twenty-one times from all other metaphysical writers.

18. See Neuman, "Cultic Origins of Word-Faith Theology," 33–44.

19. Ibid., 106.

20. Ibid., citing Mary Baker Eddy, *Science and Health with Key to the Scriptures* (Boston: Trustees, 1934), 274, 590.

21. Eddy, *Science and Health*, 475, 557.

22. E. W. Kenyon, *The Bible in the Light of Our Redemption: Basic Bible Course*, ed. Ruth A. Kenyon (Lynnwood, Wash.: Kenyon's Gospel Publishing Society, 1969), 18.

23. Compare DeArteaga, *Quenching the Spirit* (1992 ed.), 223–24; (1996 ed.), 236–37. I agree with DeArteaga that Kenyon was not a Gnostic, but I disagree with his claim that Kenyon's theology was faithfully based on the teachings of the apostle Paul.

24. McConnell, *Different Gospel*, 106–7.

25. E. W. Kenyon, *Two Kinds of Knowledge* (Lynnwood, Wash.: Kenyon's Gospel Publishing Society, 1966), 50–53.

26. E. W. Kenyon, *Identification: A Romance in Redemption* (Lynnwood, Wash.: Kenyon's Gospel Publishing Society, 1968), 52–54.

27. McConnell, *Different Gospel*, 107 n. 25–26.

28. Ralph Waldo Trine, *In Tune with the Infinite* (1897; reprint, New York: Bobbs-Merrill, 1970), 35–36, emphasis in original.

29. McConnell, *Different Gospel*, 51.

30. Ibid., 118.

31. Kenyon, *Two Kinds of Knowledge*, 22.

32. Eddy, *Science and Health*, 468.

33. Trine, *In Tune with the Infinite*, 46.

34. Kenyon, *Hidden Man*, 7.

35. Trine, *In Tune with the Infinite*, 16, emphasis in original.

36. Eddy, *Science and Health*, 330, cited in McConnell, *Different Gospel*, 120.

37. Kenyon, *Hidden Man*, 26, cited in McConnell, *Different Gospel*, 121.

38. McConnell, *Different Gospel*, 122, citing Trine, *In Tune with the Infinite*, 20 n. 49.

39. Ibid., n. 50.

40. Trine, *In Tune with the Infinite*, 20–21, emphasis in original.

41. McConnell, *Different Gospel*, 136.

42. On deism and pantheism, see especially Norman L. Geisler and William D. Watkins, *Worlds Apart: A Handbook on World Views*, 2d ed. (Grand Rapids: Baker, 1989), 75–106, 147–85.

43. Kenyon, *Two Kinds of Faith*, 20; *Hidden Man*, 35; cited in McConnell, *Different Gospel*, 135, 137.

44. McConnell, *Different Gospel*, 137.

45. Ibid.

46. Hanegraaff, *Christianity in Crisis*, 93. Hanegraaff does not reference McConnell's nearly identical statement.

47. Ibid., 111.

48. Kenyon, *Identification*, 15.

49. McConnell, *Different Gospel*, 150, citing both P. P. Quimby and Ralph Waldo Trine.

50. Ibid., 151–53.

51. Kenyon, *Jesus the Healer* (Lynnwood, Wash.: Kenyon's Gospel Publishing Society, 1968), 67, cited in McConnell, *Different Gospel*, 174.

52. McConnell repeats Ern Baxter's assertion that Kenyon "did not have biblical propositionalism as the basis of his faith" (*Different Gospel*, 26). However, no evidence to back up this assertion is offered from Kenyon's writings. It is obvious to anyone reading Kenyon that he took the Bible at face value as truth (however badly he misinterpreted it).

53. Kenyon, *Two Kinds of Faith*, 17, quoted in DeArteaga, *Quenching the Spirit* (1992 ed.), 204; (1996 ed.), 214–15.

54. See Kenyon, *The Bible in the Light of Redemption*, 13. Keep in mind that I am not saying that Kenyon's understanding of the Trinity was completely sound, but only that he accepted the doctrine of the Trinity as traditionally conceived.

Chapter 4
Kenyon's "Pentecostal" Context

1. McConnell, *Different Gospel* (1995 ed.), 204–5.

2. Simmons, *E. W. Kenyon*, 304.

3. Dale H. Simmons, "The Postbellum Pursuit of Peace, Power, and Plenty: As Seen in the Writings of Essek William Kenyon" (Ph.D. dissertation, Drew University, 1990).

4. Ibid., xiii.

5. DeArteaga, *Quenching the Spirit* (1996 ed.), 235–36, 319 n. 2. DeArteaga does not mention the fact that Simmons is highly criti-

cal of both the Higher Christian Life movement and Kenyon.

6. The historical facts discussed in this section have been presented in several other works. For a convenient summary, see Paul G. Chappell, "Healing Movements," in *Dictionary of Pentecostal and Charismatic Movements*, 353–74, especially 357–67. For even more detail see Chappell's Ph.D. dissertation, "The Divine Healing Movement in America" (Drew University, 1983). In addition, see Raymond J. Cunningham, "From Holiness to Healing: The Faith Cure in America, 1872– 1892," *Church History* 43 (1974): 499–513; DeArteaga, *Quenching the Spirit* (1996 ed.), 104–15; and Simmons, *E. W. Kenyon*, 17–23, 86–95, 152–64, 218–34.

7. See Phoebe Palmer, *The Devotional Writings of Phoebe Palmer* (New York: Garland, 1986); *Selected Writings of Phoebe Palmer*, ed. Thomas C. Oden (New York: Paulist Press, 1988). Works discussing her thought include DeArteaga, *Quenching the Spirit* (1996 ed.), 109–12; Harold E. Raser, *Phoebe Palmer: Her Life and Thought* (Lewiston, N.Y.: Edwin Mellen Press, 1987); Charles Edward White, *The Beauty of Holiness: Phoebe Palmer as Theologian, Revivalist, Feminist, and Humanitarian* (Grand Rapids: Francis Asbury Press, 1986).

8. An excellent introduction to the Keswick movement and its teaching is Steven Barabas, *So Great Salvation: The History and Message of the Keswick Convention* (Westwood, N.J.: Revell, 1952). For a brief article on the subject, see D. D. Bundy, "Keswick Higher Life Movement," in *Dictionary of Pentecostal and Charismatic Movements*, 518–19.

9. Chappell, "Healing Movements," 358.

10. George Müller, *The Life of Trust: Being a Narrative of the Lord's Dealings with George Müller*, introduction and concluding chapter by J. R. Miller (New York: Thomas Y. Crowell, 1898).

11. Chappell, "Healing Movements," 359.

12. See Ernest B. Gordon, *Adoniram Judson Gordon: A Biography with Letters and Illustrative Extracts Drawn from Unpublished or Uncollected Sermons and Addresses* (New York: Revell, 1896); Russell C. Allyn, "Adoniram Judson Gordon: Nineteenth-Century Fundamentalist," *American Baptist Quarterly* 4 (1985): 61–89.

13. See A. J. Gordon, *The Ministry of Healing: Or, Miracles of Cure in All Ages*, 2d ed. (1882; reprint, Harrisburg, Pa.: Christian Publications, 1961).

14. Edith L. Blumhofer, "Dowie, John Alexander," in *Dictionary of Pentecostal and Charismatic Movements*, 248–49.

15. Ibid., 368.

16. Compare Harrell, *All Things Are Possible: The Healing and Charismatic Revivals in Modern America* (Bloomington, Ind.: Indiana University Press, 1975), 14–15.

17. For some enlightening discussions of Parham, the 1901 upsurge of Pentecostalism, and Parham's theology, see Robert Mapes Anderson, *Vision of the Disinherited: The Making of American Pentecostalism* (New York: Oxford University Press, 1979), 47–61, 81–91; Edith L. Blumhofer, *Restoring the Faith: The Assemblies of God, Pentecostalism, and American Culture* (Urbana, Ill.: University of Illinois Press, 1993), 43–56. A briefer treatment can be found in J. R. Goff Jr., "Parham, Charles Fox," in *Dictionary of Pentecostal and Charismatic Movements*, 660–61.

18. Walter J. Hollenweger, *The Pentecostals: The Charismatic Movement in the Churches* (Minneapolis: Augsburg, 1972), 22.

19. Ibid., 83.

20. Anderson, *Vision*, 48.

21. Ibid., 84.

22. Ibid., 49; Blumhofer, *Restoring the Faith*, 45.

23. Anderson, *Vision*, 49; Blumhofer, *Restoring the Faith*, 47.

24. Hollenweger, *Pentecostals*, 22; Anderson, *Vision*, 82–83.

25. McConnell, *Different Gospel*, 22, 24.

26. Simmons, *E. W. Kenyon*, 5–7, 46–47 n. 25.

27. Ibid., 15.

28. After Kenyon left the school, Bethel Bible Institute went through many changes. Eventually it was renamed Barrington College when it moved to Barrington, Rhode Island (McConnell, *Different Gospel*, 32–33). Barrington College later merged with Gordon College, founded by A. J. Gordon.

29. McConnell, *Different Gospel*, 32.

30. W. H. Daniels, *Dr. Cullis and His Work* (Boston: Willard Tract Repository, 1885).

31. Simmons, *E. W. Kenyon,* 17, 21.

32. F. F. Bosworth, *Christ the Healer,* 8th ed. (1924, 1948; reprint, Old Tappan, N.J.: Revell, 1973), 148.

33. Simmons, *E. W. Kenyon,* 192 n. 172, 236, 274 n. 184, 292–96, 310 nn. 26–27.

34. Cecil M. Robeck Jr., "McPherson, Aimee Semple," in *Dictionary of Pentecostal and Charismatic Movements,* 569.

35. Simmons, *E. W. Kenyon,* 101, 294.

36. McConnell, *Different Gospel,* 33.

37. Ibid., 23.

38. Kenyon, *Wonderful Name of Jesus,* 70.

39. On this subject, see especially David A. Reed, "Origins and Development of the Theology of Oneness Pentecostalism in the United States" (Ph.D. dissertation, Boston University, 1978), 6–85. It is interesting to note that Reed did his doctorate in Boston and that his undergraduate education was at Barrington College (McConnell, *Different Gospel,* 32–33).

40. Simmons, *E. W. Kenyon,* 103.

41. Reed, "Origins and Development of the Theology of Oneness Pentecostalism," 39.

42. Note the discussion of this point in Simmons, *E. W. Kenyon,* 166–68.

43. Kenyon, *Wonderful Name of Jesus,* 9.

44. Richard M. Riss, "Kenyon, Essek William," in *Dictionary of Pentecostal and Charismatic Movements,* 517.

45. E. W. Kenyon, *In His Presence: The Secret of Prayer. A Revelation of What We Are in Christ* (Lynnwood, Wash.: Kenyon's Gospel Publishing Society, 1969), 121.

46. A. B. Simpson, *The Lord for the Body,* rev. ed. (Harrisburg, Pa.: Christian Publications, 1959), 123.

47. Kenyon, *Two Kinds of Faith,* 103, cited in McConnell, *Different Gospel,* 141.

48. A. B. Simpson, *Himself* (Harrisburg, Pa.: Christian Publications, n.d.), 7–8.

49. A. B. Simpson, *The Gospel of Healing* (Harrisburg, Pa.: Christian Publications, 1915), 142–43.

50. John G. Lake, "Incarnation," in *John G. Lake: His Life, His Sermons, His Boldness of Faith,* rev. printing (Fort Worth: Kenneth Copeland Ministries, 1995), 199.

51. Kenyon, *Hidden Man,* 7, 26, quoted in McConnell, *Different Gospel,* 118, 121 nn. 3, 40.

52. Simpson, *The Lord for the Body,* 17–18.

53. R. A. Torrey, *How to Obtain Fulness of Power in Christian Life and Service* (New York: Revell, 1897), 12, quoted in Simmons, *E. W. Kenyon,* 86.

54. John G. Lake, *John G. Lake Sermons on Dominion over Demons, Disease, and Death,* ed. Gordon Lindsay (Dallas: Christ for the Nations, 1949), 22.

55. John G. Lake, *Spiritual Hunger, the God-men and Other Sermons by John G. Lake,* ed. Gordon Lindsay (reprint, Dallas: Christ for the Nations, 1976), quoted in Leonard Lovett, "Positive Confession Theology," in *Dictionary of Pentecostal and Charismatic Movements,* 719.

56. Lake, "Incarnation," in *John G. Lake: His Life, His Sermons,* 196–97, 200.

57. A. J. Gordon, quoted in Kenyon, *The Father and His Family,* 146; quoted in Simmons, *E. W. Kenyon,* 132 n. 148.

58. Simpson, *The Lord for the Body,* 57.

59. Simpson, *Gospel of Healing,* 130–31.

60. Quoted from an 1874 address by Smith, in Simmons, *E. W. Kenyon,* 152.

61. Lake, *John G. Lake Sermons,* 62.

62. Ibid., 47, 56.

63. Ibid., 56.

64. See Simmons, *E. W Kenyon,* 154–57.

65. Simpson, *The Lord for the Body,* 23–24.

66. Ibid., 130–31. The reference is to Job 3:25.

67. Simpson, *Gospel of Healing,* 98.

68. Simpson, *The Lord for the Body,* 66.

69. Ibid., 133.

70. Lake, *The John G. Lake Sermons,* 15.

71. Ibid., 105.

72. Ibid., 115.

73. Simpson, *The Lord for the Body,* 102.

74. Assemblies of God statement of faith, quoted in Hollenweger, *Pentecostals,* 515.

75. Hollenweger, *Pentecostals,* 35.

76. Kenyon, *Hidden Man,* 99.

77. Simpson, *The Lord for the Body,* 132.

78. Simpson, *Gospel of Healing,* 90–91.

79. Kenyon, *Jesus the Healer,* 65, cited in McConnell, *Different Gospel,* 157 (who also cites Kenyon, *Two Kinds of Faith,* 109).

80. Simpson, *The Lord for the Body,* 115–16.

81. Frederick K. C. Price, on "Ever Increasing Faith," TBN, 16 November 1990, cited in Hanegraaff, *Christianity in Crisis*, 271, 346, 384; cf. 286.

82. Kenyon, *In His Presence*, 153.

83. Lilian B. Yeomans, *Healing from Heaven* (Springfield, Mo.: Gospel Publishing House, 1926), 22ff., quoted in Hollenweger, *Pentecostals*, 35, and again, 358.

84. Simpson, *Gospel of Healing*, 76–78.

85. Lake, *John G. Lake Sermons*, 131. Compare "Have Christians a Right to Pray 'If It Be Thy Will' Concerning Sickness?" in *John G. Lake: His Life, His Sermons*, 173–81.

86. Kenneth Hagin, *Right and Wrong Thinking* (Tulsa: Kenneth Hagin Ministries, 1966), 18–19, cited in McConnell, *Different Gospel*, 15.

87. McConnell, *Different Gospel*, 43, 45.

88. Kenyon, *Hidden Man*, 35, 74 (also 137), cited in McConnell, *Different Gospel*, 45.

89. Simpson, *The Lord for the Body*, 85.

90. Simpson, *Gospel of Healing*, 53.

91. Ibid., 185.

92. John G. Lake, "Lake's Reply to Dr. Elwood Bulgin" (1920), in *John G. Lake: His Life, His Sermons*, 160, 163–64. These are just a few of Lake's statements in this letter referring to Christian Science and related cults.

93. Hollenweger, *Pentecostals*, 119.

94. Charles Fox Parham, *Kol Kare Bomidbar: A Voice Crying in the Wilderness* (Baxter Springs, Kans.: Joplin Printing Co., 1944), 26, quoted in Anderson, *Vision*, 87–88.

95. Blumhofer, *Restoring the Faith*, 37 n. 32.

96. Ibid., 19.

97. Hanegraaff, *Christianity in Crisis*, 47–48.

98. Hank Hanegraaff, *Counterfeit Revival* (Dallas: Word, 1997), 26–28, 38–39, 93–94, 165–66, 170–74.

99. Ibid., 38–39, 125–42, 165–75.

Chapter 5
Fathers of the Word-Faith Movement

1. Hanegraaff, *Christianity in Crisis*, 30.

2. DeArteaga, *Quenching the Spirit* (1996 ed.), 270.

3. McConnell briefly notes the significance of the Latter-Rain healing revivals for Hagin's thought; see McConnell, *Different Gospel*, 69.

4. See Vinson Synan, *In the Latter Days: The Outpouring of the Holy Spirit in the Twentieth Century* (Ann Arbor, Mich.: Servant, 1984), 5–7.

5. For accounts of these events from various perspectives, see Richard Riss, "The Latter Rain Movement of 1948," *Pneuma* 4 (spring 1982): 32–45; idem, "Latter Rain Movement," in *Dictionary of Pentecostal and Charismatic Movements*, 532–34; L. Thomas Holdcroft, "The New Order of the Latter Rain," *Pneuma* 2 (fall 1980): 46–60; William W. Menzies, *Anointed to Serve: The Story of the Assemblies of God* (Springfield, Mo.: Gospel Publishing House, 1971), 321–25; David Edwin Harrell Jr., *All Things Are Possible*, 3–132, especially 25–52.

6. On Hall, see Harrell, *All Things Are Possible*, 80–82, 212–14; 49–53 (highly critical); S. Shemeth, "Hall, Franklin," in *Dictionary of Pentecostal and Charismatic Movements*, 345–46.

7. On Branham, see C. Douglas Weaver, *The Healer Prophet, William Marrion Branham: A Study of the Prophetic in American Pentecostalism* (Macon, Ga.: Mercer University Press, 1987); also Harrell, *All Things Are Possible*, 27–41; Carl Dyck, *William Branham: The Man and His Message* (Saskatoon, Saskatchewan: Western Tract Mission, 1984) (extremely critical); D. J. Wilson, "Branham, William Marrion," in *Dictionary of Pentecostal and Charismatic Movements*, 95–97; Dager, *Vengeance*, 53–59 (highly critical); Eric Pement, "William Branham: An American Legend?" *Cornerstone* 81 (1987): 14–17 (moderately critical); see my corrective letter, *Cornerstone* 82 (1987).

8. Hagin, *Understanding the Anointing*, 41–42.

9. Richard M. Riss, "Osborn, Tommy Lee," in *Dictionary of Pentecostal and Charismatic Movements*, 655–56; Simmons, *E. W. Kenyon*, 296–98.

10. See above, n. 6. Strangely, the *Dictionary* does include a harshly critical article on "Positive Confession" by Leonard Lovett (719–20) that specifically criticizes Kenyon,

Hagin, and Copeland, presumably in the interests of "balance." Unfortunately, the result is that readers are confused, since the articles on these three men (written by Richard M. Riss) are all thoroughly uncritical and laudatory.

11. Kenneth Hagin, *Ministry of a Prophet* (Tulsa: Kenneth Hagin Ministries, 1978), 8, cited in Pement, "William Branham," 16.

12. For material about Oral Roberts, see David Edwin Harrell Jr., *Oral Roberts: An American Life* (San Francisco: Harper & Row, 1985), especially 422–27, 439–68.

13. Where I was born, ten years later!

14. This is not to say that Roberts was the very first televangelist; that honor apparently goes to Rex Humbard, who was broadcasting as early as 1952. Compare James Randi, *The Faith Healers* (Buffalo: Prometheus Books, 1987), 52.

15. Ibid., 389.

16. Kenneth E. Hagin, *Don't Blame God!* (Tulsa: Kenneth Hagin Ministries, 1979), 4.

17. Kenneth E. Hagin, *How God Taught Me About Prosperity* (Tulsa: Kenneth Hagin Ministries, 1985), 1; *Words* (Tulsa: Kenneth Hagin Ministries, 1979), 27–28; *I Believe in Visions* (Old Tappan, N.J.: Revell, 1972), 11.

18. McConnell, *Different Gospel*, 74 n. 7.

19. Hagin, *I Believe in Visions*, 11–16.

20. Ibid., 18–30; also Kenneth Hagin *"You Can Have What You Say!"* (Tulsa: Kenneth Hagin Ministries, 1979), 13–16; *Understanding the Anointing*, 25.

21. Hagin, *Don't Blame God*, 7–8.

22. Hagin, *Words*, 6–7.

23. Kenneth Hagin, *The Name of Jesus* (Tulsa: Kenneth Hagin Ministries, 1979), 44.

24. Ibid., 133.

25. Hagin, *I Believe in Visions*, 30–39; *Understanding the Anointing*, 26–29.

26. Hagin, *Understanding the Anointing*, 53.

27. Ibid., 42, 60–61.

28. Ibid., 132.

29. Hagin, *How God Taught Me about Prosperity*, 5, 10–15.

30. Hagin, *Name of Jesus*, 9–11 (preface); compare McConnell, *Different Gospel*, 6. McConnell points out that there is some evidence that Hagin had read Kenyon even before 1950.

31. McConnell, *Different Gospel*, 6–12.

32. Hagin, *Name of Jesus*, 9.

33. McConnell, *Different Gospel*, 63–66 (quote on 65–66).

34. Hagin, *I Believe in Visions*, 46–47, 96–97, 101–2.

Chapter 6
Real Men Don't Use Reason

1. Kenneth Hagin, *New Thresholds of Faith* (Tulsa: Kenneth Hagin Ministries, 1972), 31–32.

2. Brian A. Onken, "Dangers of the 'Trinity' in Man," in *C.R.I. Speaks Out on the Errors of the Word-Faith Movement*, ed. Robert M. Bowman Jr. (San Juan Capistrano, Calif.: Christian Research Institute, 1991), 62.

3. Kenyon, *The Father and His Family* (Lynnwood, Wash.: Kenyon's Gospel Publishing Society, 1937), 56 (compare 1964 printing, 45–46); Kenyon, *Two Kinds of Knowledge*, 8; Hagin, *New Thresholds of Faith*, 26.

4. Kenneth Copeland, *The Force of Faith* (Fort Worth: Kenneth Copeland Ministries, n.d.), 6–9.

5. Kenyon, *The Father and His Family* (1937), 56.

6. Kenyon, *Two Kinds of Knowledge*, 22.

7. Ibid., 16; Copeland, *Force of Faith*, 6–9.

8. Kenyon, *Two Kinds of Knowledge*, 18.

9. Hagin, *New Thresholds of Faith*, 28, 31–32.

10. Capps, *Authority in Three Worlds*, 17–18.

11. Compare John W. Cooper, *Body, Soul, and Life Everlasting: Biblical Anthropology and the Monism-Dualism Debate* (Grand Rapids: Eerdmans, 1989), 108. This is probably the best book on the subject of monism and dichotomy and is highly recommended for serious students.

12. Compare Onken, "The Dangers of the 'Trinity' in Man," 60–64.

Chapter 7
Does God Have Faith?

1. Capps, *God's Creative Power Will Work for You . . .* (Tulsa: Harrison House, 1976), 2, 25.

2. McConnell, *Different Gospel*, 143–44.

3. Kenyon, *Two Kinds of Knowledge*, 14–15 (compare 17–18); see also Kenyon, *The Bible in the Light of Our Redemption*, 15; *Two Kinds of Faith*, 20.

4. Hagin, *New Thresholds of Faith*, 74–76.

5. Copeland, *Force of Faith*, 16–17.

6. Kenneth Copeland, *The Laws of Prosperity* (Greensburg, Pa.: Kenneth Copeland Ministries, Manna Christian Outreach, 1974), 18–19.

7. Charles Capps, *God's Creative Power*, 2, 25; compare Capps, *Authority in Three Worlds*, 24–25.

8. Frederick K. C. Price, *How Faith Works* (Tulsa: Harrison House, 1976), 93.

9. Ibid., 99, 101.

10. A. T. Robertson, *A Grammar of the Greek New Testament in the Light of Historical Research* (Nashville: Broadman, 1934), 500.

11. Ibid.

12. Price, *How Faith Works*, 99.

13. Hagin, *New Thresholds of Faith*, 8.

14. Price, *How Faith Works*, 51. Admittedly, some Christians today do not believe that God transcends time or that he knows the future completely, but surely all Christians agree that God knows with certainty whatever *he* has determined to do in the future. Once this point is granted, the first three reasons given for denying that God has faith are enough to prove the point.

Chapter 8
The God with a Bod

1. Copeland, "Spirit, Soul, and Body," tape #1.

2. Hanegraaff, *Christianity in Crisis*, 126.

3. Kenyon, *The Bible in the Light of Our Redemption*, 19.

4. Hagin, *New Thresholds of Faith*, 30.

5. Letter from Kenneth Copeland to Larry Smith, 21 July 1977.

6. Copeland, "Spirit, Soul, and Body," tape #1.

7. Ibid.

8. Copeland, "Following the Faith of Abraham," tape #01-3001.

9. Jimmy Swaggart, *Questions & Answers: Bible-Based Answers to Your Questions about Life* (Baton Rouge: Jimmy Swaggart Ministries, 1985); see 147–57 for his criticisms of the Word-Faith doctrines, and 199–202 for his advocacy of the doctrine of three divine bodies.

10. Benny Hinn, *Good Morning, Holy Spirit* (Nashville: Thomas Nelson, 1990).

Chapter 9
Big God, Little Gods

1. Earl Paulk, *Satan Unmasked* (Atlanta: Kingdom Publishers, 1985), 96–97.

2. Earl Paulk, *That the World May Know* (Atlanta: Kingdom, 1987), 132.

3. Kenyon, *The Father and His Family*, 32–33.

4. Kenyon, *Two Kinds of Knowledge*, 17, 22.

5. Kenyon, *The Bible in the Light of Our Redemption*, 21.

6. Kenneth Hagin, *Zoe: The God-Kind of Life* (Tulsa: Kenneth Hagin Ministries, 1981), 3.

7. Hagin, *New Thresholds of Faith*, 53–54.

8. Hagin, *The Believer's Authority*, 19; compare Hagin, *Plead Your Case* (Tulsa: Kenneth Hagin Ministries, 1979), 3; *Paul's Revelation: The Gospel of Reconciliation* (Tulsa: Kenneth Hagin Ministries, 1983), 24–25.

9. Kenneth Copeland, *Our Covenant with God* (Fort Worth: Kenneth Copeland Publications, 1987), 7.

10. Copeland, "Praise the Lord," TBN, 6 February 1986.

11. Copeland, "Authority of the Believer," tape #1, cited in Greg Durand, "In God We Trust? Exposing the Neo-Gnostic 'Gospel' of the Faith Movement, Part Two," *The Expositor* 5, no. 3 (fall 1991): 25, with minor typographical changes.

12. Copeland, "Following the Faith of Abraham," tape #01–3001, cited in Durand, "In God We Trust . . . Part Two," 25.

13. Kenneth Copeland, *Walking in the Realm of the Miraculous* (Fort Worth: Kenneth Copeland Ministries, n.d.), 15–16.

14. Paulk, *Satan Unmasked*, 96–97; compare 287–88.

15. Earl Paulk, *Held in the Heavens Until* (Atlanta: Kingdom, 1985), 171.

16. Earl Paulk, *That the World May Know* (Atlanta: Kingdom, 1987), 73.

17. Ibid., 27, 50–52, 73, 132, 134–40, 145–46.

18. Ibid., 132.

19. Paulk, "Paulk Answers," *Thy Kingdom Come* (November 1987): 3.

20. Capps, *Authority in Three Worlds*, 110.

21. James A. Laine, "Critique of *The Seduction of Christianity*," in Thomas Reid et al., *Seduction?? A Biblical Response* (New Wilmington, Pa.: Son-Rise, 1986), 24.

22. Hagin, *Zoe: The God-Kind of Life*, 3.

23. Kenneth Copeland, "Following the Faith of Abraham," tape #01–3001, cited in Durand, "In God We Trust . . . Part Two," 25.

24. See Benny Hinn's notorious sermon on the nine parts of the Godhead, TBN, 13 October 1990.

25. Kenneth E. Hagin, *Exceedingly Growing Faith* (Tulsa: Kenneth Hagin Ministries, 1983), 32–33, cited in Durand, "In God We Trust . . . Part Two," 27; also *New Thresholds of Faith*, 28.

26. Durand, "In God We Trust . . . Part Two," 27.

27. For a detailed overview of the various views, see G. C. Berkouwer, *Man: The Image of God*, Studies in Dogmatics (Grand Rapids: Eerdmans, 1962), 37–118.

Chapter 10
Dominion and the Devil

1. Copeland, "Following the Faith of Abraham," tape #01–3001.

2. Michael G. Moriarty, *The New Charismatics* (Grand Rapids: Zondervan, 1992), 361.

3. Copeland, *The Power of the Tongue*, 6.

4. Kenyon, *The Father and His Family*, 34–35 (1937 ed., 42–43); compare 69–70.

5. Ibid., 36.

6. Ibid., 40; see also 37–38, 57–58.

7. Ibid., 59–60; see also 37.

8. Hagin, *New Thresholds of Faith*, 53–54.

9. Hagin, *Believer's Authority*, 19.

10. Hagin, *Plead Your Case*, 3.

11. Copeland, *The Force of Faith*, 13–14.

12. Copeland, "Following the Faith of Abraham," tape #01–3001.

13. Copeland, "What Happened from the Cross to the Throne," tape #02–0017; compare Copeland, *Our Covenant with God* (Fort Worth: Kenneth Copeland Ministries, 1976), 8–9.

14. Copeland, TBN, recorded in 1988; cited in Durand, "In God We Trust . . . Part Three," *The Expositor* 6, no. 1 (winter 1992): 22.

15. Capps, *Authority in Three Worlds*, 49–51.

16. Copeland, TBN, recorded in 1988; cited in Durand, "In God We Trust . . . Part Three," 22.

Chapter 11
Confessing Jesus—A New Twist

1. Hanegraaff, *Christianity in Crisis*, 142.

2. Michael Bruno, *Christianity in Power* (Slippery Rock, Pa.: Abba Ministries, 1994), 232.

3. Ibid., 112.

4. Ibid, 112–13.

5. Ibid., 112–14.

6. Hanegraaff, *Christianity in Crisis*, 124, emphasis in original; referred to but with no direct citation in Bruno, *Christianity in Power*, 114.

7. Bruno, *Christianity in Power*, 115.

8. Kenyon, *Wonderful Name of Jesus*, 52.

9. Kenneth E. Hagin, *Prayer Secrets* (Tulsa: Kenneth Hagin Ministries, n.d.), 3, 8; compare *Name of Jesus*, 73–74; *Believer's Authority*, 22–23.

10. Hagin, *Understanding the Anointing*, 4–6; compare *Healing Belongs to Us*, 5.

11. Copeland, *Our Covenant with God*, 32–34.

12. Copeland, "Take Time to Pray," *Believer's Voice of Victory* (February 1987): 9.

13. Walter Martin, "The Warnings of God (Kenneth Copeland's False Prophecy)," tape #C–210 (San Juan Capistrano, Calif.: Christian Research Institute, 1987), side 1. The statement is quoted, for example, in Hanegraaff, *Christianity in Crisis*, 360.

14. Walter Martin, "Ye Shall Be as Gods," in *Agony of Deceit*, ed. Michael Horton (Chicago: Moody, 1990), 102, 104. Ironically, this essay by Martin was based almost entirely on an article I wrote titled "Ye Are Gods? Orthodox and Heretical Views on the Deification of Man," *Christian Research Journal* (winter/spring 1987), commended by Martin as "thorough" and "penetrating" ("Ye Shall Be as Gods," 93), although he came to a different conclusion than I did.

15. Copeland, "Question & Answer," *Believer's Voice of Victory* (August 1988): 8.

16. Martin, "Ye Shall Be as Gods," 102.

17. Hanegraaff, *Christianity in Crisis*, 138–39.

18. See especially Robert M. Bowman Jr., *Why You Should Believe in the Trinity: An Answer to Jehovah's Witnesses* (Grand Rapids: Baker, 1989).

19. Walter Martin, *Essential Christianity: A Handbook of Basic Christian Doctrines* (Santa Ana: Vision House, 1962), 37–38.

20. Hanegraaff, *Christianity in Crisis*, 140.

21. I trust the reader will understand why I choose not to give the man's name.

22. Martin, *Essential Christianity*, 38.

23. Copeland, "Take Time to Pray," 9, emphasis added.

24. Hagin, "The Incarnation," *The Word of Faith* (December 1980): 14.

25. Kenyon, *The Father and His Family*, 118.

26. Copeland, "What Happened from the Cross to the Throne."

27. Kenneth Copeland, "God's Covenants with Man I," tape 01–4403 (Fort Worth: Kenneth Copeland Ministries, 1982 [recorded 1981]), side 1.

28. Copeland, TBN, 9 August 1987.

29. Copeland, "The Incarnation," quoted in Hanegraaff, *Christianity in Crisis*, 138.

30. Hanegraaff, *Christianity in Crisis*, 138–39.

31. Copeland, "The Incarnation," quoted in DeArteaga, *Quenching the Spirit*, 272.

32. DeArteaga, *Quenching the Spirit*, 272.

33. Kenyon, *The Father and His Family*, 135–36.

34. Ibid., 211–12.

35. Ibid., 28, 32.

36. Charles Capps, *Faith and Confession* (Tulsa: Harrison House, 1987), 84–87, 105.

37. Copeland, "Faith in the Blood of Jesus," tape 01–4402 (Fort Worth: Kenneth Copeland Ministries, 1982).

38. Copeland, "What Happened from the Cross to the Throne," tape 02–0017.

39. E. W. Kenyon, *New Creation Realities: A Revelation of Redemption* (Lynnwood, Wash.: Kenyon's Gospel Publishing Society, 1945), 11.

Chapter 12
The Fall and Rise of the Born-Again Jesus

1. Copeland, "What Happened from the Cross to the Throne."

2. Hanegraaff, *Christianity in Crisis*, 174.

3. Kenyon, *Identification*, 16.

4. E. W. Kenyon, *What Happened from the Cross to the Throne* (Lynnwood, Wash.: Kenyon's Gospel Publishing Society, 1969), 47.

5. Kenneth Hagin, *His Name Shall Be Called Wonderful* (Tulsa: Kenneth Hagin Ministries, 1983), 18.

6. Kenyon, *Identification*, 12.

7. Hagin, *Name of Jesus*, 31.

8. Hagin, attachment to letter from Kenneth Hagin Jr. to Hendrik H. Hanegraaff, 4 January 1991.

9. Copeland, "What Happened from the Cross to the Throne," tape #02-0017.

10. Kenyon, *What Happened from the Cross to the Throne*, 64.

11. Hagin, *Name of Jesus*, 28.

12. Ibid., 29–30.

13. Copeland, "What Happened from the Cross to the Throne."

14. I have quoted the RSV in these texts because in my opinion its rendering of the passage is more accurate than either the NASB or the NIV.

15. The NASB adds the word *now* in italics before the words *in prison*, apparently to avoid the implication that the preaching of Christ took place while he was physically dead. However, there is no justification for this addition.

16. Kenyon, *What Happened from the Cross to the Throne*, 60.

17. Ibid., 74–75. In this regard Kenyon's position differs substantially from the Adventist position, which is that the thief would not be with Jesus until the second coming.

18. I have given a detailed study of this text in *Understanding Jehovah's Witnesses: Why They Read the Bible the Way They Do* (Grand Rapids: Baker, 1991), 97–108. The Jehovah's Witnesses take a position similar to that of the Adventists.

19. Hagin, *Name of Jesus*, 29.

20. Ibid., 31.

21. Ibid.

22. Hagin, *Redeemed: From Poverty, Sickness, and Spiritual Death*, 2d ed. (Tulsa: Kenneth Hagin Ministries, 1989), 26.

23. Ibid., 28.

24. Spencer, *Heresy Hunters*, 101–4; DeArteaga, *Quenching the Spirit* (1996 ed.), 240–41, 271. Spencer exaggerates when he claims that the ransom theory "was held by the entire Church during its first thousand years," 102.

25. On this doctrine, see Bowman, *Why You Should Believe in the Trinity*, 76–78.

26. Hanegraaff, "A Summary Critique: *The Anointing* [Benny Hinn]," *Christian Research Journal* (fall 1992): 38, cited in Spencer, *Heresy Hunters*, 101; DeArteaga, *Quenching the Spirit* (1996 ed.), 270–71.

27. John Calvin, *Institutes of the Christian Religion*, ed. John T. McNeill, trans. Ford Lewis Battles; Library of Christian Classics 20–21 (Philadelphia: Westminster Press, 1960), 1:515, 517; compare DeArteaga, *Quenching the Spirit* (1996 ed.), 242. The following citations from Calvin in parentheses refer to book, chapter, and section or paragraph.

28. DeArteaga, *Quenching the Spirit* (1996 ed.), 242–43.

29. Calvin, *Institutes*, 1:518 (2.16.12).

30. Ibid., 1:516 (2.16.10).

31. Ibid. (2.16.11, emphasis added).

32. Ibid., 1:518 (2.16.12).

33. Ibid., 1:519 (2.16.12).

34. Ibid., 1:517 (2.16.11).

Chapter 13
Just Like Jesus?

1. Copeland, "Substitution and Identification," tape #00-0202 (Fort Worth: Kenneth Copeland Ministries, 1989).

2. MacArthur, *Charismatic Chaos*, 277.

3. See p. 239, notes 24, 25.

4. Hagin, *Believer's Authority*, 14–16.

5. Hagin, *Name of Jesus*, 66.

6. Ibid., 105–06.

7. Hagin, *Believer's Authority*, 27–28.

8. Ibid., 30.

9. Ibid., 32; see also Kenneth Hagin, *Knowing What Belongs to Us* (Tulsa: Kenneth Hagin Ministries, 1989), 25; *Paul's Revelation: The Gospel of Reconciliation* (Tulsa: Kenneth Hagin Ministries, 1983), 16.

10. Ibid., 48.

11. Hagin, *Paul's Revelation*, 16.

12. Hagin, *Understanding the Anointing*, 4–6.

13. Copeland, "What Happened from the Cross to the Throne."

14. Copeland, "The Force of Love," tape #02–0028.

15. Copeland, TBN, 9 August 1987.

16. Kenneth Copeland, *The Force of Righteousness* (Fort Worth: Kenneth Copeland Ministries, 1984), 8–9.

17. Copeland, "Substitution and Identification."

18. "Praise the Lord," TBN, 7 July 1986.

19. "Praise the Lord," TBN, 15 November 1990.

20. The Greek word is *monogenēs*, which though always used in the New Testament to describe a son or daughter has the meaning "only" or "one of a kind," and thus, "unique" (or even "special"), not "only begotten" as found in the KJV and several other translations.

21. I made this point earlier in *Why You Should Believe in the Trinity*, 72.

22. Kenneth E. Hagin, "The Incarnation," *The Word of Faith* (December 1980): 14.

23. I am quoting here from the NASB, slightly modified to be more literal.

Chapter 14
The Faith Debate

1. Kenneth E. Hagin, *You Can Write Your Own Ticket with God* (Tulsa: Kenneth Hagin Ministries, 1979), 18.

2. Demos Shakarian, *A New Wave of Revival . . . In Your Finances!* (Costa Mesa, Calif.: Full Gospel Business Men's Fellowship International, n.d.), 10, quoted in James M. Kinnebrew, "The Charismatic Doctrine of Positive Confession: A Historical, Exegetical, and Theological Critique" (Th.D. dissertation, Mid-America Baptist Theological Seminary, 1988), 257.

3. Hagin, *New Thresholds of Faith*, 74–76; Copeland, *The Laws of Prosperity*, 18–19.

4. Hagin, *New Thresholds of Faith*, 75; Copeland, *Force of Faith*, 15; Price, *How Faith Works*, 103.

5. Hagin, *Having Faith in Your Faith* (Tulsa: Kenneth Hagin Ministries, 1980), 3–5.

6. Charles Capps, *The Tongue: A Creative Force* (Tulsa: Harrison House, 1976), 132.

7. Hagin, *Having Faith in Your Faith*, 3–4.

8. Ibid., 5.

9. Copeland, *The Force of Faith*, especially 13–14, 19; Capps, *Faith and Confession*, 44.

10. Hagin, *New Thresholds of Faith*, 7–8; *Right and Wrong Thinking*, 8; Copeland, *Our Covenant with God*, 38–39.

11. Hagin, *Real Faith*, 26; *Knowing What Belongs to Us*, 6–7, 10, 29; Price, *How Faith Works*, 25.

12. Price, *How Faith Works*, 31.

13. Hagin, *Words*, 32; *New Thresholds of Faith*, 9, 30; Price, *How Faith Works*, 21.

14. Copeland, *The Force of Faith*, 10–14; Price, *How Faith Works*, 48.

15. Hagin, *New Thresholds of Faith*, 9–12; Price, *How Faith Works*, 41–42; Capps, *Faith and Confession*, 15.

16. Hagin, *The Real Faith* (Tulsa: Kenneth Hagin Ministries, n.d.), 25.

17. Hagin, *New Thresholds of Faith*, 43; Price, *How Faith Works*, 111.

18. Hagin, *New Thresholds of Faith*, 10.

19. Ibid., 77; Capps, *The Tongue*, 12–14; Price, *How Faith Works*, 58.

20. See especially Hagin, *Words;* also Price, *How Faith Works*, 58.

21. Hagin, *You Can Write Your Own Ticket with God*, 18; Capps, *Faith and Confession*, 15.

22. Hagin, *Name of Jesus*, 73–74; compare *Believer's Authority*, 22–23; Kenneth Copeland, "Origin of the Blood Covenant," tape 01–4401 (Fort Worth: Kenneth Copeland Ministries, 1982 [recorded 1981]), side 2.

23. Copeland, *Our Covenant with God*, 40–41.

24. Hagin, *Understanding Our Confession*, 4, cited in Kinnebrew, "Charismatic Doctrine of Positive Confession," 199.

25. Anthony C. Thiselton, "The Supposed Power of Words in the Biblical Writings," *Journal of Theological Studies* NS 25 (1974): 291.

26. Derek Kidner, *Proverbs: An Introduction and Commentary*, Tyndale Old Testament Commentaries Series (Downers Grove, Ill.: InterVarsity Press, 1964), 47, cited in Thiselton, "Supposed Power," 298; and also in Kinnebrew, "Charismatic Doctrine of Positive Confession," 92.

27. Capps, *Faith and Confession*, 33–34.

28. Kinnebrew, "Charismatic Doctrine of Positive Confession," 99.

Chapter 15
On Being Healthy, Wealthy, and Wise

1. Capps, *Faith and Confession*, 12.

2. Kinnebrew, "Charismatic Doctrine of Positive Confession," 260.

3. Hagin, *Redeemed: From Poverty, Sickness, Death*, 2d ed., 1.

4. Copeland, *Our Covenant with God*, 28.

5. Hagin, *Real Faith*, 9, 20.

6. Ibid., 25.

7. Hagin, *New Thresholds of Faith*, 53–54.

8. C. Marvin Pate, *The End of the Ages Has Come: The Theology of Paul* (Grand Rapids: Zondervan, 1995).

9. Hagin, *Understanding the Anointing*, 25.

10. B. B. Warfield, *Counterfeit Miracles* (1918; reprint, London: Banner of Truth Trust, 1972), 170.

Conclusion: By Their Fruits

1. Bowman, *Orthodoxy and Heresy.*
2. See "The Gospel according to Paulk: A Critique of 'Kingdom Theology,'" and "Ye Are Gods? Orthodox and Heretical Views on the Deification of Man," in *C.R.I. Speaks Out on the Errors of the Word-Faith Movement,* by Bowman and Onken, 35–59.

Select Bibliography

The purpose of this bibliography is to offer some suggestions for further study of the issues discussed here. I have tried to list only the best, most influential, or most representative works from different points of view.

Background Studies

Barabas, Steven. *So Great Salvation: The History and Message of the Keswick Convention*. London: Marshall, Morgan & Scott, 1952. Excellent overview of the Keswick wing of the Holiness movement by an advocate.

Burgess, Stanley M., Gary B. McGee, and Patrick H. Alexander, eds. *Dictionary of Pentecostal and Charismatic Movements*. Grand Rapids: Zondervan, 1988. Includes articles on many of the individuals mentioned in this book (Kenyon, Branham, Hagin, etc.), as well as Paul G. Chappell's important article, "Healing Movements" (353–74).

Ehrenborg, Todd. *Mind Sciences*. Zondervan Guide to Cults and Religious Movements. Grand Rapids: Zondervan, 1995. Probably the best evangelical analysis and critique of the metaphysical cults; important for comparing those cults to the Word-Faith movement.

Meyer, Donald E. *The Positive Thinkers: Religion as Pop Psychology from Mary Baker Eddy to Oral Roberts*. New York: Pantheon Books, 1980. Chronicles the history of positive thinking in American religion throughout the past century plus. The book shows that such an approach to religion is not limited to one tradition but is pervasive in American culture.

Simmons, Dale H. *E. W. Kenyon and the Postbellum Pursuit of Peace, Power, and Plenty*. Studies in Evangelicalism 13. Lanham, Md., and London: Scarecrow Press, 1997. Essential scholarly study (originally a doctoral dissertation); Simmons rightly emphasizes Kenyon's debt to the evangelical faith-cure tradition but sees more commonality between that tradition and the metaphysical religions than I would.

Forerunners of the Word-Faith Movement

Bosworth, F. F. *Christ the Healer*. 8th ed. 1924, 1948. Reprint, Old Tappan, N.J.: Revell, 1973. Extremely popular defense of evangelical faith-healing theology by a Latter-Rain preacher influenced by Kenyon.

Gordon, Adoniram Judson. *The Ministry of Healing: Or, Miracles of Cure in All Ages*. 2d ed. 1882. Reprint, Harrisburg, Pa.: Christian Publications, 1961. The Baptist pastor whose preaching brought Kenyon into the evangelical faith-cure movement offers a defense of the movement's beliefs.

Kenyon, E. W. *The Father and His Family: The Story of Man's Redemption*. Lynnwood, Wash.: Kenyon's Gospel Publishing Society, 1964. Offers a sweeping account of God's work in creation and redemption as Kenyon understood it.

———. *What Happened from the Cross to the Throne*. Lynnwood, Wash.: Kenyon's Gospel Publishing Society, 1969. This book presents the fullest exposition of Kenyon's distinctive views on Christ's spiritual death and new birth that are the cornerstone of Word-Faith teaching.

Lake, John G. *The John G. Lake Sermons on Dominion over Demons, Disease, and Death*. Edited by Gordon Lindsay. Dallas: Christ for the Nations, 1949. The sermons of a faith-healing evangelist who was widely influential in Pentecostalism. Despite no apparent direct influence from Kenyon, Lake's sermons contain striking parallels to Kenyon's teaching.

Murray, Andrew. *Divine Healing*. Springdale, Pa.: Whitaker House, 1982. Murray is perhaps the most influential of the nineteenth-century Keswick writers; this book presents a passionate argument for divine healing as a fruit of holy living in Christ.

Simpson, A. B. *The Gospel of Healing*. Harrisburg, Pa.: Christian Publications, 1915. An influential defense of the evangelical faith-cure movement by one of its most dynamic leaders. Simpson's position on healing is even more radical than that of the Word-Faith teachers, since he openly condemned all use of medicine.

Modern Word-Faith Teachers

Most of the books and booklets written by Word-Faith teachers repeat the same themes over and over again. Thus, one can read a handful of such books almost at random and pick up the major ideas of the movement. The following are perhaps some of the more representative and often-cited works by these teachers.

Capps, Charles. *Faith and Confession*. Tulsa: Harrison House, 1987. Title page: *Dynamics of Faith and Confession*. Notable for Capps's exposition of the idea that Mary confessed Jesus into being, as well as for its detailed presentation of standard Word-Faith ideas.

Copeland, Kenneth. *The Blood Covenant*. Tape series. Fort Worth: Kenneth Copeland Ministries, 1982. Copeland has written comparatively little. Most of his in-depth teaching is available only in cassette tapes. This series is one in which many of his most disturbing teachings are found.

―――. "What Happened from the Cross to the Throne." Tape #02–0017. Fort Worth: Kenneth Copeland Ministries, 1990. Copeland's own radical interpretation of the doctrine presented in Kenyon's book bearing the same title.

Hagin, Kenneth E. *The Name of Jesus.* Tulsa: Kenneth Hagin Ministries, 1979. One of Hagin's most popular writings, containing significant exposition of the born-again Jesus doctrine.

―――. *New Thresholds of Faith.* 2d ed. Tulsa: Kenneth Hagin Ministries, 1989. The closest thing to a systematic presentation of Word-Faith theology, by the movement's father.

Price, Frederick K. C. *Name It and Claim It! The Power of Positive Confession.* Tulsa: Harrison House, 1992. Characteristic presentation of the Word-Faith teaching, by its best-known African-American teacher.

The Word Study Bible. Tulsa: Harrison House, 1990. A study Bible published by a major Word-Faith publishing house, with notes by leading teachers in the movement.

Works Defending the Word-Faith Movement

Bruno, Michael. *Christianity in Power.* Slippery Rock, Pa.: Abba Ministries, 1994. A response to Hanegraaff's *Christianity in Crisis,* written by a Word-Faith pastor. Bruno seems more orthodox than the leading lights of the movement, but problems remain.

DeArteaga, William L. *Quenching the Spirit: Discover the REAL Spirit behind the Charismatic Controversy.* Lake Mary, Fla.: Creation House, 1996. A substantially revised edition of his 1992 book that includes a response to Hanegraaff's *Christianity in Crisis.* DeArteaga agrees that there are some doctrinal excesses in the Word-Faith movement (he likes Kenyon better than the modern teachers), but he considers wholesale rejection of the movement to be a form of Pharisaism. So far, DeArteaga's book is the only scholarly work defending the Word-Faith movement.

Spencer, James R. *Heresy Hunters: Character Assassination in the Church.* Lafayette, La.: Huntington House, 1993. Unusual because Spencer is a former Mormon and active in countercult ministry, yet he defends the Word-Faith teachers (and others) against those he considers "heresy hunters." Spencer takes basically the same view as DeArteaga but makes his case in a more popular and less accurate fashion.

Works Critiquing the Word-Faith Movement

Barron, Bruce. *The Health and Wealth Gospel.* Downers Grove, Ill.: InterVarsity Press, 1987. A sympathetic critique, viewing the Word-Faith movement as an extreme Pentecostalism.

Farah, Charles, Jr. *From the Pinnacle of the Temple: Faith vs. Presumption*. Plainfield, N.J.: Logos International, 1979. A Pentecostal critique of what the author regards as the radical excesses of the Word-Faith movement.

Fee, Gordon D. *The Disease of the Health and Wealth Gospels*. Costa Mesa, Calif.: The Word for Today, 1979. A short but incisive, popularly written critique by a renowned Pentecostal New Testament scholar.

Hanegraaff, Hank. *Christianity in Crisis*. Eugene, Ore.: Harvest House, 1993. Massively documented but sensationalized critique of the Word-Faith movement, characterizing it as a metaphysical cancer that has invaded the charismatic tradition.

———. *Counterfeit Revival*. Dallas: Word, 1997. A critique of the Toronto Blessing and related revivals; Hanegraaff identifies the evangelical faith-cure and Pentecostal roots of the revival but fails to note their connection to the Word-Faith movement.

Horton, Michael, ed. *The Agony of Deceit*. Chicago: Moody, 1990. Hard-hitting but uneven collection of essays critiquing the Word-Faith televangelists; includes an article by Walter Martin on the Word-Faith "little gods" doctrine.

Hunt, Dave, and T. A. MacMahon. *The Seduction of Christianity*. Eugene, Ore.: Harvest House, 1985. Argues that a variety of religious trends, including the Word-Faith movement, signal the coming of a widespread apostasy leading to the end times. Hunt's books, especially this one, have been enormously influential.

Kinnebrew, James M. "The Charismatic Doctrine of Positive Confession: A Historical, Exegetical, and Theological Critique." Th.D. diss., Mid-America Baptist Theological Seminary, 1988. A sober analysis of the Word-Faith views on faith, healing, and prosperity, followed by a discussion of numerous misinterpreted biblical texts.

MacArthur, John. *Charismatic Chaos*. Grand Rapids: Zondervan, 1992. Wide-ranging critique of charismatic and Pentecostal theology and practice, including the Word-Faith movement.

McConnell, D. R. *A Different Gospel: A Historical and Biblical Analysis of the Modern Faith Movement*. Updated ed. Foreword by Hank Hanegraaff. Peabody, Mass.: Hendrickson Publishers, 1995. Argues that Kenyon was the real father of the Word-Faith movement and that his theology was essentially that of the New Thought wing of the metaphysical cults.

Moo, Douglas, gen. ed. *The Gospel and Contemporary Perspectives: Viewpoints from Trinity Journal*. Biblical Forum Series 2. Grand Rapids: Kregel, 1991. Includes five articles from the 1988 *Trinity Journal* critiquing the Word-Faith teachings.

Biblical Interpretation and Theology

Bowman, Robert M., Jr. *Orthodoxy and Heresy: A Biblical Guide to Doctrinal Discernment*. Grand Rapids: Baker, 1992. Explains the importance of discerning orthodox from heretical teaching and sets forth a broad evangelical approach to doing so.

Horton, Stanley, ed. *Systematic Theology: A Pentecostal Perspective*. Springfield, Mo.: Gospel Publishing House, 1994. Collection of essays from noted Pentecostal theologians on a range of doctrinal topics.

Stein, Robert H. *A Basic Guide to Interpreting the Bible: Playing by the Rules*. Grand Rapids: Baker, 1994. One of the best textbooks on biblical interpretation, emphasizing the importance of reading passages in the light of the kind of writing in which they appear.

Stott, John R. W. *Baptism and Fullness: The Work of the Holy Spirit Today*. Downers Grove, Ill.: InterVarsity Press, 1976. Makes the case for a noncharismatic theology that is open to miraculous healing and other supernatural occurrences as God wills.

Williams, J. Rodman. *Renewal Theology: Systematic Theology from a Charismatic Perspective*. 2 vols. Grand Rapids: Zondervan, 1988, 1990. Perhaps the best textbook on Pentecostal systematic theology; highly recommended as an example of good theology from a Pentecostal perspective.

Name Index

Allen, A. A., 83
Avanzini, John, 8, 222

Barabas, Steven, 243
Barron, Bruce, 39, *230*, 245
Baxter, Ern, 231, *232*
Blumhofer, Edith, 80, 82, *233, 235*
Boardman, William, 57
Bosworth, F. F., 62, 65, 87–88, *234*, 244
Braden, Charles S., *231*
Branham, William M., 62, 83, 86–90, 92, 93, 94, 99, *235*
Bright, Bill, 81
Bruno, Michael, 147–49, *238*, 245
Bullinger, E. W., 87

Calvin, John, 177–78, *240*
Capps, Charles, 8, 14–15, 32, 84, 99, 105, 106, 132, 140, 141, 143, 155–58, 162, 201, 205, 227, 228, *229, 236–39, 241*, 244
Chappell, Paul, 60, *233*, 243
Coe, Jack, 83
Copeland, Kenneth, 8, 14–16, 30–32, 38, 40, 48, 72, 83, 84, 89, 90, 98, 99, 106, 115–20, 124–26, 129, 131, 133, 134, 136–43, 145, 147, 150–63, 175, 179, 182–84, 196, 206, 221, 223, 225, 227, 228, *229, 236–41*, 244–45
Crenshaw, Curtis, 39, *231*
Crouch, Paul, 8, 17, 183–84, 223–24
Cullis, Charles, 57, 60–61, 65, *234*

Dager, Albert James, 18, *229, 235*
Dake, Finis Jennings, 120

DeArteaga, William, 10, 25–26, 36, 39, 43, 44, 58, 85, 154–55, 176–78, *230–33, 235, 239, 240*, 245
Dicks, Donald, 12
Dowie, John Alexander, 61–63, 65, 77, 80, 81, 91, *233*
Du Plessis, David, 83
Durham, William H., 65–66

Eddy, Mary Baker, 40, 44–45, 48–51, *231–32*
Ehrenborg, Todd, 243
Emerson, Charles Wesley, 65, 81

Farah, Charles, 9, 39, *230*, 246
Fee, Gordon D., 246
Fénelon, 81
Finney, Charles, 60, 81

Gordon, Adoniram Judson, 57, 61, 65–66, 71, *233–34*, 244
Guyon, Madame, 81

Hagin, Kenneth, 8–11, 14–16, 23, 25, 26, 29–32, 36–40, 43, 48, 52, 78, 83, 84, 86, 88–90, 92–94, 97–99, 106–8, 111, 116, 120, 124, 125, 129, 133–35, 139, 141, 145, 149–50, 153, 155, 160–63, 167–68, 174, 180–82, 188–90, 193–95, 200, 206–8, 211, 215, 216, 222, 223, 225, *229–30, 235–42*, 245
Hall, Franklin, 87, 89, 235
Hanegraaff, Hank, 10, 12, 13, 18, 19, 23, 30, 36, 39, 52–53, 83–84, 85, 115, 147–149,

151–52, 154–55, 159, 176, 178, *229–32,*
    235, 245–46
Hawtin, George and Ern, 86
Hinn, Benny, 13, 15–17, 30, 83, 120, 148,
    220, 221, *229, 237, 238*
Hollenweger, Walter, 76, *233, 235*
Holt, Herrick, 86
Horton, Michael S., 246
Humbard, Rex, 222, *236*
Hunt, Dave, 9, 18, 39, 43, 127, 132, 178,
    229, 231, 246

Irving, Edward, 61

Jackson, Robert, 39, *231*
Judah, J. Stillson, *231*

Kenyon, E. W., 9–11, 18, 25, 26, 35, 36–59,
    64–82, 84–89, 92–94, 98–99, 106, 109,
    110, 116, 124–25, 136, 138–39, 141, 149,
    153, 155, 156, 160–62, 167, 170, 177,
    178, 180, 222, 225, *230–40,* 243–45
Kinnebrew, James, 199, 201, 205, *241,* 246
Kuhlman, Kathryn, 83

Laine, James A., 132–33, *238*
Lake, John G., 62, 69–75, 78, 79, 91, *234,*
    235, 244
Larson, Martin A., *231*
Lindsay, Gordon, 62, 88, 93
Lindsey, Hal, 9
Luther, Martin, 63

MacArthur, John, 18–19, 39–40, 44, 83,
    179, *229–31, 240,* 246
MacMillan, John A., 26
Martin, Walter, 12, 150–53, 157, 225, *239*
Matta, Judith, 18, *229*
McConnell, Daniel R., 9–10, 18, 25, 26,
    35–37, 39–40, 44–45, 47–53, 57, 64–66,
    71, 78, 79, 92–94, 105, 178, *229–37,* 246
McPherson, Aimee S., 37, 66, 68, 77, 83
Meyer, Donald E., 243
Montgomery, Carrie, 57
Moo, Douglas, 246
Moody, Dwight L., 81
Moon, Sun Myung, 19
Moriarty, Michael G., 137, *238*
Müller, George, 57, 61, 65, *233*

Murray, Andrew, 57, 60, 244

Neuman, H. Terris, *230–31*

Onken, Brian A., 97, *236, 237, 242*
Osborn, T. L., 8, 88, 222
Osteen, John, 8

Palmer, Phoebe, 60, *233*
Parham, Charles Fox, 62–64, 80, 81, 83, 91,
    233, 235
Paulk, Earl, 123, 126–28, 190, 228, *237, 238,*
    242
Price, Frederick, 8, 15, 30, 77, 106, 110,
    221, 223, *229, 235, 237, 241,* 245

Roberts, Oral, 8, 86, 87, 89–91, 92, 94, 119,
    236
Robertson, A. T., 108, *237*
Rosenbladt, Rod, 18, *229*

Seiss, Joseph A., 87
Seymour, William J., 63
Shakarian, Demos, 193, *241*
Simmons, Dale, 40–41, 57–58, *231–34, 236,*
    243
Simpson, A. B., 57, 61–63, 66–77, 79, 81,
    91, *234–35,* 244
Smith, Hannah Whitehall, 60, 72
Spencer, James, 14, 176, *229, 240,* 245
Spong, John Shelby, 19, 228
Stanley, Charles, 8
Swaggart, Jimmy, 120, *237*

Thiselton, Anthony, 200, *241*
Tilton, Robert, 8
Tinney, James S., *231*
Torrey, R. A., 57, 71, *234*
Trine, Ralph Waldo, 44, 49–51, 81, *231–32*

Walker, James, 12
Warfield, B. B., 217, *242*
Webb-Peploe, H. W., 57
Wesley, Charles, 68
Wesley, John, 63, 64, 68
Wigglesworth, Smith, 83
Woodworth-Etter, Maria B., 83

Yeomans, Lilian B., 77

Scripture Index

Old Testament

Genesis

1–2—112, 127, 134–136
1:1—131
1:3—195
1:26–27—124, 135
1:28–30—136
1:31—75
2:1–4—119
2:4—165
2:7—100, 135
3:19—134
5:1—135
9:6—135, 145
45:8–9—143
50:20—143

Exodus

1:5—100
4:16; 7:1—131
21:6; 22:8, 9, 28—131–132
31:17—119

Deuteronomy

4:35—130, 165
4:39—130
6:4–5—223
18:22—150
19:17—131
28—206–207, 209

30:15, 19—164
32:39—130

1 Samuel

2:25—131–132

2 Samuel

22:32—130

1 Kings

8:27—115, 119

Job

Book—75, 213–15
1:21–22; 2:10—214
3:25—74, 214
40:3–5; 42:1–7—214

Psalms

2:7—174–175, 187
8:3–4—124
8:5–8—136
11:4—118
16:8–10—167, 173–174
18:8—118
19:1–3—113
22—171–173

24:1—142
33:6–9—113–114, 131, 195, 200
33:10–11—143, 200
33:16–22—200
45:6—131
68:20—164
78:39—134
82—131–133, 191
82:1—131
82:6—130, 131–133
102:25–27—131
103:2–4—208, 213
103:14—134
107:18–20—208, 213
139:7–8—167, 173
148:3–8—113

Proverbs

3:1–7—198
3:5—195, 198
3:13–16—224
6:1–2—195, 200–201
14:23—200
15:1–2—13
16:1, 4, 9—144
16:32—103
16:33—143
17:10—200
18:6–7—201

18:13—19, 23, 24
18:17—35
18:21—164, 195, 201
21:1—144
26:23, 26—200
27:6—219
29:19—200

Isaiah

9:6—131
10:5–15—143
14:24–27—143
31:3—131, 134
40:12—117–118
40:22—131
40:24—114
40:28—119
41:22–23—144
42:9—144
43:10—130, 142
44:6–8—130, 144
44:24—131
45:1—144
45:5–7—142
45:5, 14, 21–22—130
46:9—130
53:4–5—207, 210–211
53:9—160, 164–165
53:10—144

251

53:12—165
55:6-13—200
55:11—200
66:1—119

Jeremiah

8:3—164
10:6-7—131
10:13—113
21:8—164
23:23-24—119, 131

29:10-11—144
49:20—143

Ezekiel

28:2, 9—131
28:8, 10—165

31:11—131
32:21—131

Hosea

1:10—186

New Testament

Matthew

3:17—178
4:5—9
5:9—186, 187
5:34-35—119
5:45—186, 187
6:8-10—187
6:13, 29-31—143
6:32—187
6:34—143
7:7-11—202
7:11—187
7:12—19, 30
7:15—217
7:16, 20—27
7:20-22—27, 217,
   220
7:21—187
7:24-27—27-28
8:16-17—76, 80,
   207, 210-211
8:29—138, 141,
   143
9:1-7—211
9:28-29—195, 200
9:34—25
10:28—100
12:15-16—207
12:24—25
12:31-32—201
12:36-37—195, 201
17:1-9—158
18:20—119
21:21—196
22:29—27
22:37-38—97
22:41-46—148
24:24—217

26:1-5, 14-16, 24,
   42—144
27:46—171
27:57-60—165
28:18-19—182, 189
28:20—119

Mark

2:1-12—158
10:29-30—208,
   212-213
11:22-24—199, 202
11:22—70,
   106-109, 112,
   194
11:23—194-196
11:24—92
12:30—101, 223
15:34—171

Luke

1:35, 38—157, 174,
   187
1:46-47—101
2:11—175
3:22—151, 187
3:38—186
4:9—9
6:12—109
6:24-25—220
6:35—186
9:35—187
12:15-34—220
16:13-14, 19-31—
   220
18:22-30—220
20:24—136

21:24—138, 141,
   143
22:3, 22, 42—144
23:23—202
23:43—167
23:52—202

John

1:1-2—227
1:1—155, 156, 158
1:3—131
1:12—186
1:13—144, 186
1:14—156, 158,
   186, 187, 190,
   227
1:18—186
3:5-6—186
3:14—80
3:16, 18—186, 187
5:14—215
5:17-18—151
5:19, 30—152
6:44—144
7:20—25
7:24—57
8:28—152
8:44—137, 141,
   145, 169
8:48, 52—25
8:58-59—151
9:1-3—215
10:17-18—144, 173
10:20—25
10:30-33—151-152
10:34-35—130-132
10:37-38—152
11:47-53—144
11:52—186

13:2—144
13:3—156
13:27—144
14:10—152
14:13-14—149,
   196, 202
14:28—151
14:30—141, 142
15:7—196, 202
16:28—156
16:30—158
17:3—142
17:23—183
20:17—187

Acts

2—63
2:23—144
2:24-27—173
2:36—175
2:41—100
3:13-15—144
3:16—109
4:28—144
7:48-49—119
7:59—149
10:38—92
12:22—131
13:33—162, 174,
   175, 187
14:15—123
17:11—27
17:24-28—131
17:28—119, 186
17:29—192
17:31—157
18:21—143
20:28—147
28:6—131

Romans

1:3–4—174–175, 187
1:9—103
1:10—143
1:20—192
1:25—131
1:26–27—192
2:14, 27—192
2:28–29—101
3:18—109
3:30—130
4:17—74, 194, 195, 197
4:19—195
5:8–9—159
6:3–8—188
6:9—175
7:18–25—101, 102
8:9–11—188, 190, 212
8:14–23—186, 209
8:14–17—187
8:14—103
8:15, 23—186
8:29—136, 159, 162
9:6–24—144
9:8—186
9:26—186
10:9–10—195, 199
11:21, 24—192
11:25—138, 141, 143
11:36—131
12:1–2—100, 102, 212
12:3—194, 196
12:4–6—188, 189, 196
15:4—133
15:13—111, 199
15:32—143
16:27—130

1 Corinthians

1:10—102
2:10–16—102
3:16—188

4:8–13—211
5:5—101
6:17–20—188
6:17—180, 190–191
7:1—198
7:34—101
8:4–6—130, 142
10:13—143
10:20—134, 142
11:7—135
11:14—192
12:4–6—196
12:9—196, 214
12:11—144, 196
12:12–27—188
12:12—180, 188–189
12:14–19, 29–30—196
12:27—189
12:30—214
13:2—196
14:1—144
14:14–15—102, 103
15—100, 199
15:3–5—165–166
15:20, 23—175, 190
15:42–49—209
15:47—157
15:49—136

2 Corinthians

1:7—191
1:9—105
3:18—136
4:3–4—135, 141, 142
4:16—101, 198
4:18—195, 198
5:1–8—198
5:7—111, 195, 198
5:18–19—171
5:21—161, 169–171
6:14–15—180, 188
6:18—186
7:1—101
11:4—160
13:5—188
13:14—191

Galatians

1:4—212
1:6–9—160
2:15—192
2:20—188
3:6—208–209
3:13—206, 208–209
3:14–15—208–209
3:20—130
3:26—186
4:5–7—186, 187
4:8—134, 142, 192
5:18—103
5:22–6:4—219

Ephesians

1:3–12—144, 197, 209
1:3—195, 197
1:13–14—210
1:13—197
1:22–23—119, 188, 189
2:1—176
2:3—192
2:5–6—188
2:8—194, 196
3:16–17—188
4:6—130
4:10—119
4:12—188, 189
4:15—20, 226
4:23—102
4:24—136
4:30—210
5:20—149

Philippians

1:12–14—209
1:27—109
2:2—190
2:5–11—152
2:5—102
2:6–7—157–158
2:9—192
3:10—191
3:21—136

Colossians

1:15—135
1:16—101
1:18—175, 188, 189
1:19–20—179
2:8—43
3:4—188
3:10—136
3:11—119

1 Thessalonians

4:13–17—210
4:14—199
5:20–22—222
5:23—101

2 Thessalonians

2:4—131
2:9—217
2:13—109

1 Timothy

1:3–7—224
1:7—223
1:17—130
2:5—130, 142, 157
5:22—191
6:9–10, 17—222

2 Timothy

1:12—199
2:18—224
3:16—27, 133

Titus

2:6–8—85

Hebrews

1:2—131
1:3—124
1:5—174, 175, 187
1:8—131, 148
2:9—168
2:14—192

4:12—101
7:26–27—171
8:10—101
10:5—119
10:16—101
10:33—191
11:1—111, 195, 198
11:3–31—110
11:3—70, 106–107, 109–112, 131, 194, 195
11:6—110, 199
11:8–10—199
11:13–16—199
11:13—193
12:23—101

James

1:3–4—214
1:6–8—216
1:5—217
1:17—217
2:19—130, 142

2:26—101
3:1—29
3:7—192
3:9—135, 145
4:3—202, 216
4:6–10—202
4:15—202, 216
5:10–20—208, 213
5:10–11—213–215
5:13–17—214–217
5:15—208

1 Peter

1:3—176
1:20—144
2:19—109
2:24—207, 210
3:4—101
3:7—202
3:17—143
3:18–19—166
4:1—166
4:13—191

2 Peter

1:3—192
1:4—183, 186, 191–192
1:16–18—158
2:12—192

1 John

1:5—75
2:20, 27—223
2:29—186, 187
3:1–2, 9–10—186, 187
4:7—186, 187
4:9—175, 186
4:17—190
5:1–5—187
5:1, 2, 4—186
5:14—202
5:18—186
5:19—141, 142
5:20—142

2 John

11—191

3 John

2—208, 212

Jude

10—192
25—130

Revelation

1:5—159, 162, 175
3:17—201
6:9–11—101
12:12—138, 141, 143
13:8—144
20:10–15—167
21:7—186

Robert M. Bowman Jr. is the president of the Institute for the Development of Evangelical Apologetics (IDEA). Previously he served as a researcher and editor for the Christian Research Institute, the Atlanta Christian Apologetics Project, and Watchman Fellowship. For five years he taught apologetics, cult studies, theology, and biblical studies at Luther Rice Seminary. Bowman has authored or coauthored seven other books, including *Orthodoxy and Heresy* and *Why You Should Believe in the Trinity*. Mr. Bowman may be contacted at IDEA, P.O. Box 60511, Pasadena, CA 91116, or by e-mail at acts17@hotmail.com.